INDUSTRIAL COOPERATION BETWEEN EAST AND WEST

INDUSTRIAL COOPERATION BETWEEN EAST AND WEST

FRIEDRICH LEVCIK AND JAN STANKOVSKY

M.E. SHARPE, INC., WHITE PLAINS, N.Y.

Translated by Michel Vale.

Published simultaneously as Vol. XIV, No. 1-2 of
Soviet and Eastern European Foreign Trade

Library of Congress Catalog Card Number: LC 78-73222
International Standard Book Number: 0-87332-126-X

Printed in the United States of America

Contents

List of Tables

ix

Introduction

A number of valuable and interesting publications have appeared in the last few years on East-West cooperation. These studies, which by means of interviews and direct contacts with the firms concerned have shed some light on a subject that in the past had remained little known, also provided us with extremely valuable incentives. Most of these studies dealt only with individual aspects of cooperation, particularly the legal and microeconomic aspects. The quantitative data used, however, did not easily lend themselves to comparison. Eastern European studies more often contained the views of the respective governments than the experiences of enterprises involved in cooperative undertakings.

In this book we have attempted to provide a unified picture of the most important problems of East-West cooperation. The motivations and goals of those concerned, in all their microeconomic, macroeconomic, commercial, and political aspects, are brought together with the pertinent legal and institutional factors and are analyzed. We found that an analysis of East-West cooperation cannot be carried out in isolation but must be seen as part of the total context of East-West relations. This is true of both exchange of goods and the transfer of technology, financing, and legal and institutional factors.

Future opportunities for cooperation must also be seen within the broader framework of the development of the world economy and of East-West trade. Crucial to these opportunities is the state of the world economy and the establishment of a viable balance of interests between the industrial nations, the oil-producing nations, and the developing countries that have few raw material resources. East-West industrial cooperation could be a useful instrument here. The process of integration in East and West, although beset with difficulties and numerous setbacks, is nevertheless not without significance for the future of East-West cooperation. In our view the endeavors on both sides toward integration need not come into conflict with East-West cooperation. On the contrary, trading partners, strengthened by regional integration measures, should provide better conditions for interfirm East-West cooperation in the areas of production, technology, price formation, and financial viability.

We have drawn on all available data for our quantitative stock taking of East-West cooperation, and as far as possible we have reduced all to a common denominator; even where no quantitative data was available, we have tried to draw a few general conclusions.

Our study is meant primarily for firms and economic policy makers interested in East-West trade, but it should also find ready acceptance among a broader readership. We have therefore avoided using an excessively specialized terminology. The authors hope that their book will prove interesting and useful to economists as well.

The authors owe their thanks to a number of people, first and foremost, Dr. Franz Nemschak, director of the Vienna Institute for Comparative International Economics, who gave his encouragement to this study not only in his capacity as editor of the series Comparative Studies of Economic Systems, but also as the chairman of the Workshop on East-West European Interaction.

Of particular value were the research studies on interfirm cooperation by Dr. K. Bolz, HWWA Institute for Economic Research, Hamburg; Professor P. Marer, Indiana University; Professor C. H. McMillan, Carleton University, Ottawa. Dr. H. Machowski, DIW Berlin, B. Askanas, and Dr. G. Fink provided important suggestions for the first draft of this manuscript. The authors are, of course, wholly responsible for any mistakes or misinterpretations.

G. Kramarics compiled the list of cooperation ventures in Appendix 2. Dr. B. Ott gets credit for preparing the manuscript. F. Prager receives our thanks for technical and language editing and for checking and supplementing the references.

INDUSTRIAL COOPERATION BETWEEN EAST AND WEST

1

General aims and definitions

East-West cooperation is a relatively new element in economic relations between the Western (capitalist) market economies and the Eastern (socialist) planned economies. Studies of the problems and prospects of East-West cooperation often overlook the fact that cooperation between firms has long existed in the Western market economies (and in the Eastern nations as well). East-West cooperation, although it is a special form of cooperation between enterprises set in different economic systems and possessing their own specific features, still has a number of features in common with the Western, market-based form of interfirm cooperation. It shares some underlying motives as well as potential forms and areas of application. A few remarks, therefore, on the form of cooperation practiced within the Western nations might be useful for an analysis of East-West cooperation.

Cooperation in the West

Economic and technical development constantly makes new demands on all who take part in the economic process. Some of the most important problems are: the need for large-scale production in many branches of the economy and the attendant growing demand for capital; the rising cost of research and development and the difficulties involved in catching up in these areas; the expansion of markets; further development in the international division of labor; long-term tendencies toward shortages and higher costs of labor, raw materials, and energy; the growing financial burden of environmental protection against industrial hazards.

Enterprises must of necessity adapt to changing conditions of competition. Market-oriented firms can respond in two basic

3

ways to an increase in the pressure for higher efficiency: they may move to reduce that pressure, or they may increase their efficiency.

A particularly effective means of achieving either of these aims is through economic cooperation between firms, which may be defined as follows:

Economic cooperation means organized collaboration between economic entities in order to achieve jointly economic means under noncompetitive conditions [1].

In German usage "interfirm cooperation" is sometimes used as a synonym for economic cooperation, although it usually refers only to certain aspects of that process. The following distinctions are expedient:

— "Lower" forms of cooperation (subcontracts, job processing, utilization of the partner firm as an "extended work bench," simple sale of licenses) are often not considered cooperation in the Western industrial countries; the term "cooperation" is usually reserved for those cases where these simple relationships are entered into on a long-term or at least iterative basis.
— "Higher" forms of cooperation, e.g.:
  — cartel arrangements aimed principally at restricting competition, at least in certain areas;
  — forms of cooperation aimed at increasing enterprise efficiency and productivity.

The following definition of cooperation roughly covers these distinctions:

Enterprise cooperation is collaboration between independent firms for an unspecified number of business transactions, this cooperation being undertaken on a contractual, voluntary, and partnership basis, in which the parties involved pool all or some of their functions in order to increase their productive and competitive capacities and hence to promote economic progress [2].

The next stage of economic cooperation (sometimes also counted as one of the higher forms of cooperation) is merger between firms or one firm's acquisition of a controlling interest in another. On an international level the multinational corporations are the product of such developments.

"Merger," "cartel," and "cooperation" may also be distinguished

4

in the following way: merger means total consolidation of all enterprise functions, while cartels and cooperation involve only partial consolidation. A cooperative undertaking is further distinguished from a cartel by the fact that "it is not aimed at reducing competition, which therefore is only an incidental effect" [3].[1]

The difference between a cooperative undertaking and a cartel depends not so much on the form or purpose of the cooperation as on the market situation. Cooperation might be defined as collaboration between independent enterprises in a growing market, and cartel formation as collaboration in a (chronically) stagnant or declining market; hence a cooperative venture could conceivably degenerate into a cartel, or conversely, a cartel could be "regenerated" into a cooperative relationship.

In the market economies business activities at both the national and international levels are regulated mainly through the market and the price system. In large concerns or multinationals, however, control through the market is supplemented or even replaced by the decisions of a central management. Economic collaboration, especially interfirm cooperation, represents a middle course between these two steering mechanisms. Which of these steering mechanisms will be opted for depends on a number of factors, including legal conditions, the state of the market, and production technology. Ultimately it is cost which decides [4].

Cooperation may also be seen as ensuing from conflicting company goals. Disparate company aims, such as maximization of profits, consolidation and expansion of the firm's sales and share of the market, and guarantee of the firm's continued existence (which also has its political and technological aspects), often can only be achieved through sacrifice of the firm's independence, which is also a company goal.[2] Sometimes "optimization" of different, and occasionally divergent, aims can best be achieved through cooperation, with independence being retained in all essential respects.

East-West Cooperation

East-West Cooperation is a result of new worldwide trends and processes in industrial societies (see Chapter 2) and of active endeavors to increase economic relations between the market and planned economies and their respective enterprises. The different economic and social systems in which the cooperating parties exercise their activities afford East-West cooperation certain special features.

There are many different forms of cooperation, which is defined in different ways depending on the initial situation, goals, and particular interests involved.

Levels of East-West Cooperation Agreements

In East-West economic relations cooperation often refers to different things. A convenient classificatory criterion is that of level, i.e., the level at which agreements are made. For example:
At the government level:
— Agreements promoting cooperation concluded by sovereign states. Agreements of this sort are examined in more detail in Chapter 8.
At the enterprise level:
— Industrial cooperation between firms and enterprises in East and West; it is with this form we shall be principally dealing in this study.[3]
At the nonprofit research institution level:
— Scientific cooperation in research and development between research institutes or government or university institutions, oriented principally toward basic research. We shall generally pay only cursory attention to scientific cooperation.[4]

Definition and Delimitation of East-West Industrial Cooperation

A precise definition and delimitation of East-West industrial cooperation is neither possible nor meaningful inasmuch as new forms of cooperation are continuously evolving. It is important to keep in mind that governments, as well as the respective enterprises, have a significant hand in shaping East-West industrial cooperation.

The following definition of East-West industrial cooperation, worked out by the ECE and approved by East and West alike, is meant only for orientation and is not intended to introduce any sharp demarcation between that form and other forms of East-West economic relations:

Industrial co-operation in an East-West context denotes the economic relationships and activities arising from (a) contracts

6

extending over a number of years between partners belonging to different economic systems which go beyond the straightforward sale or purchase of goods and services to include a set of complementary or reciprocally matching operations (in production, in the development and transfer of technology, in marketing, etc.) and from (b) contracts between such partners which have been identified as industrial co-operation contracts by Governments in bilateral or multilateral agreements [5].[5]

In the Final Act of the Helsinki Conference on Security and Cooperation in Europe (CSCE), an even broader definition of industrial cooperation is used:

...Industrial cooperation (comprises) a number of forms of economic cooperation that extend beyond traditional commercial transactions [6].

In another section of the Final Act large-scale projects of common interest are mentioned as a separate category.

In this book we shall deal pragmatically with the term "industrial cooperation," relying on the factual evidence. The various forms of East-West industrial cooperation are examined in Chapters 3 and 6 (joint ventures); Chapters 10 and 11 take stock of available experience and statistics.

Notes

1. A much broader definition of cooperation is used by E. Boettcher: "Cooperation is the deliberate activity of economic entities ... in pursuit of a common objective in which the particular activities of each of the involved parties are coordinated in negotiation and agreements. This definition is broader than market coordination and plan coordination, and is distinct from both" [3].

2. The partial sacrifice of sovereignty entailed by integration is the counterpart of this problem at the national level.

3. The term "industry" includes mining, construction, and public utilities. Agricultural cooperation is also de facto included in this term; it takes place mainly in agrobusiness (i.e., cooperation of the canned goods industry with fruit and vegetable growers).

4. In the Eastern nations the term "scientific and technical cooperation" (STC) is often used. It usually comprises both scientific cooperation and that portion of industrial cooperation involving research and development and licensing agreements.

5. Section (b) of the ECE definition is patently influenced by the very broad Soviet definition of cooperation (see Chapter 10, "USSR," pp. 201-2).

References

[1] F. Romig, Theorie der wirtschaftlichen Zusammenarbeit, Berlin 1966, cited in Institut für Gewerbeforschung, Wirtschaftliche Zusammenarbeit zwischen Gewerbe und Industrie in Österreich, Studie im Auftrag des Bundesministeriums für Handel, Gewerbe und Industrie, Vienna, 1973.

[2] CEPES/RKW, Grenzüberschreitende Unternehmenskooperation in der EWG, Stuttgart, 1968.

[3] E. Boettcher, Kooperation und Demokratie in der Wirtschaft, J. C. B. Mohr, Tübingen 1974.

[4] C. H. McMillan, "The International Organization of Inter-firm Co-operation (with special reference to East-West relationship)," IEA Conference on "Economic Relations between East and West," Dresden, June 29-July 3, 1976.

[5] ECE, Analytical Report on Industrial Co-operation Among ECE Countries, Geneva, United Nations, 1973.

[6] Final Act of the Conference on Security and Cooperation in Europe of August 1, 1975, Department of State Bulletin, September 1, 1975, pp. 331-33.

2

New trends in the world economy as a basis for East-West cooperation

Since the midsixties studies of East-West economic relations have repeatedly called attention to the growing importance of industrial and scientific-technical cooperation between Western and Eastern partners. The number of cooperation agreements concluded and negotiations begun between firms and enterprises in East and West shows a steady rise. At the governmental level traditional trade agreements between Eastern and Western countries are generally being complemented by intergovernmental agreements for the promotion of scientific-technical and industrial cooperation (see Chapter 8).

This naturally brings up the question of the magnitude and significance of East-West industrial cooperation for East-West trade and for economic relations in general. For a variety of reasons statistical information is extremely inadequate (see the first section on Chapter 10). Estimates of the share of cooperative deliveries in East-West trade are quite rough, varying from 2% to 15%; moreover, they usually have no identifiable basis [1, 2, 3]. At present the magnitude of this cooperation, measured in terms of volume of East-West trade, is of very minor importance [4]. If one considers further that East-West trade makes up only 3-5% of the total foreign trade of the Western industrial countries, [1] one could easily conclude that it does not merit the attention paid it, which is considerable even in the Western nations.

However, these considerations — quite apart from the questionable basis of the quantitative estimates — do not provide a complete and objective picture of the prospects and potential of East-West industrial cooperation.

Over the relatively short period of ten years that industrial East-West cooperation has existed, a remarkable development has taken place. Almost all intergovernmental agreements on the pro-

9

motion of industrial and scientific-technical cooperation between Eastern and Western trading partners have been concluded only in the last five years, and initiatives in this direction have intensified especially markedly in the last two to three years. There are various reasons for this which will be discussed in more detail in Chapter 8. For the time-being let the mention of just one suffice: Whereas in the initial stages of East-West industrial cooperation the Soviet Union and the United States had adopted a skeptical and waiting posture toward this development, since 1972 the USSR has shown a clear interest in developing economic relations with the West in general and in concluding cooperation agreements in particular. In the United States the giant multinationals have stepped up pressure on the government to assist them in opening up the potentially vast Eastern market and to adopt an export-oriented trade policy toward Eastern Europe.

For all these reasons the prospects and potential of East-West industrial cooperation seem more promising than the purely quantitative statistics on the scope of East-West cooperation agreements might indicate; indeed, to a certain extent such agreements even serve as a catalyst for the expansion of East-West economic relations.

In this regard attention is being drawn to various trends discernible in the organization of industry at the national and international levels, and in the structure of world trade in general, that are contributing to the expansion of East-West industrial cooperation.

General Structural Trends
in Industrial Nations

Various statistical studies [5, 6, 7] have shown that profound changes have taken place in the structure of production and foreign trade in the developed industrial countries during the last twenty-five years. These changes have been instigated by technical progress which, occurring under generally favorable conditions, was itself spurred on by these changes as they took place. The structural changes may be characterized as follows. In the last twenty to thirty years the manufacturing industries have grown more rapidly than basic industries, and more rapidly still than the national product. Within the manufacturing industries growth has been most pronounced in the innovation-intensive branches. Foreign trade has been growing faster than production, with a marked shift toward export of finished products [1, 8, 9].

These developments have given rise to adaptive processes in the organization of industry that have led to concentration, specialization, and internationalization of production, spurred by the possibility, and even necessity, of reducing fixed costs by increasing the volume of production. Economies of scale are attainable not only in production but also in the pre- and postproduction operations and in management.

Concentration

Despite various legislative measures against control of the market (antitrust legislation, cartel prohibition, etc.) that have been used in the market economies to safeguard competition, industrial concentration continues. Since the sixties economic policy has shifted emphasis from broadening the general conditions for competition to giving active support to the rationalization of industrial organization. This has meant a concentration of industrial power on both a national and an international scale. The average size of firms and the number of large companies (measured in terms of number of employees, size of capital stock, or volume of sales) have been on the increase [7]. Some branches of industry are controlled by monopolies or by a few oligopolistically organized firms. This trend prevails in both the market economies and the centrally planned economies of Eastern Europe and in the USSR [7, 10].

It is enhanced by the technical conditions of production, but also by the rising costs of research and development, as well as by the costs of sales and service. These fixed costs can be kept within tolerable limits only by maintaining mass production and lot size at a given level. Not even in the biggest economies is the domestic market large enough, let alone in the small and medium-sized countries. Industry is organized across national borders, and multinationals are growing in importance. Even the centrally planned economies of Eastern Europe and the USSR are now establishing international economic organizations and enterprises in line with their Comprehensive Program [11].[2]

Specialization

The process of concentration has gone hand in hand with endeavors to achieve economies of scale through specialization, in which the market for each product remaining in production is widened by reducing the range of products offered. Specialization does not stand in opposition to concentration. At the company or corporation level concentration is often accompanied by factory specialization on the one hand and product diversification on the other.

Job contracting is also increasing in importance, especially in the vehicle and transport equipment industry. It is a unique kind of specialization that enables small and medium-sized firms to achieve economies of scale despite their limited production output by concentrating and simultaneously stabilizing orders with one or a few principals.

Closely connected with these trends is the shift in foreign trade from specialization by branch to specialization within the same branch and product group. The growing share of exports in proportion to the gross production output, along with a simultaneous increase in the share of imports in apparent consumption[3] in the same branch, is a sign of international specialization of products [1, 6].

The figures in Table 1 clearly show a growing trend toward product specialization in the sixties in Western Europe in all the branches listed. This trend will probably continue. Understandably the degree of specialization in the smaller industrial nations of Western Europe is particularly high. The figures are not adequate to state with certainty whether product specialization is also increasing in Eastern Europe, although in the light of other information, this is very likely.[4] However, the degree of specialization in the Eastern European nations by the end of the sixties was not so high as in the smaller and medium-sized industrial nations of Western Europe. This was even more the case with the USSR as compared with the major Western European nations.

The CMEA nations have recently stepped up their promotion of product specialization in intra-CMEA trade. In 1973 the share of exports of specialized articles in total intra-CMEA exports was 10% in Eastern Europe and 6% in the USSR. Bulgaria, with almost 20%, had the largest share, and Romania, with 3.5%, the smallest share of specialized products[5] in proportion to their total exports to the other CMEA countries. For 1974 the individual CMEA countries were expecting a general increase in the share of specialized products in total intra-CMEA export (see Table 2) as a consequence

12

Table 1

Product Specialization in Western and Eastern
Europe in Terms of Foreign Trade Shares
as Reflected in Trade Proportion

	Western Europe				Eastern Europe			
	4 large*		7 small†		4 countries‡		USSR	
	industrial nations							
	export	import	export	import	export	import	export	import
Industrial branch	Export in % of gross output; import in % of consumption							
Textiles								
Late 50s	16	8	33	36				
Late 60s	23	17	59	61	15	13	–	–
Chemicals								
Late 50s	19	10	34	40			3	4
Late 60s	26	18	53	56	18	29	3	4
Base metals								
Late 50s	18	17	70	64				
Late 60s	21	22	74	66	29	44	12	5
Machinery, nonelectric								
Late 50s	28	12	30	40				
Late 60s	42	26	41	48				
Machinery, electric								
Late 50s	18	5	30	35			6	5
Late 60s	21	13	40	44	27	32	3	5
Transport equipment								
Late 50s	23	4	22	34				
Late 60s	27	11	43	50				

Source: Analytical Report on Industrial Cooperation among ECE Countries,
UN, Geneva, 1973, p. 23.
*Federal Republic of Germany, France, Italy, United Kingdom.
†Austria, Belgium-Luxembourg, Denmark, Finland, Netherlands, Norway,
Sweden.
‡Bulgaria, Czechoslovakia, Hungary, Poland.

of trade agreements, and indeed a one-third increase did occur.
This trend has quite likely continued into 1975 [12].

Similar Structural Changes —
Different Means and Forms to Implement Them

The foregoing discussion has demonstrated how similar factors have led to profound structural changes in both West and East, although these changes have proceeded along different lines and have been manifested in different ways as a result of differences in economic systems.

Table 2

Specialized Products in Intra-CMEA Trade

	Total exports	Exports of specialized products	Share of specialized products in total exports		Share of countries in exports of specialized products	
	Millions of transferable rubles		in %		in %	
	1973	1973	1973	1974*	1973	1974*
Bulgaria	1,904	367.4	19.3	24.9	18.4	19.9
CSSR	2,920	265.0	9.1	11.5	13.2	13.9
GDR	3,923	347.5	8.9	13.4	17.4	20.3
Poland	2,794	321.5	11.5	11.8	16.1	14.3
Romania	1,268	44.6	3.5	5.2	2.2	2.4
Hungary	2,082	164.0	7.9	10.7	8.2	8.3
Eastern Europe, without USSR	14,891	1,505.0	10.1	–	75.5	79.1
USSR	8,311	489.0	5.9	6.1	24.5	20.9
CMEA countries[†]	23,202	1,997.0	8.6	–	100.0	100.0

Source: J. Bethkenhagen and H. Machowski "Integration im Rat für gegenseitige Wirtschaftshilfe," Berlin, 1976, p. 52; CMEA Statistical Annual, 1974; own calculations.
*Target based on trade agreement.
†Only European CMEA countries.

In the market economies, with their many economic units that have autonomous decision-making powers, concentration and specialization are promoted through interfirm agreements and measures taken at the national and international levels, through mergers, firm takeovers, formation of trusts and corporations, cartel agreements, and more recently, through the multinationals. In these processes the ways in which control is exercised over the economic decisions of the partner enterprise are of major importance. The mode of control peculiar to market economies is capital participation or the pooling of capital. Cooperation between firms on a contractual basis without capital participation is possible in principle but is regarded as a relatively primitive form of cooperation.

In the centrally planned economies of Eastern Europe and in the

USSR, concentration and specialization take place through planned steering and administrative measures. At the national level they are usually the result of a restructuring of the economy in accordance with a government decision. Enterprises are brought together in various ways: e.g., in trusts, combines, or associations (branch administrative boards). At the same time, the production programs of the formerly independent enterprises are streamlined and simplified. A far-reaching specialization in individual merchandise groups, individual products, and even parts and components of such products is sought.

In the East the predominant form of control at the international level is intra-CMEA or bilateral coordination of middle-term (usually five-year) economic plans implemented through intergovernmental specialization agreements and through binding protocols on reciprocal delivery of stipulated quantities or values of products or product groups. This principal form of concentration and specialization of production is now complemented by joint forecasts and joint development plans in selected areas and branches, as well as by the creation of international economic organizations and large-scale enterprises. Even in these new forms, however, cooperation between enterprises still requires a government decision or an agreement between governments; the respective enterprises cannot set it into motion on their own [11].

Regional Integration

The realization that these processes raise overall economic efficiency has spurred integration efforts at the government level in both East and West. Pertinent measures, implemented initially at the regional level, are taken to support these processes or to create favorable conditions. In the West this happens under the auspices of the European Economic Community, on the basis of the Treaty of Rome; in the East integration is promoted within the Council for Mutual Economic Assistance (CMEA or Comecon), and in particular — since the early seventies — within the framework of the "Comprehensive Programme" [11].[6]

In the West the most important integration instrument is the elimination of trade restrictions by abolishing intraregional tariff barriers. In the East the CMEA, through international agreements and accords, enables the individual countries to effectuate integration measures at the national level.

Such measures on the part of the respective governments have been geared toward promoting the internationalization of innovation, production, trade, and financing within the integration area. They have, however, not been able to go beyond the confines of regional integration, even with regard to third countries belonging to the same economic system. The different economic systems in the East and West are an additional obstacle to the further internationalization of the world economy.

Industrial Cooperation — A New Element in Economic Relations between East and West

There is an increasing realization in both blocs that all would tend to benefit from stepped-up mutual economic relations. In the last ten to fifteen years, until the recession in 1975, East-West trade increased steadily, at a faster pace than any other trade flows (although, of course, the initial level was extremely modest) [13]. This trend demonstrates that the establishment of closer and more involved relationships between these two systems fulfills an objective need that has made itself felt despite existing trade obstacles.

Various difficulties, which have become increasingly apparent in trade between East and West in recent years, indicate that the expansion of East-West trade will reach the limits of its potential if normal commodity exchange is not backed up by more active economic relations and ties at the enterprise level. The differences existing between the economic and social systems, however, do not permit either bloc to impose its own forms for international division of labor on the other bloc. The West could not hope to succeed if it tried to make inroads into Eastern Europe by means of mergers, firm takeovers, or capital investments by the multinationals. Since all major enterprises in the East are state property and their management fulfills only administrative functions and has no right of property over them, capital acquisition or capital participation is in principle ruled out a priori (see Chapter 6).

On the other hand, the East is equally unable to impose its methods on the West. Attempts to achieve a more effective international division of labor by coordinating planning at the regional level and through attendant organizational measures at the international level are doomed to failure simply by the fact that the Western governments have no power to take on such far-reaching commitments on behalf of private enterprises. Even in the simple negotiations prefatory to normal trade agreements, Western representatives often find themselves faced with the incomprehension of their Eastern partners when they try to explain that they cannot assume any commitment to accept delivery on predetermined quantities of products, since such decisions are up to the importers, not the government. They are even less able to shoulder the commitments entailed by plan coordination on behalf of private firms. Furthermore this principle is applicable to most of the state-owned enterprises in the West as well, since they too are usually run on business principles without government interference.

Under these circumstances East-West cooperation at the enterprise level, based on agreements between interested firms in the two blocs, is a fitting means to achieve further economies of scale on a European and global scale, within the bounds permitted by the differences between the two economic systems. The forms of East-West industrial cooperation that have emerged over the relatively short period of the past ten years are so manifold that while taking into account the peculiarities of both systems, they yet can produce results in the interests of both partners.

Notes

1. The share of the Eastern nations in total OECD exports and imports in 1974 was, respectively, 3.6% and 2.9% (the corresponding figures for Western Europe were 4.8% and 3.8%).
2. The "Comprehensive Program" for the further expansion and improvement of cooperation and development of socialist economic integration of the CMEA member nations was adopted in Bucharest in July 1971 at the Twenty-fifth Meeting of the Council for Mutual Economic Assistance after long preparations by the member nations.
3. Gross production minus exports plus imports.
4. The following proportions for specialized products were attained in exports of machinery to other CMEA countries: Bulgaria 41%, GDR 26%, Poland 30%, Hungary 15%, Czechoslovakia 19%, and USSR 37% [1].
5. Of products for which specialization agreements between Eastern European countries were set up.
6. Intergovernmental specialization agreements on a bilateral basis or on the basis of CMEA recommendations had already been in practice before the adoption of the Comprehensive Program.

References

[1] ECE, Analytical Report on Industrial Co-operation Among ECE Countries, Geneva, United Nations, 1973.

[2] P. Knirsch, "Vom Ost-West-Handel zur Wirtschaftskooperation," Europa-Archiv, 1973, no. 2.

[3] Berliner Bank, Mitteilungen für den Aussenhandel, 1973, no. 11-12.

[4] ECE, "Preparations for the Second Meeting of Experts on Industrial Cooperation," Committee on the Development of Trade, TRADE/R. 320, August 26, 1975 (mimeographed).

[5] A. Maizels, Industrial Growth and World Trade, Cambridge University Press, 1965.

[6] ECE, "The European Economy from the 1950's to the 1970's," Economic Survey of Europe in 1971, part 1, New York, United Nations, 1972.

[7] ECE, "Industrial Co-operation," Economic Bulletin for Europe, vol. 21, no. 1, New York, United Nations, 1970.

[8] ECE, Analytical Report on the State of Intra-European Trade, New York, United Nations, 1970.

[9] C. T. Saunders, From Free Trade to Integration in Western Europe, London, Chatham House, PEP, 1975.

[10] ECE, "Industrial Organisation and Policy," Economic Survey of Europe in 1970, Part 1, chap. 2, provisional version (mimeographed).

[11] Comprehensive Programme for the Further Extension and Improvement of Co-operation and the Development of Socialist Economic Integration by the CMEA Member Countries, Moscow, CMEA Secretariat, 1971.

[12] ECE, "Recent Changes in Europe's Trade," Economic Bulletin for Europe, vol. 27, New York, United Nations, 1975.

[13] B. Askanas, H. Askanas, and F. Levcik, "Structural Developments in CMEA Foreign Trade over the Last Fifteen Years (1960-1974)," Forschungsberichte des Wiener Institutes für Internationale Wirtschaftsvergleiche, 1975, no. 23.

3

Types of industrial cooperation between East and West

The types of industrial cooperation between East and West may be classified in different ways, and a number of systems have been proposed [1, 2]. The first section of this chapter provides one possible classification; the second section discusses the way industrial cooperation is actually delimited in practice; and the third section examines the most important types of cooperation.

Cooperation According to Enterprise Activity and Type of Relationship

The various types of industrial cooperation between East and West may be classified according to the particular area of the production process involved or according to the type of relations established between the respective firms; finally, they may be classified according to geographic location. The categories delimited below partly overlap, yet they can be combined to form a cooperation matrix (see Table 3).

Any classification has both static and dynamic aspects: types of cooperation change according to needs, especially if they prove viable and they give way to other, often higher, forms.

Types of cooperation by activity and object:
— Cooperation in production:
  — concerning individual articles or their parts and components: job processing, subcontracting, coproduction, specialization;
  — concerning deliveries of complete industrial plants (product pay-back instead of payment);
— Cooperation involving patents, licenses, and know-how;
— Cooperation in industrial research and development;

19

Table 3

Cooperation Matrix

Cooperation by activity	Specific form of cooperation			
	Cooperation in partner countries			Cooperation in third countries
	Contribution of partner in same form (stage)	Contribution of partners in different form (stage)		
		material connection in the object of cooperation		
		with	without	
In production	specialization coproduction joint venture	plant delivery* job processing subcontracting	plant delivery for compensation‡	joint venture, furnishing of machinery, parts or technical know-how
In sales	sales in both countries a) joint sales (sales organization) b) separate sales but cooperation in marketing and service	sale of a product manufactured cooperatively	pure sales cooperation; use of partner's sales and service network	joint tendering, joint marketing organizations, sale and service of partner's product
In research and development	exchange of researchers and engineers; exchange of documentation	licensing agreement†	licensing agreement paid in money or compensation‡	

*Repayment (part or whole) with products manufactured in newly installed plant.
†Repayment (part or whole) with products manufactured by license.
‡Long-term relations between partners only.

20

— Cooperation in prospecting for and utilization of natural resources;
— Cooperation in the supply of raw materials and primary products;
— Cooperation in distribution, marketing, and service;
— Cooperation in other services.

Types of cooperation by legal relations between partners:
— Contractual functional relations, including:
  — simple contractual relations;
  — advanced contractual relations;
— Institutional relations (joint ventures).

Types of cooperation by geographic location:
— In the participating countries;
— In third countries.

Delimitation of Industrial Cooperation in Practice

The most important, constituent element in East-West industrial cooperation is, as defined in the ECE Convention and various bilateral agreements, the long-term nature of such relations, which go beyond simple sale and purchase and are based on reciprocity.

Moreover, contracts specifically identified as cooperation in intergovernmental cooperation agreements must be viewed as forms of cooperation. The delimitation of cooperation is not merely of academic interest, since cooperation agreements may be promoted by various economic policy measures (exemptions from quota restrictions in the West, easier credit terms to cooperating enterprises in the East, etc.). Defining the types of East-West cooperation is also important for the Eastern trade policy of the EEC (see the second section of Chapter 7). It is understandable, therefore, that governments have reserved to themselves the final say in deciding which transactions will be promoted.

Excerpts from agreements promoting cooperation between the FRG and Hungary, Romania, and the USSR are given below as examples.

Types of cooperation in the FRG-Hungary agreement of October 27, 1970, include:
— mutual deliveries of raw materials, semifinished products, primary products, parts and elements for their processing and handling (including job processing) or installation in one country or in both countries, and the sale of the manufactured products

21

on the market of one country, both countries, or third countries, independently of where these products are manufactured or finished;

— the expansion and modernization of existing plants or the construction of new plants; modernization of techniques and technological processes in one of the countries through the supply of machinery and equipment or licenses and know-how or technical and technological documentation by enterprises from the other country which have a continuing interest in procuring or joint or coordinated sale of goods produced by means of the delivered equipment, licenses, and technical and technological documentation;

— collaboration in the use or improvement of existing technical and technological procedures or in the development of new ones; joint drafting and design; the exchange of specialists if the relevant enterprises of the two countries have an interest in the production or joint or coordinated sale of the object of this cooperative undertaking;

— mutual deliveries of raw materials, semifinished products, primary products, parts, elements, or final products for the current output of enterprises of the other country for the purpose of expanding or supplementing its production and sales program;

— joint planning and designing of industrial, agricultural, and other ventures in third countries and their joint management; joint exploring or processing of raw materials in third countries and cooperation in the sale of these materials.

Types of cooperation in the FRG-Romania agreement of May 19, 1973, include:

— construction of new and the expansion and modernization of existing industrial plants;

— joint production and joint sale of articles and specialization in production and sales;

— the establishment of joint corporations for production and sales;

— the exchange of know-how, technical information, patents, and licenses; the use and improvement of existing or the development of new technological procedures, and the training and exchange of specialists and trainees;

— exchange of experience and agreements on standards, norms, and material testing.

Types of cooperation in the FRG-USSR agreement of June 29, 1973, include:

— construction of industrial plants in the economic interests of both; the expansion and modernization of existing industrial enterprises;

— cooperation in the production of equipment and other products;

— cooperation in raw materials production;

— exchange of patents, licenses, know-how, and technological information; the use and improvement of existing and the development of new technological processes; and dispatch of specialists for technical services or training.

The cooperation agreements of the FRG with East European countries vary considerably in their enumeration of the forms of cooperation deemed especially worthy of promotion. In the agreement with Hungary a maximum number of types of cooperation are enumerated, and the introduction stresses the long-term nature of the relations; in the agreement with Romania the establishment of joint production companies is mentioned; while in the agreement with the USSR relatively few types of cooperation are listed. The FRG's agreements with Bulgaria and Poland are similar to the agreement with Hungary (in the Bulgarian agreement cooperation in agriculture is stressed), and in the agreement with Czechoslovakia a distinction is made between scientific-technical (licenses, standardization, and norms) and economic cooperation.

The Major Types of East-West Industrial Cooperation

Specialization and coproduction, which represent an advanced form of collaboration, are always considered forms of cooperation. Collaboration between enterprises in research and development and the formation of joint ventures are also generally regarded as cooperation. It is a matter of debate, however, whether job processing and subcontracting ventures, which are only simple forms of collaboration, represent cooperation in the formal sense. There are also differences of opinion on how licensing agreements and the delivery of complete plants are to be classified: according to the ECE concept these transactions are counted as cooperation only if there exists a "material" relationship between the delivery and the counter-delivery, i.e., if licenses are paid with licensed products, or plants with products manufactured in them.[1] According to this definition payment with other products would be called compensation.

In most Eastern European sources and in studies on cooperative ventures of the FRG and the United States with the East [3], however, licensing agreements are in principle considered cooperation; but in many cases this is so only if they rest on long-term relations. In the Hungarian view [5] East-West cooperative undertakings are classified according to their form as technical service arrangements or management arrangements, whereas a classification based on the content of the agreement distinguishes between various areas of enterprise activity.

A classification of agreements on East-West industrial cooperation according to type can only be made on a statistical basis. The ECE Secretariat in Geneva maintains a "cooperation file" that contains detailed information on a representative selection of agreements of this type. The ECE publications provide a classification of East-West cooperation agreements by type for the years 1972 and 1975 [2, 6].[2]

In addition, national statistics on cooperation, classified by form, are available for the FRG for 1972 [3], the United States for 1975 [4], Poland for 1968 [7], and Hungary for 1974 [8]. Table 4 sums up the results of all these studies. Tables 5 and 6 give figures for East-West cooperation in 1975 (ECE statistics) classified by type and by country. Tables 7, 8, and 9 contain further details on U.S. cooperative ventures with the East.

Coproduction and Specialization[3]

Agreements on specialization and coproduction may be regarded as forms of industrial cooperation in the strict sense. They are usually based on long years of relationships between the partners; in many cases specialization and coproduction have grown out of previous cooperation agreements on licensing, job processing, and collaboration in research and development.

a) According to the ECE studies [2, 6], 30% in 1972, and 33% in 1975, of all East-West cooperative ventures were in the area of coproduction and specialization (including cooperation in marketing). The following types of agreements are of importance:
— Coproduction of the final product, involving collaboration in the manufacture of its parts. Both partners produce parts that are then put together in the final product by one or by both partners. Agreements of this type usually provide that the Eastern partner manufacture the simpler parts, the Western the more intricate or more capital-intensive parts (e.g., in numerically controlled machine tools the Eastern partner manufactures the machinery,

24

Table 4

Structure of East-West Cooperation by Type of Cooperation

Total (1972, 1975) and Agreements of FRG (1973), USA (1975), Poland (1968), and Hungary (1974)

Type of cooperation	East-West, total (1972)	East-West, total (1975)	FRG (1973)	USA ## (1975)	Poland (1968)	Hungary (1974)
	Share of each type of cooperation in total number of cooperation agreements, in %					
Licensing agreements*						
"Broad definition"	–	–	40.3	48.3***	10	–
"Narrow definition"	28.2	26.1	–	8.2	–	43
Supply of complete plants	11.9†	21.7†	–	32.1	35	19
Specialization	4.0‡	2.9‡	ca. 23‖	–	–	–
Coproduction	26.2§	30.4§	–	4.1	30	30‖‖‖‖
Research and development	6.9	–#	19	11.6	–	–
Joint ventures	14.9	2.9**	–††	1.3	2.5	–
Only marketing	9.4	#	–	–	–	–
Including production	–	2.9	–	–	–	–
Subcontracting	7.9	6.8	–	2.6	17.5	–
Job-processing	–	–	10	–	–	–
Cooperation in third countries	–	7.2‡‡	ca. 7	–	5	8
Joint projects	–	1.9§§	–	–	–	–
Total	100.0	100.0	100.0	100.0	100.0	100.0

Sources: East-West total (1972): ECE, Analytical Report on Industrial Cooperation among ECE Countries, Geneva, 1974. Based on 202 agreements recorded in 1972.

East-West total (1975): ECE, TRADE/R.320, Geneva, August 26, 1975. Based on a selection of 207 from a total of 340 agreements recorded in 1975. Cooperation agreements on research and development and joint ventures not involving production were excluded as compared with 1972.

25

FRG: K. Bolz and O. Plötz, Erfahrungen aus der Ost-West-Kooperation, HWWA-Institut für Wirtschaftsforschung, Hamburg, 1974.

USA: The U.S. Perspective on East-West Industrial Cooperation (preliminary), Bloomington, International Development Research Center of Indiana University, Team of Researchers, June 1975.

Poland: J. Olszynski, "Kooperacja przemystowa Polski z wysoko rozwiniętymi krajami Europy Zachodniej," SGPiS, Zeszyty Naukowe, (Warsaw), 1973, no. 94.

Hungary: F. Horchler, "The Future of Austro-Hungarian Foreign Trade," Forschungsberichte des Wiener Institutes für Internationale Wirtschaftsvergleiche, June 1975, no. 27.

*Broad definition: all licensing agreements; narrow definition: only licensing agreements in which repayment is by licensed products.

†Only plants in which repayment is by products manufactured in the plant.

‡Specialization in manufacture of final product.

§Coproduction of final product by cooperation in manufacture of parts.

‖Including 16% specialization agreements; about 7% joint production; the definition of these two types of cooperation may not be entirely commensurate with the ECE definition.

#This form of cooperation was not taken into account in 1975.

**Not comparable with 1972.

††Not shown because negligible.

‡‡Joint projects and joint tendering for customers in third countries

§§Joint projects and joint tendering for customers in partner countries.

‖‖Including subcontracts and joint ventures.

##In 18% of the contracts U.S. firms are only indirect partners (i.e., the agreements are with subsidiaries in Western Europe and Canada).

***Including know-how agreement (8.2%) and licensing and know-how agreements in which the Eastern countries are the licensers (3.9%).

26

Table 5

Structure of East-West Cooperation by Type of Cooperation,
Total (1975) by Eastern Country

Type of cooperation	USSR	Hungary	Poland	Romania	Bulgaria	CSSR	GDR	Eastern countries*
				Share of individual Eastern countries in total number of East-West cooperation agreements, in %				
Licensing	—	40.7	25.9	14.8	9.3	9.3	—	100.0
Supply of complete plants	28.9	20.0	20.0	26.7	4.4	—	—	100.0
Specialization	—	50.0	16.7	16.7	16.7	—	—	100.0
Coproduction	12.7	42.9	31.7	3.2	—	6.3	3.2	100.0
Joint ventures	—	—	16.7	83.3	—	—	—	100.0
Cooperation in third countries	—	13.3	40.0	13.3	—	26.7	6.7	100.0
Joint projects	25.0	—	75.0	—	—	—	—	100.0
Subcontracting	—	12.5	25.0	50.0	—	12.5	—	100.0
Total	11.1	32.8	27.1	16.9	3.9	6.8	1.4	100.0

Source: ECE, TRADE/R, 320, August 26, 1975.

27

Table 6

Structure of East-West Cooperation by Type of Cooperation,
Total (1975) by type of cooperation

Type of cooperation	USSR	Hungary	Poland	Romania	Bulgaria	CSSR	GDR	Eastern countries*
			Share of each type of cooperation in total number of East-West cooperation agreements, in %					
Licensing	–	32.3	25.0	22.8	62.5	35.7	–	26.1
Supply of complete plants	56.6	13.2	16.1	34.3	25.0	–	–	21.7
Specialization	–	4.4	1.8	2.9	12.5	–	–	2.9
Coproduction	34.8	39.7	35.7	5.7	–	28.6	66.7	30.4
Joint ventures	–	–	1.8	14.3	–	–	–	2.9
Cooperation in third countries	–	3.0	10.6	5.7	–	28.6	33.3	7.2
Joint projects	4.3	–	5.4	–	–	–	–	1.9
Subcontracting	4.3	7.4	3.6	14.3	–	7.1	–	6.8
Total	100.0	100.0	100.0	100.0	100.0	100.0	100.0	100.0

Source: ECE, TRADE/R. 320, August 26, 1975.
*Corresponds to Column 2 in Table 4.

28

Table 7

Cooperation of U.S. Firms with the CMEA Collectively
and with Individual CMEA Countries, 1975,
by Type of Cooperation, in %

	USSR	Bulgaria	CSSR	GDR	Poland	Romania	Hungary	Country unknown	Total Eastern countries
I. Agreements in force or expired									
Total number	136	23	34	13	71	51	31	30	389
Licensing agreements, total*	24.3	65.2	64.7	53.8	57.7	49.0	64.5	83.4	48.3
(of which, narrow definition)†	(2.2)	(13.0)	(2.9)	(7.7)	(22.5)	(3.9)	(16.1)	(3.3)	(8.2)
Turnkey plants	39.7	26.1	29.4	38.5	28.2	43.1	16.1	10.0	32.1
(of which U.S. firms as prime contractor)	(9.6)	(17.4)	(14.7)	(30.8)	(9.9)	(11.8)	(6.5)	(3.3)	(10.8)
Coproduction	1.5	8.7	5.9	–	8.5	2.0	9.7	–	4.1
Joint ventures	–	–	–	–	–	3.9	6.5	3.3	1.3
Subcontracting	2.2	–	–	7.7	5.6	–	3.2	3.3	2.6
Scientific-technical agreements	32.4	–	–	–	–	2.0	–	–	11.6
Total	100.0	100.0	100.0	100.0	100.0	100.0	100.0	100.0	100.0
Of which, large U.S. corporations‡	78.7	73.9	73.5	84.6	81.7	74.5	71.0	60.0	76.1
other U.S. companies	21.3	26.1	26.5	15.4	18.3	25.5	29.0	40.0	23.9
II. Projects									
Total number	112	33	13	5	54	47	31	107	402
Of which, U.S. large corporations in %‡	67.0	57.6	53.8	0	66.7	68.1	58.1	40.2	57.2
other U.S. firms in %	33.0	42.4	46.2	100.0	33.3	31.9	41.9	59.8	42.8

Source: The U.S. Perspective on East-West Industrial Co-operation (preliminary), Bloomington, International Development Research Center of Indiana University, Team of Researchers, 1975.

* Including know-how agreements; see Table 9.

† Licensing fee paid by deliveries of licensed product.

‡ Fortune's list of 500 largest U.S. firms in 1975.

Table 8

Cooperation of U.S. Firms with the CMEA* Collectively and with Individual CMEA Countries, 1975, by CMEA Country, in %

	USSR	Bulgaria	CSSR	GDR	Poland	Romania	Hungary	Country unknown	Eastern countries	Total number
I. Agreements in force or expired										
Licensing agreements, total†	17.6	8.0	11.7	3.7	21.8	13.3	10.6	13.3	100.0	188
(of which, narrow definition)‡	(9.4)	(9.4)	(3.1)	(3.1)	(50.0)	(6.3)	(15.6)	(3.1)	(100.0)	(32)
Turnkey plants	43.2	4.8	8.0	4.0	16.0	17.6	4.0	2.4	100.0	125
(of which, U.S. firms as prime contractor)	(31.0)	(9.5)	(11.9)	(9.5)	(16.7)	(14.3)	(4.8)	(2.4)	(100.0)	(42)
Coproduction	12.5	12.5	12.5	0	37.5	6.3	18.8	–	100.0	16
Joint ventures	–	–	–	–	–	40.0	40.0	20.0	100.0	5
Subcontracting	30.0	–	–	10.0	40.0	–	10.0	10.0	100.0	10
Scientific-technical agreements	97.8	–	–	–	–	2.2	–	–	100.0	45
Total	35.0	5.9	8.7	3.3	18.3	13.1	8.0	7.7	100.0	389
Of which, large U.S. corporations§	36.1	5.7	8.4	3.7	19.6	12.8	7.4	6.1	100.0	294
other U.S. companies	31.2	6.5	9.7	2.2	14.0	14.0	9.7	12.9	100.0	95
II. Projects										
Total	27.9	8.2	3.2	1.2	13.4	11.7	7.7	26.6	100.0	402
Of which, large U.S. corporations§	32.6	8.3	3.0	–	15.7	13.9	7.8	18.7	100.0	230
other U.S. firms	21.5	8.1	3.5	2.9	10.5	8.7	7.6	37.2	100.0	172

Source: The U.S. Perspective on East-West Industrial Co-operation (preliminary), Bloomington, International Development Research Center of Indiana University, Team of Researchers, 1975.

*Including indirect agreements, i.e., in which European or Canadian subsidiaries of U.S. firms participate. Share of indirect agreements in all agreements in force, 18.0%; in projects, 6.5%.

†Including know-how agreements; see Table 9.

‡Licensing fee paid by deliveries of licensed product.

§Fortune's list of 500 largest U.S. firms in 1975.

Licensing Agreements of U.S. Firms with Individual CMEA Countries and the CMEA Collectively, 1975

	USSR	Bulgaria	CSSR	GDR	Poland	Romania	Hungary	Country unknown	Eastern countries	Total in %
			Number of Agreements							
I. Agreements in force or expired										
Licensing to East:										
Narrow definition*	10	5	15	6	14	8	7	22	87	46.3
Broad definition†	3	3	1	1	16	2	5	1	32	17.0
Total‡	14	9	17	7	34	18	17	25	141	75.0
Of which, direct	11	8	15	6	25	15	16	25	121	64.4
indirect§	3	1	2	1	9	3	1	–	20	10.6
Know-how agreements	6	4	5	–	7	7	3	–	32	17.0
Licensing to USA‖	13	2	–	–	–	–	–	–	15	8.0
Total	33	15	22	7	41	25	20	25	188	100.0
in %	17.6	8.0	11.7	3.7	21.8	13.3	10.6	13.3	100.0	–
II. Projects										
Licensing to East:										
Narrow definition*	4	4	2	–	8	–	2	1	95	42.8
Broad definition†	18	6	–	2	–	–	–	2	31	14.0
Total‡	43	18	6	4	29	20	18	55	193	86.9
Of which, direct	42	16	5	4	28	20	18	52	185	83.3
indirect§	1	2	1	–	1	–	–	3	8	3.6
Know-how agreements	8	2	1	–	2	–	–	–	13	5.9
Licensing to USA‖	13	–	1	–	1	–	1	–	16	7.2
Total	64	20	8	4	32	20	19	55	222	100.0
in %	28.8	9.0	3.6	1.8	14.4	9.0	8.6	24.8	100.0	–

Source: The U.S. Perspective on East-West Industrial Co-operation (preliminary), Bloomington, International Development Research Center of Indiana University, Team of Researchers, 1975.
*Licensing fee paid by deliveries of licensed product.
†Licensing fee paid in foreign exchange.
‡Including licensing agreements not further specified.
§Agreements in which European and Canadian subsidiaries of U.S. firms participate.
‖Including supplying of know-how to USA.

the Western partner the control equipment).
— Specialization within the range of final products. In agreements of this type the partners divide production into different items of the manufacturing program (e.g., section [shape] specialization in the steel industry). In some situations subsidiary agreements are reached on specialization in the production of parts. In 1973 26%, and in 1975 30%, of all cooperation agreements involved coproduction, while specialization was the subject of only 4% and 3%, respectively. In Eastern Europe almost three fourths of all East-West coproduction undertakings involved Hungary and Poland. Hungary was involved in half of all specialization agreements (Table 5). Coproduction was especially important in Hungary, Poland, and the USSR, where 35-40% of all cooperation agreements were of this type. For Romania and Bulgaria — countries at a low level of economic development — this figure was much lower (Table 6).

b) In a study of the FRG's cooperative undertakings with the East [3], a distinction is made between "joint production" and specialization.[4]
— The term "joint production" refers to agreements stipulating the joint production of an article in which the Eastern partner usually provides the plant and the Western partner the know-how, machinery, and perhaps the technical personnel. Joint sales are usually stipulated contractually.
— In specialization agreements either the production technology is provided by one partner, or each partner uses his own procedure. In some situations the technology is the product of joint research and development. In joint production and specialization special agreements must be concluded to define sales territories and trademark rights. In the FRG's specialization agreements with the Eastern countries, the West German partner in most cases has the right to sell the joint product on all markets, and the Eastern partner only domestically or in other socialist countries, and more rarely, in the developing countries. For sales in the West the German trademark is mainly used, while for Eastern sales and sales in the developing countries either the German trademark or a combined trademark is used.

The financial aspects of joint production and specialization agreements are cleared by dividing the jointly produced goods. If the end product of a specialization agreement is manufactured by only one partner (the case with most such agreements), that partner receives the greater share of the output.

About 7% of all of the FRG's cooperative undertakings with the East involve agreements on joint production, while 16% involve specialization, making a total of 23%.

c) Only a small portion, 4.1%, of U.S. cooperative undertakings with the East involve coproduction. For the GDR no coproduction ventures exist, while the figure for the USSR is 1.5%. Coproduction is somewhat more common in relations with Hungary and Bulgaria (9.7% and 8.7%, respectively). More than one third (37.5%) of American coproduction agreements with the East are with Poland.

d) According to Hungarian statistics [8] 19% of all cooperative undertakings with the West in 1974 involved specialization, while 30% involved production sharing (a term which also evidently includes subcontracts).

e) According to Polish statistics [7] specialization agreements and coproduction made up 35% and 30% of all cooperative undertakings with the West.

Licensing Agreements [9, 10]

Licensing agreements are among the most important forms of East-West cooperation. A simple sale of licenses is not in itself an instance of cooperation, although experience has shown that in East-West relations licensing transactions are usually linked with additional agreements. Licensing agreements are often the first step toward further cooperative ventures: if, for example, the licenser continues to purchase the product manufactured by the licensee after the licensing fee has been paid off, the cooperative agreement becomes a subcontract.

a) The ECE report reserves the term cooperation only for those licensing agreements in which the licensing fee is paid at least partially in the products manufactured on the basis of the licenses in question. In 1972 28%, and in 1975 26%, of all East-West cooperative ventures stemmed from licensing agreements, and in 11% and 7%, respectively, of these the licenser also supplied components of the end product. Licensing agreements are the most important form of cooperative venture in Bulgaria and Czechoslovakia (in some of its agreements Czechoslovakia is apparently the licenser) and the second most important in Hungary, Poland, and Romania. The ECE statistics suggest that the USSR is not inter-

33

ested in licensing agreements; it evidently prefers deliveries of complete plants and scientific-technical cooperation as a means of technology transfer. These forms better fit the USSR notion of planning by directive, which as it now stands usually provides no room for direct contact between the Soviet enterprise and the foreign partner.

b) A study of U.S. cooperative undertakings with the East [4] contains detailed information on licensing agreements. About 48% of all American cooperative ventures are licensing agreements, with only about 8%[5] of all these providing for repayment with the product for which the license was obtained; half of the latter are with Poland. American firms are the licensers in 92%, and the licensees in only 8% of all licensing agreements, most of which are with the Soviet Union (Table 9). According to the U.S. study most of the licenses are granted directly to the Eastern countries by the American parent concern; the foreign subsidiary was involved in only twenty cases. It is noteworthy that there is even a greater preponderance of such direct licensing in projects.[6]

c) In a study on the FRG's cooperative ventures with the East [3], all licensing agreements are included that involve long-term collaboration; these make up 40% of all agreements. In most licensing agreements FRG firms are the licensers. Supplementary services are often tied to the sale of licenses; in 70% of the cases the East European partner is furnished the needed know-how in the form of additional documentation, and in 70% in the form of technical personnel. In 40% of all cases machinery is also supplied; in 70% the German licensers agree to pass on new development in the area of licenses to their Eastern European partners. In addition arrangements concerning quality control of the licensed product are included in 80% of licensing agreements.

In 80% of all such agreements it is stipulated that the licensing fee is to be paid in foreign exchange, usually in lump sums.[7] In about 20% of such agreements payment is made with the products manufactured under the license. In 50% of the agreements the quantity of the licensed product to be manufactured is limited. In about 70% the Eastern European licensee is authorized to export the product, although in most cases only to the other socialist countries. Among the FRG's Eastern European partners, Hungary is to a certain extent an exception: Hungarian firms are permitted in many cases to pay the license fee in licensed products, especially when the licenser is a small German firm.

34

d) In 1974 more than 40% of all cooperation agreements between Hungary and the West were licensing agreements (only those agreements stipulating payment in the licensed product were considered cooperative). For Poland this figure was only 10%.

Job Processing

It is debatable whether job processing is a form of East-West cooperation. In various agreements promoting cooperation (e.g., in the agreement between Hungary and the FRG), job processing within a long-term context is explicitly recognized as a form of cooperation. Job processing is a simple form of economic collaboration that can be a first step toward closer economic cooperation. At least 10% of FRG cooperation arrangements with the Eastern countries involve job processing (the actual proportion is most likely larger, since many firms do not regard job processing as a form of cooperation), with the principal weight in the machinery and electric industries. The Eastern European contractor is usually given the intermediate products and technical accessories by the Western principal; less often, machinery and personnel are provided. Payment for manufacturing is often made with a portion of the manufactured product [3].

There are two types of job processing: drawback and processing in bond. These are customs terms and need not correspond with the cooperative terms. In the case of drawback a producer is authorized to import foreign goods without payment of import duty (customs, import turnover tax) if they are used for a product that is to be reexported (for example, a new drive for a locomotive or cotton for textile fabric). In bond processing an enterprise is authorized to send goods abroad for processing (e.g., printing or finishing of fabric manufactured domestically) and then to reimport it; the import fees are then paid only on the additional value accrued from the processing, not on the total value of the item. In all countries permission must be obtained for job processing and is usually only granted under certain specified conditions.

Subcontracts

Subcontracts are another borderline case of cooperation. In many instances the only difference between subcontracts and job processing is that the former is more independent. In both cases a long-term contractual relationship must exist. For example, in agreements in which the Eastern partner manufactures automobile tires according to Western specifications (and perhaps by means of Western equipment and accessories), job processing is the right term when the manufacturer obtains the intermediate product from the principal; while subcontract is the correct term when the manufacturer himself procures the materials. Subcontracts also overlap with licensing, coproduction, and specialization agreements. Of the total number of East-West cooperative undertakings in 1972 and 1975, 8% and 7%, respectively, were subcontracts, with Romania showing the greatest preference for this form of cooperation. American cooperative undertakings with the East included 2.6% subcontracts, while the figure for Polish subcontracts with the West was 18%.

Supplying of Complete Plants

Supplying complete plants is not always counted as a form of cooperation.[8]

a) In the ECE study the term cooperation was reserved only for plant deliveries in which at least some of the repayment was made with products or parts manufactured by the plant. In addition this category includes predelivery project studies on the exploitation of natural resources and minerals and feasibility studies of various technological processes.

In 1972 12%, and in 1975 22%, of the total number of East-West cooperative ventures involved whole plant deliveries. The USSR and Romania were involved in most agreements of this kind. In these countries delivery of whole plants is the most important form of cooperation.

b) In the United States 32% of all cooperative undertakings were deliveries of turnkey plants; in only one of every three projects were U.S. firms the principal supplier. In most cases (43%) the partner was the USSR, followed by Poland and Romania.

Sales Cooperation

Agreements on sales cooperation are frequently tacked on to other already existing cooperative arrangements as addenda (licenses, specialization, etc.). Sales cooperation also includes joint publicity, market research, etc., usually in the country of the Western partner, often also in other Western third-party nations, and

less frequently in socialist countries. Cooperative sales undertakings independent of cooperative ventures in production usually
involve the utilization of the sales and service network and the
marketing knowledge of the Western partner. About 6% of the
FRG's cooperative arrangements involve sales. From time to
time joint sales promotion companies are formed in the Western
countries with capital participation by both the Western and Eastern partner.

Cooperation in Third Countries

Cooperation in third countries is often a joint venture for joint
sales (see Case Study 2 in Appendix I), so that overlaps with other
forms of cooperation are unavoidable.

The ECE report lists joint tendering of offers and joint projects
as a special form of cooperation; joint projects for customers
in third countries make up 7% of all cooperation agreements,
with Poland and Czechoslovakia being the main East European
countries involved. [9]

For the FRG, third country cooperative undertakings constitute
about 7% of all forms of cooperation with the East, especially in
the capital goods industry.

East-West cooperation with participation of the developing countries occupies a special place (see the fourth section of Chapter 7,
pp. 121-29). The collaboration of Eastern and Western firms in
projects in the developing countries in many cases enables various
problems (financing, repayment with the goods produced in the developing country, transfer of technology, management) to be solved
more easily than if either Western or Eastern enterprises were
involved alone. In FRG experience this "tripartite" cooperation is
still in the developing stages and is used almost exclusively in setting up joint plants in the developing countries.

Cooperation in Research and Development

Industrial cooperation in research and development is an important area of East-West cooperation and is preferred by the
Eastern nations. It is especially promoted by the Soviet Union, [10]
and in all major cooperative undertakings the State Committee for
Science and Technology of the USSR Council of Ministers (GKNT)
acts as the Soviet representative.

In 1972, 7% of all East-West cooperative agreements involved

industrial cooperation in research and development; this figure
was somewhat higher for FRG cooperative undertakings with the
Eastern countries (19%), reflecting the high esteem in which West
German research is held in Eastern Europe. FRG experience shows
a concentration of research and development cooperation on problems of applied production technology, although in both the FRG and
in the Eastern countries industrial enterprises engage occasionally
in basic research. In most cases research results are further developed in common; only very seldom is the objective the development of completely new technology. West German firms are usually willing to make larger material contributions than their Eastern partners to joint research projects; on the other hand, the number of West German experts on the joint research teams is usually less than the number supplied by the Eastern nations. West
German enterprises enter into cooperative undertakings in research and development with Eastern partners primarily for sales
reasons; of course, the utilization of Eastern European research
capacity plays some role, although not the primary one [13, 14].

Research and development is the subject of 11.5% of all U.S.
cooperative ventures with the East. In almost all cases the partner is the Soviet Union; there are almost no such undertakings
with the other Eastern nations.

Joint Ventures

Joint ventures (see Chapter 6) with participation of both Eastern and Western firms formerly could only be undertaken in
the Western country or in a third country. It was only a few
years ago that joint ventures became possible in Hungary and
Romania; in Yugoslavia the possibility has existed for some years.
Joint ventures in Western countries were usually established for
purposes of sales, marketing, and other services, and less frequently for joint production.

According to the findings of the ECE study, 15% of all East-West
cooperative undertakings in 1972 were joint ventures, of which about
two thirds (over 9%) were joint institutions founded in the West for
marketing products usually of East European origin. In 1975, 3%
of all agreements concerned joint ventures in production (other
joint ventures were not taken into account in 1975).

Joint ventures make up 6% of all the cooperative undertakings
of the FRG, and only 1.3% of all U.S. efforts. About 50% of American joint ventures were with Romania and Hungary.

38

Types of Cooperation

Summary

Considering the broad differences in the definition of cooperation used in the existing studies, only a very few general conclusions may be drawn: The most frequent form of cooperation in East-West relations are licensing agreements, although only a fraction of them can be considered genuine cooperation (i.e., with delivery of the licensed product in payment). Only one third of the agreements (for the United States even fewer) involved specialization and coproduction. The significance of joint ventures is still small; in most cases joint ventures are not built in the Eastern country. The FRG is a preferred partner of the Eastern countries in research and development cooperation thanks to its fine reputation.

Notes

1. The pipeline-natural gas agreements between Austria, the FRG, and the Soviet Union are also counted as cooperative undertakings, since there is a material connection between delivery and the goods supplied in payment.
2. In 1972 and 1975, 202 and 207, respectively, of 340 agreements registered (in both cases excepting Yugoslavia) were evaluated; in 1975 certain types of cooperation that had existed in 1972 (research and development, joint ventures involving no production arrangement) were eliminated. This restriction should not, however, notably impair the comparability of the 1972 and 1975 statistics.
3. Specialization and coproduction are defined differently in different studies; often no distinction at all is made between them [see 2, 3].
4. In the FRG, specialization agreements are also called "subcontractings," but the type of agreements meant here are not subcontracts in the sense used in this study (see the section on subcontracts, pp. 35-36).
5. The American study also includes licensing agreements, which are not ordinarily classified as cooperation.
6. There is very little information on the amount of the licensing fee, which can vary considerably depending on circumstances. In East-West cooperation in the machine-tool industry, figures ranging from 4 to 12% of the sales price of the licensed product have been quoted [11].
7. It should be borne in mind that in most Eastern European countries, foreign exchange transfers for licensing fees are taxed at a rate of 15-20%; a contract clause stipulating that the licensee shall assume this tax can be employed to avoid this expense.
8. See, e.g., the observation of the FRG ambassador in Poland, H. Ructe; "The ordering and construction of complete plants from Western countries, which are then paid for with products made in these same plants, cannot be called cooperation; it is rather a form of long-term compensation" [12].
9. Two percent of all East-West cooperative undertakings involve joint projects for clients in the country of the cooperating firms.

10. In Soviet terminology this form of cooperation is usually extended to include "designing and building prototypes."

References

[1] D. P. St. Charles, "East-West Business Arrangements: A Typology," in C. H. McMillan, ed., Changing Perspectives in East-West Commerce, Toronto-London, Lexington Books, 1974.

[2] ECE, Analytical Report on Industrial Co-operation Among ECE Countries, Geneva, United Nations, 1973.

[3] K. Bolz and P. Plötz, Erfahrungen aus der Ost-West-Kooperation, Hamburg, HWWA-Institut für Wirtschaftsforschung, 1974.

[4] The U.S. Perspective on East-West Industrial Co-operation (preliminary), Bloomington, International Development Research Center of Indiana University, Team of Researchers, June 1975.

[5] E. Kemenes, "Einige juristische und finanzielle Aspekte der industriellen Kooperation," Marketing in Ungarn, 1974, no. 3.

[6] ECE, "Preparations for the Second Meeting of Experts on Industrial Co-operation," Committee on the Development of Trade, TRADE/R. 320, Geneva, United Nations, August 26, 1975 (mimeographed).

[7] J. Olszynski, "Kooperacja przemysłowa Polski z wysoko rozwiniętymi krajami Europy Zachodniej," SGPiS, Zeszyty Naukowe, Warsaw, 1973, no. 94.

[8] F. Horchler, "The Future of Austro-Hungarian Foreign Trade," Forschungsberichte des Wiener Institutes für Internationale Wirtschaftsvergleiche, June 1975, no. 27.

[9] A. Wolf, "Licence Trade with CMEA States," Intereconomics, 1975, no. 11.

[10] B. Klümper and N. Leise, "Lizenzgeschäfte mit Staatshandelsländern," Forschungsbericht, no. 6, Hamburg, Institut für Aussenhandel und Überseewirtschaft, 1976.

[11] Die Presse, Vienna, November 12, 1974.

[12] Interview with H. Ruete, in Co-operation, 1975, no. 6, p. 20.

[13] W. Beitel, "Die wirtschaftlich-technische Kooperation aus sowjetischer Sicht," in G. Leptin, ed., Handelspartner Osteuropa, Berlin, Duncker & Humblot, 1974.

[14] K. H. Standke, "Technologischer Transfer und die Kooperation westlicher Industrieländer mit Ostmitteleuropa," in G. Leptin, ed., Handelspartner Osteuropa, Duncker & Humblot, Berlin, 1974.

4

Motives for cooperation

Expectations in East and West

Different levels and different motives of interest may be distinguished in East-West industrial cooperation. The interested parties are the various central state bodies and the enterprises imme-
diately concerned. The motives behind an interest in industrial
cooperation may be political, commercial policy, macro- or microeconomic considerations.

In the West government interests are as a rule clearly differentiated from enterprise interests. A government body usually
places political, trade, or national economic interests above the
interests of individual enterprises. There will often be conflicting
interests between different groups of enterprises. Export industries generally promote East-West cooperation, while branches of
industry that supply principally the domestic market, and hence
feel themselves threatened by counter-deliveries of Eastern European products stemming from cooperative agreements, will tend
to reject East-West cooperation. A conflict of interests occurs,
for example, on the question of easier import terms for cooperation products.

In the East the situation is more complicated. State ownership
of the means of production might lead one to suppose that an identity of interests existed at all levels of the economic and administrative apparatus. In reality, however, the Eastern European system has spawned a central administrative and economic planning
apparatus that claims to represent the state's interests; at the other
end of the scale is a network of economic enterprises. Differences of
interest may arise between these two domains.[1] The party agencies, whose function is to mediate between the various interests,
usually express the interests of those areas in which they function,
or they have their own vested interests.

Enterprise activity is steered in two ways: directly, by the terms of the plan, and indirectly, by a number of control instruments.[2] The enterprises respond to these prescribed conditions in a way designed to promote to the utmost the interests of the enterprise management, and perhaps the personnel in general, but which often runs counter to the intentions of the central authorities. An often criticized flaw here is that the enterprises consider their cardinal interest to lie in the fulfillment of quantitative planning indicators, which guarantees planned wage increases and management awards.

For this same reason, however, the enterprises often have no interest in the introduction of new, improved production procedures, since these initially mean only losses due to reorganization, so that in some situations improvements are simply a disadvantage to the enterprises. For this reason objectives such as a rise in productivity, cost reductions, the initiation or expansion of exports, etc., must often be taken care of by the central authorities, sometimes against the will of the enterprise. This problem is of major importance for East-West cooperation.

The following survey provides a rough picture of state and enterprise interests in the East and West in industrial cooperation between the two blocs with reference to motive.

Interest in East-West Cooperation

	East		West	
	state	enterprise	state	enterprise
Political motives	+ +	0	+ +	0
Commercial policy motives	+ + +	0	+ +	0
National economic policy motives	+ + +	0	+	0
Individual enterprise motives	+ +	±	+	+ +

+ + + Great interest.   − Negative interest.
 + + Moderate interest.   0 Not relevant.
  + Slight interest.

Political Motives

An analysis of the political interests of the East in industrial cooperation with the West must treat the USSR and the smaller Eastern European countries separately. Obviously, a few Eastern

European countries (Romania, Poland) attach some importance to the political aspects of cooperation with the West, since for them it means a greater degree of independence from the CMEA. Also, political détente means a better climate for increased trade with the West; this was easy to see at the Helsinki Conference for Security and Cooperation in Europe. In the case of the USSR considerations of power politics, e.g., catching up with and overtaking the capitalist West, cannot be ruled out. In general, however, the immediate political aspect of cooperation is not a major source of motivation for the East.

For the West the political component of East-West cooperation is of some importance. This interest may derive from:
— the assumption that political détente can be strengthened by broadening economic relations (this was the basic consideration in the Security and Cooperation Conference negotiations);
— the belief that political concessions can be wrested from the East in exchange for Western accommodation in the economic sphere;
— the pursuit of special political interests.

Motives of Commercial Policy

For the East trade matters, especially the abolition of quota restrictions and tariff barriers, are one of the most important reasons for cooperation [2]. With regard to quota restrictions the Eastern countries have for the most part achieved their objectives [3] (for nonliberalized items products of cooperative ventures are not subject to quantitative quotas in many countries); tariffs still remain a major obstacle, however. True, most of the Western countries (with the exception of the United States) have granted in agreements lower conventional tariffs to the Eastern countries (even those not GATT members), but the latter have not yet succeeded in overcoming the much-lamented customs barrier to integration (which by mid-1977 embraces paractically the whole of Western Europe). In this respect the position of the Eastern countries vis-à-vis Western Europe is the same as that of any other third country (United States, Japan). Trade objectives are also the reason behind the Eastern countries' efforts to get around the common commercial policy of the EEC by making long-term cooperation agreements with the individual EEC countries, thereby continuing to enjoy the advantages that previous bilateral trade agreements had offered.

Industrial Cooperation between East and West

The trade policy of the Western nations expects East-West cooperation to improve their ability to compete in the East; export interests are primarily concerned here, but lately the securing of (mainly Soviet) sources of raw materials and fuels has been a growing interest.

Soviet-Japanese cooperation in opening up the Soviet Far East should be seen in the light of Japanese efforts to obtain a source of raw materials and fuel [4]. In some countries (Canada) a prominent factor in the promotion of East-West cooperation is the desire for broader diversification in foreign trade. The individual EEC countries have used intergovernmental cooperation agreements to retain their hold on some independent instrument of commercial policy after the transfer of policy-making powers in questions of commercial relations to the respective EEC bodies.

National Economic Policy Motives

The East's national economic interests in the expansion of East-West cooperation might be summarized as follows:
— Stimulation of economic growth by broader participation in the international division of labor and by the use of modern Western technology and management methods; industrial cooperation seems to be the most effective way to import Western technology [5];
— Improvement in the balance of payments by procuring long-term capital and by expanding the production of goods that can replace imports or promote exports;
— Improvement of the branch and product structure.

In the West national economic objectives now play only a secondary role as a motive for promotion of East-West cooperation, in view of the relatively minor importance of Eastern trade (4% on the average). In some smaller countries that are relatively active in trade with the East (e.g., Austria and Finland), the expansion of cooperative relations with the Eastern countries could boost some branches of industry.

Individual Enterprise Motives

In the East (see pp. 48-53 in this chapter) both the enterprises and state agencies have comparable microeconomic interests in

cooperation. The reasons may be described as follows:
— Expansion of production, raising the technical level of production processes and of the product, and increasing productivity through the procurement of modern Western technology. This is probably the most important motive of the Eastern countries for cooperating with the West.
— The system of material incentives in the Eastern countries is often structured in such a way that enterprise managers are not interested in or even reject cooperation (which would perforce entail changes in the most diverse areas). The reason for this can be a general fear of novelty or even an actual worsening of efficiency indicators as a consequence of cooperation. In some situations conflicts may arise between an enterprise and the higher-level agency promoting cooperation agreements; enterprises which feel that such cooperative arrangements have been imposed on them are often dilatory or even remiss in carrying them out [6].

Many export enterprises in the smaller Eastern European nations dispose of a large part of their output in the Soviet Union. Export to the Soviet Union has been (at least so far) possible even if the product was of inferior quality and of a low technical level. Enterprises are therefore not very interested in cooperative agreements with the West, since they must expend a considerable amount of effort on development, care, and control for only a fraction of their output. The expectation that the Western partner will force the Eastern European enterprise to strive for higher product quality and a better accommodation to demand is one of the principal motives for cooperation in the East, although, to be sure, the bearer of this interest is a higher-level agency of the state rather than an enterprise.
— Easier access to Western markets through utilization of Western sales organizations; the enterprises are interested in cooperation to the extent that export is regarded as an explicit success criterion.

Western enterprises are mainly interested in East-West cooperation for the profit opportunities it offers. Most enterprises, however, are prepared to gear their calculations to a more distant future in view of the expected potential of the Eastern markets. The possibility of relieving the pressure of competition with other Western firms by means of cooperation also plays a role. Further reasons motivating Western firms to enter into cooperative arrangements with Eastern firms are:
— The opening up of new markets, not only in the partner country,

45

but also in the other CMEA countries, and even in the developing countries.

— Increasing one's own production capacity through the procurement of well-trained, relatively cheap labor either on a temporary (if the domestic plant is running at capacity) or long-term basis. Such solutions are especially attractive when there is a shortage of labor, e.g., no social burdens are involved, as there are when foreign labor is hired. Fixed costs (investments) can be transformed into proportional costs; hence the availment of an Eastern enterprise is often referred to as "obtaining an 'extended' work bench" [6].

— Access to Eastern technology and research potential, which often is brought into use only after great delay or not at all because of the cumbrousness of the planning system in these economies. Research results can sometimes be put to use quickly and flexibly by cooperation with a Western firm.

— The possibilities of product specialization and expansion of long runs, which means an increase in productivity and economies of scale.

A study of the motives of West German firms [7, 8] for entering into cooperative agreements with Eastern European partners showed sales objectives to be the most prominent reasons. Many enterprises openly stated that cooperation was the price one had to pay for achieving the more basic objective of greater sales. This attitude is frequently criticized by the Eastern European countries. West German firms have also often entered into a cooperation agreement in order to gain access to the market of a country with which they had had no previous contact or even to enter, with the help of an old partner in the East, markets in other socialist countires. In about 30% of the West German cooperation agreements, expansion of the existing market share has been the motive. License agreements with Eastern countries have had sales as the basic motive in as many as two thirds of the cases (opening up or expansion of market share).[3] In many cases license agreements must be concluded in order for a firm not to be pushed out of the market. Sales considerations also play a role in job processing.

Only about 30% of the FRG's cooperation agreements with the East have been motivated by a desire for "real" cooperation. In another 30% cost advantages, particularly lower labor costs in the Eastern countries, were important, especially in specialization agreements and job processing — as could be expected.

Further important factors motivating the cooperation of West

German firms with the Eastern countries are:
— utilization of the unused productive capacity of the Eastern
  European partner (job processing and specialization);
— making up for domestic shortage of labor;
— relief of bottlenecks in productive capacity;
— increase in the range of goods without increasing capacity;
— commercial utilization of one's own licenses (in 44% of the licensing agreements);
— utilization of the research and development potential and the
  know-how of the partner;
— reduction of delivery time;
— utilization of the sales network of the partner;
— no strike hazards in the Eastern countries; this eliminates one
  uncertainty factor affecting delivery time.
Obtaining a source of raw materials is usually only a secondary factor that shapes East-West cooperation in the FRG.

Specific Motives of the East

The Eastern countries see the following specific advantages in
industrial cooperation with the West:

Promotion of Exports from East to West

Although foreign trade had developed at a fast pace in both
West and East until the outbreak of the Western recession in 1974,
there was still a fundamental difference between the two economic
systems with regard to the driving force behind the movement of
foreign trade. In the West export is the active component in the
expansion of foreign trade and is often referred to as the engine
of growth. Competition forces market-oriented firms to expand
their sales, and often this can only be achieved with the help of
exports. In the planned economies, on the other hand, import is
the decisive component in foreign trade. In a recently published
study by a Czechoslovak trade journal it is noted that the study is
concerned with exports, "although the objective of foreign trade
is imports.... Exported products are rated primarily for their
ability to bring in a maximum of the foreign exchange needed to
pay for imported goods required by the nation's economy for the
planned satisfaction of social needs" [9].
Of course, the importance of imports is not entirely overlooked

in the West, nor are exports in the East; but the determining factors in the expansion of foreign trade are different in the two systems. The flow of goods from West to East is hence stimulated more forcefully than the flow in the opposite direction, thus leading to one of the most difficult problems of East-West trade: the imbalance in trade and payments. Industrial cooperation is intended to restore this balance.

Facilitation of Technology Transfer and Improvement in Efficiency

Although the Eastern European countries use a large portion of their national product for investments in plant and equipment and for outlays on research and development, the results achieved often are not commensurate with the funds expended. The economic efficiency of investments and research usually lags behind the corresponding parameters in the West [10, 11].

The translation of research results into practice has proven to be an especially unwieldy task (the innovation question). This is essentially a consequence of the centralized, predominantly administrative and directive system in a planned economy. Apart from major fields (armaments, space) and a few minor sectors of production, the Eastern countries are generally behind the developed Western industrial countries both technically and technologically. The reason for this is of course not only the low economic efficiency of investments and research but also the relatively backward situation from which the Eastern countries started: after World War II only the GDR and Czechoslovakia could be counted among the developed industrial nations.

In the early sixties the flaws in the existing system of management and planning in the Eastern countries had brought about structural and growth crises that led to the adoption of a series of economic reforms in these countries [12]. One way to stimulate growth, it was thought, was through the import of "technical progress" from the West, i.e., the import of highly developed industrial technology[4] in the form of machinery and equipment and licenses and patents [13].[5]

Expansion of these imports, however, was severely limited by balance-of-payments difficulties: exports of raw materials and food could not be substantially expanded by the Eastern countries because of their own increasing need; in many cases export of finished products was hindered by poor marketing and the inferior

Table 10

Enterprise's Evaluation of Own Product Quality,*
1974, in % of All Products

Industrial branch	meets standards fully	Measured against Western standards, the product does not meet standards of which,		
		total	meets about half of Western standards	meets only a few Western standards	totally inadequate

Industrial branch	meets standards fully	total	meets about half of Western standards	meets only a few Western standards	totally inadequate
Mechanical engineering	17.9	82.1	39.5	25.3	17.3
Consumer goods	26.0	74.0	34.4	22.6	17.0
Chemicals	27.8	72.2	40.3	17.4	14.5
Foodstuffs	31.3	68.7	29.7	23.5	15.5
Metallurgy	33.8	66.2	35.9	18.1	12.2
Industry total	24.3	75.7	36.7	22.9	16.1

Source: Business International, Eastern European Report No. 12, 1974, p. 186, in Hospodářské noviny, Prague
*Managers from Hungary, CSSR, and Poland.

quality of the products offered by the Eastern nations. Poor quality was the most serious obstacle: Table 10 shows how managers from Hungary, Czechoslovakia, and Poland assessed the quality of products manufactured in their own firms in 1974. Only 23.3% of the products conformed to Western standards, 36.7% of the products met half of the Western standards, and 22.9% met only a few standards; 16.1% were totally unacceptable. Eastern European metallurgical products did best, while the products of the engineering industry were rated the worst.

Another difficulty in the import of technical progress (mainly of licenses and know-how) arose in the translation of the technology and procedures thus acquired into production, which sometimes took a long time.

This problem may be illustrated with the case of Poland [15, 16]. From 1948 through 1970 Poland acquired 227 licenses for technological procedures and designs from Western countries (with almost one third of this number falling in the period from 1966 to 1970). From 1971 to 1973 another 126 licenses were acquired. In 1970, 182 licenses were in force, with 131 in heavy industry and the engineering and chemical industry. The foreign exchange spent for license imports between 1948 and 1970 amounted to 1.6 billion zlotys. According to Polish figures only 5% of this outlay went to pay for the licenses, while 80% was spent for the import of capital goods needed to make use of the licenses. The share of licensed production in Polish total industrial production was 3.1% in 1970 (1.3% in 1966). Only 112 (62%) of the 182 licenses legally valid in 1970 were actually used in production; the time elapsed between the acquisition of the license and actual production start-up was two years for 40%, more than three years for 33%, and more than six years for 2% of the licenses; in 1969 this time reached more than six years for 8% of all the licenses (see Tables 11 and 12). In 1970 only the products resulting from 32% of the licenses in force were exported. We should call attention here to one aspect of technology transfer to which the Eastern states have so far paid inadequate attention. Technology transfer involves considerable costs in addition to expenditures for machinery and licensing fees; for example, the costs involved in the adaptation of technological processes, etc. These costs ran between 11% and 59% (average 36%) for machinery and electric equipment, between 2% and 22% (average 10%) of total costs in the chemical industry and for oil refineries in twenty-six American case studies of international technology transfer [17].

Poland obtained the majority of its licenses before 1970 from

Motives for Cooperation

Table 11

Poland's Licensing Agreements with Western Nations, 1966-70

	End of 1966		End of 1970		Increase,* 1966-70	
	number	in %	number	in %	number	in %
Valid licenses, total	87	100	182	100	+ 95	+ 109.2
Of which, from:						
Great Britain	26	30	48	26	+ 22	+ 84.6
FRG	19	22	38	21	+ 19	+ 100.0
Italy	8	9	19	10	+ 11	+ 137.5
France	7	8	18	10	+ 11	+ 157.1
Switzerland	6	7	14	8	+ 8	+ 133.3
Others	21	24	45	25	+ 24	+ 114.3
Used:						
in production	52	60	112	62	+ 60	+ 115.4
in production and export	–	–	64	32	–	

Source: W. Brzost, "Podstawowe cele i warunki realizacji polityki licencyjnej Polski w latach 1966-70," SGPIS, Zeszyty Naukowe (Warsaw), 1973, no. 94.
*Net increase, i.e., after subtraction of expired license agreements.

Table 12

Time Required for Start-up and Period of Validity
of Licenses from Western Countries in Poland, 1966-70

	End of 1966	End of 1970
	share in %*	
Time between acquisition of license and production start-up		
1 year	31	37
2 years	27	40
3 - 5 years	38	21
6 - 10 years	4	2
Period of validity of licenses		
4 years or fewer	3.8	9.8
5 - 7 years	15.4	25.9
8 - 10 years	42.3	35.7
Over 11 years	13.5	14.3
Unlimited	25.0	14.3

Source: W. Brzost, "Podstawowe cele i warunki realizacji polityki licencyjnej Polski w latach 1966-70," SGPIS, Zeszyty Naukowe (Warsaw), 1973, no. 94.
*In total number of licenses valid in each year.

Great Britain and the FRG. Since 1966 the pattern has changed
little. It is interesting that, according to Polish calculations, there
were differences in the number of licenses actually put to use depending on the country of origin: in 1970 an average of 62% of existing licenses were actually in use in production; for British licenses this figure was 67%; for West German and French licenses,
76%; but for Swiss licenses, only 43%. There were also differences
in the export of licensed products: in 1970 the proportion of licenses
for which the licensed product was also exported was 32% as an
overall average: 45% for German and French licenses, 39% for
British licenses, but only 14% to 13% for Swiss and Italian licenses.

This Polish example illustrates problems with putting the acquired technical know-how to actual practical use that perhaps exist to an even greater extent in the other Eastern countries. In
1967 Bulgaria obtained a license from the Kassbohrer Company for
Setra buses, including know-how, diverse equipment, and two prototypes. Five years were required before actual production was begun. The Romanian head of state and party leader Ceausescu called
attention in May 1974 to the case of an enterprise in Brasov that obtained a license for a motor. Production was scheduled to begin in
1970 or 1971 but was delayed until 1974 [18]. Czechoslovakia purchased forty licenses in 1972 (40% for the machine-building industry). The central Czechoslovak authorities reprimanded some enterprises for acquiring licenses without bothering about the machinery and equipment necessary to use the licenses. The gap between the acquisition of licenses and their use runs to four years
or more in many cases [19].

One possible way to overcome these problems, it is thought, is
industrial cooperation with the West. The interest of the Western
partner in the success of the cooperative undertaking is supposed
to accelerate technology transfer from West to East, make it cheaper, improve it, and streamline it [20, 21]. To achieve this objective the Eastern countries are ready to make concessions, but they
sometimes expect too much from their Western partners. Industrial cooperation should presumably also make it easier to solve
the balance-of-payments aspect of technology transfer.

For Western enterprises participating in Eastern cooperative
ventures, it is their own prospects rather than the expectations of
the Eastern nations that are the decisive factor.[6] For example, if
payment of the license fee is contractually stipulated in the form
of product payback, there is always the risk that the start of delivery
will be delayed, or even that product quality will be poor. If a license

contract for ten years with royalties is signed, then if production is begun only after five years (instead of the usual period of one or two years), the returns for the licenser are substantially reduced. The situation after expiration of the license period should be precisely defined in the contract. It should be pointed out that between 1966 and 1970 the percentage of agreements with short periods of validity (four to five or seven years) between Poland and the West rose substantially, while the number of agreements without any time limit decreased from 25% to 14.3% (see Table 12).

Notes

1. The realization that differences in interests and even conflicts also exist in the socialist societies, and that in the economy these can best be overcome by means of market relations, was one of the basic notions of O. Šik's design for reform in Czechoslovakia. See [1].

2. Prices, taxes, interest, etc. are included.

3. The prospect of assured Hungarian counterdeliveries was a motivating factor for cooperation only in licensing agreements with Hungary.

4. Industrial technology is defined as the sum of processes by means of which raw materials and semifinished products are transformed into a final product. Its constituent elements are: (a) capital goods (plant, machinery, and equipment); (b) modern intermediate goods (e.g., plastics); (c) procedures; (d) information, either technical (e.g., patents, licenses, know-how) or commercial; (e) trained labor; (f) final products.

5. The Eastern countries had purchased a total of 1,700 licenses from the West between 1960 and 1973 (almost three fourths of them from multinational firms) [14].

6. For the problem of license trade with the East see [22]. The license trade with the East is obviously important for only a few Western enterprises; income from license fees from the Eastern countries amounted to only 3.1% of the total income from that source in 1973 in the FRG; for the German MAN Company, however, this figure was 30% [23].

References

[1] O. Šik, Ökonomie — Interessen — Politik, Berlin (DDR), Dietz-Verlag, 1966.

[2] V. Vetrov and V. Kazakevich, in Vneshniaia torgovlia, 1972, no. 11, cited in "Mitteilung der Kommission an den Rat," in cooperation agreements between countries of the Community and the Eastern European countries, Europe-Dokumente, Brussels, no. 766, October 23, 1973.

[3] ECE, "A Review of East-West Commercial Policy Developments, 1968 to 1973," Economic Bulletin for Europe, vol. 25, Geneva, United Nations, 1974.

[4] J. Stankovsky, "Japans wirtschaftliche Beziehungen zur UdSSR und Ost-

europa," in A. Lemper, ed., Japan in der Weltwirtschaft, Munich, Weltforum-Verlag, 1975.

[5] E. Hewett, "The Economics of East European Technology Imports from the West," American Economic Review, May 1975.

[6] W. von Lingelsheim-Seibicke, Kooperation mit Unternehmen in Staatshandelsländern Osteuropas. Eine Einführung in die Praxis, Cologne, Deutscher Wirtschaftsdienst, 1974.

[7] The following statements are mainly from K. Bolz and P. Plötz, Erfahrungen aus der Ost-West-Kooperation, Hamburg, HWWA-Institut für Wirtschaftsforschung, 1974.

[8] C. H. McMillan and D. P. St. Charles, Joint Ventures in Eastern Europe: A Three Country Comparison, Montreal, Canadian Economic Policy Committee, 1974.

[9] J. Jezbera, "Efektivnost vývozu a optimalisace," Zahraniční obchod (Prague), 1975, no. 7, p. 19.

[10] V. Nešvera, Investitionen in Österreich und in der Tschechoslowakei, Vienna, Studien über Wirtschafts- und Systemvergleiche, vol. 1, 1971.

[11] J. Kosta, H. Kramer, and J. Sláma, Der technologische Fortschritt in Österreich und in der Tschechoslowakei, Vienna, Studien über Wirtschafts- und Systemvergleiche, vol. 2, 1971.

[12] ECE, "Institutional Changes," Economic Survey of Europe in 1968, chap. II, 2, New York, United Nations, 1969.

[13] P. J. Nichols, "Western Investment in Eastern Europe: the Jugoslav Example," in Joint Economic Committee, Congress of the United States, Reorientation and Commercial Relations of the Economies of Eastern Europe, Washington, U.S.G.P.O., 1974.

[14] J. Wilczynski, Multinational Corporations and the East-West Technological and Economic Relations, Manuscript, 1975.

[15] W. Brzost, "Podstawowe cele i warunki realizacji polityki licencyjnej Polski w latach 1966-1970," SGPiS, Zeszyty Naukowe (Warsaw), 1973, no. 94.

[16] Business International, Eastern Europe Report, 1974, no. 1.

[17] E. Mansfield, "International Technology Transfer: Forms, Resource Requirements, and Policies," American Economic Review, May 1975.

[18] Neue Zürcher Zeitung, July 27, 1974.

[19] ZVO-Informationen, CSSR, Information Bulletin of Siemens AG (Red. v. Heyking), Munich, December 1973.

[20] R. Campbell and P. Marer, ed., East-West-Trade and Technology Transfer, Bloomington, Indiana University, 1974.

[21] S. Wasowski, ed., East-West-Trade and the Technology Gap. A Political and Economic Appraisal, New York, 1970.

[22] A. Wolf, "Licence Trade with CMEA States," Intereconomics, 1975, no. 11.

[23] Blick durch die Wirtschaft, July 5, 1973, cited in A. Wolf, "Licence Trade with CMEA States," Intereconomics, 1975, no. 11.

5

Legal and institutional regulations for interfirm cooperation between East and West in Eastern Europe

General Legal Status of Interfirm East-West Cooperation

In Chapter 3 it was pointed out that most types of East-West cooperation consisted in a lasting, contractually agreed, functional collaboration. The relations between the parties in a cooperative undertaking are institutionalized only if there is capital participation [1]. In these cases it has proved necessary to secure these institutionalized relations by establishing a set of specific legal regulations for them (see Chapter 6).

All functional forms of East-West cooperation (without capital participation) entail a bundle of reciprocal or complementary deliveries of goods and/or services which from the legal standpoint may be regarded as a series of independent contracts or agreements. Some Eastern European countries, including the USSR, have therefore not felt it necessary to establish specific legislation for cooperative arrangements between enterprises. In principle the legal provisions governing foreign trade in general and trade with the Western market economies in particular apply to such cases [2].

Where the commitments assumed in a cooperation agreement consist wholly or in part of services (e.g., licenses, patents, trademarks), the relevant provisions for the legal protection of intellectual property and its cession against compensation apply. Since in most instances transfrontier deliveries of goods and services entail payment in foreign exchange or bilateral clearing, the legal provisions regulating foreign exchange transactions and bilateral settlement are applicable here as well. If the transfrontier transaction also requires the procurement of credit, the pertinent legal regulations apply as well to cooperative deliveries. The same holds for customs and tax regulations to the extent that no special customs or tax concessions have been made for goods exchanged as a part of cooperative undertakings. All other legal provisions (e.g., health regulations, standards, and norms) applicable to transfrontier commodity traffic also apply to deliveries made as part of cooperative undertakings.

In view of the scope and complexity of these regulations, which moreover vary from country to country, we shall have to limit our discussion to an elucidation of general legal and organizational institutions; in the final section of this chapter we shall take up in more detail the specific legal norms that have been worked out in some Eastern European countries to apply exclusively to East-West cooperative undertakings.

Legal and Organizational Principles in the Foreign Trade of the Eastern Nations

The Foreign Trade Monopoly

One of the most important organizational principles in the foreign trade of the CMEA nations is the state foreign trade monopoly. The organizational forms and the methods and means for the exercise of state control have undergone changes with time, and marked differences exist from country to country. In almost all the Eastern nations, the foreign trade monopoly has undergone a series of decentralizations and recentralizations. As the CMEA nations became more broadly integrated into the international division of labor, the tendency was to give a broader interpretation to the concept of foreign trade monopoly.

According to earlier, now somewhat obsolete definitions,[1] the state monopoly over foreign trade defines a legal situation in which all matters of foreign trade belong to the sovereign right of the state, which by means of planning manages and controls a country's entire foreign trade [4]. The state derives its monopoly on foreign trade from the state ownership of the social means of production.

Foreign Trade Planning

Just as the activities of state-owned production enterprises are steered by the central economic plan, so foreign trade is also shaped in its broad contours by this plan. The plan for foreign trade, for which the ministry of foreign trade is responsible, is an integral part of the national economic plan, into which it is integrated by means of the planned balance of foreign trade worked out by the planning office [5]. The decentralization measures that have been undertaken over the course of time in several Eastern countries have also brought about changes in the scope and content of the foreign trade plan, with marked differences sometimes emerging from country to country. In general, however, this plan sets targets in terms of quantity and value for the most important raw materials, fuels, energy, the major agricultural products and foodstuffs, and the basic consumer goods that must be imported or exported [6]. It does the same for capital goods, such as equipment for new or modernized plants, and for the most important machinery. Total import and export volumes are also planned and expressed in terms of foreign exchange. Most Eastern countries no longer use the former customary territorial breakdown by individual countries. A general territorial subdivision, distinguishing between the developed market economies, the developing countries, and the socialist countries (including CMEA members), is, however, needed; first, because the national currencies are not convertible, and hence separate trade and payments balances must be planned for these three groups of countries; and second, because in coordinating the middle-term five-year plans of the CMEA nations, binding delivery and procurement commitments must be made in long-term trade agreements and annual protocols [7, 8]. Through its various directives and communiqués, the ministry of foreign trade enjoins those enterprises authorized by special permission to engage in foreign trade to hold their foreign trade transactions within the framework provided by the foreign trade plan. Nonetheless, considerable discrepancies constantly occur between foreign trade activities and plan intentions.

Organizations Authorized to Engage in Foreign Trade

For its foreign trade operations, the state employs specialized foreign trade organizations empowered exclusively to undertake such activities. Just as the state-owned producing enterprises administer through their management the resources placed at their disposal, although those resources still remain state property, the specialized foreign trade organizations, supplied by the state with the appropriate financial and material resources, exercise their activities in the name of the state and in accordance with the tasks and objectives stipulated in the foreign trade plan. At the time a foreign trade organization is formed, the activities in which it shall engage and the particular articles and groups of articles for which it is to be exclusively responsible are specified. Originally a specific item or group of items could be exported or imported only by a specific foreign trade organization. According to the traditional conception of foreign trade, such a foreign trade organization was legally totally separated from the enterprises producing the exported item or receiving the imported commodity. In that system the prices at which the foreign trade organization delivers abroad or purchases from abroad had no direct relation to the state-controlled domestic prices. Under such conditions the outstanding balances arising out of differences between domestic and foreign prices and costs had to be offset centrally in the state budget.

This function of protecting domestic production and trade enterprises from foreign influence and foreign competition was one of the principal reasons for creating the foreign trade monopoly.

The foreign trade organizations are independent legal entities that may take various legal forms, such as state-owned enterprises, cooperatives, joint stock companies, or limited companies. Whatever the case, they may enter into contractual commitments for which they are liable up to the sum of funds placed at their disposal. The state itself cannot be made liable for the actions and commitments of a foreign trade organization, which can only exercise its activities within the framework of the concessions that have been granted to it; actions at variance with the stipulated activities have no legal force [2, 4].

The strict separation between the domestic economy and foreign operations has been modified over time in a number of different ways, with considerable differences from country to country. The former defensive and protective function they exercised within a predominantly autarkic growth model has been transformed into an offensive function, and the most important task of the foreign trade monopoly has become the expansion of exports to make possible the import of capital goods, technology, and licenses.

This changed function of foreign trade necessitated corresponding changes in the organizational forms and the legal and economic institutions of the state foreign trade monopoly. Under certain circumstances, and after obtaining the required permission, production enterprises in some Eastern countries may now also participate in foreign trade. Producer associations, such as the associations of state-owned enterprises in the GDR, or industrial concerns in Romania, or important enterprises and combines, are also authorized, along with the existing foreign trade enterprises, to export their products themselves. In other cases producers can select their own foreign trade organization, which then engages in foreign trade transactions on commission on behalf and on the account of the producer. Sometimes competition between foreign trade organizations may arise. In some cases producers are able to join to form their own foreign trade companies (joint stock or limited). In all cases the state, as representative of the foreign trade monopoly, reserves the right to grant permission for these ventures [9, 10].

Internal Conversion Factors

The strict separation between domestic and foreign prices has been considerably lessened in most CMEA countries (Bulgaria, Hungary, Poland, Czechoslovakia, and to a certain extent, the GDR in the export sector). These countries now use separate internal conversion factors for the market economies (dollar area) and for the CMEA countries (ruble area). These conversion factors have nothing in common with the official exchange rates; they reflect the average reproduction cost of the domestic currency in foreign transactions [11, 12, 13, 14, 15]. The reproduction cost, on which conversion factors are based, is computed from the ratio between the proceeds obtained for the total exports in dollars or rubles and the corresponding sum at wholesale prices (price at factory) in domestic currency. It is worth noting that in using the conversion factors, the dollar ratio is set much higher than the ruble ratio, although in the official exchange rate the ruble is rated higher than the dollar [7, 15].[2] Eastern European experts explain this discrepancy by the wider area of use of the freely convertible dollar as compared with the transferable ruble.

Now producers generally obtain a sum, calculated in domestic currency by means of the conversion factors, for their exported goods or pay for their imported goods a sum in domestic currency corresponding to the foreign sales price after conversion. In view of the extremely variable profitability of different items and groups of items (a consequence of long-term officially pegged prices set without regard to changes in costs), additional subsidies are sometimes attached to the conversion factors, and in some countries (Czechoslovakia) imposts are levied.

These circumstances have given rise to multiple shadow exchange rates intended to protect many producers from unfair, undeserved losses in converting to the new accounting procedure (or in the contrary case, to obviate windfall gains). These multiple shadow exchange rates were introduced with the intention of ultimately establishing more uniform internal exchange rates by gradually reducing the subsidies or imposed deductions. This intention was never realized, in particular because of broad price fluctuations in world trade.

In order to understand the complicated conversion system, it must be borne in mind that the factor prices are for the most part pegged for the long term by the state, so that the cost structure is extremely inelastic, and business costs can essentially be reduced only through rationalization measures. The close connection between the domestic economy and foreign prices is intended to induce the producers to improve the structure of production and shape exports more in accordance with demand. In a similar fashion foreign prices should influence business costs and in this way force the producer to be more cost conscious in decision-making. These intentions had, however, to be abandoned as a result of the Western inflation explosion of the last few years. The imported goods, especially raw materials and fuels but also machinery and equipment, had to be increasingly subsidized to somewhat shield the domestic price structure from Western inflation. The increasing burden of subsidies is now, however, forcing most of the CMEA countries to raise their industrial selling prices for the 1976-80 five-year period.

Other Regulations

In settlement and payment transactions with the West, all the Eastern countries converted, with few exceptions, from bilateral clearing systems to settlements in Western currencies as a result of the above-mentioned changes. Still each state retains control through binding foreign exchange payment plans and special foreign exchange control arrangements made necessary because the currencies of the Eastern European countries are not convertible [18].

Finally, we should say something about the legal provisions that enable foreign firms to establish a representative in Eastern European countries. Before 1974 only domestic firms could represent Western countries, except in Romania. Foreign firms hoped that they would be able to establish contact more easily with potential customers by setting up their own representative. In the last two years all the Eastern European countries have permitted foreign firms to set up their own missions. Ordinarily the mission can only perform marketing activities, such as giving out information about their products, services, prices, and contractual regulations, and find out about the desires of their prospective customers. The mission is not, however, authorized to conclude specific trade transactions [19, 20, 21, 22, 23].

In contrast to most of the other Eastern countries, the USSR has retained the original system of foreign trade monopoly with exclusive specialized foreign trade organizations and a strict separation between domestic and foreign prices. Even the Soviet Union, however, deals in the currency of the Western partner country in its foreign trade transactions [24].

Special Legal Provisions for Industrial Cooperation

Only Czechoslovakia and Bulgaria have worked out a legal framework specifically for transfrontier industrial cooperation.

Czechoslovakia

The Czechoslovak law on procedures for the conclusion of agreements on economic cooperation with foreign countries [25] deals mainly with the procedure for obtaining permission. In contrast to most foreign trade transactions, not only a foreign trade organization but also any Czechoslovak economic organization can, after obtaining permission, become a party to a transfrontier cooperation agreement. These agreements are on cooperation in production, including scientific-technical cooperation, and collaboration in the specialization of production programs. The foreign partner may be either a physical or a legal person. The law makes no distinction between foreigners from capitalist countries and foreigners from socialist countries; it is therefore applicable to cooperation agreements with CMEA partners and to East-West cooperative undertakings.

Cooperation agreements concluded without prior permission from the competent central authorities are invalid. Permission is given by the authorities (federal or republic)[3] controlling the organization that wants to conclude a transfrontier cooperation agreement. Cooperative organizations must obtain permission from the central cooperative authority. Before the competent authorities can grant permission for the conclusion of a cooperation agreement, it must be approved by the federal ministries for Foreign Trade, Investments and Technical Development, and Finances and by the

Czechoslovak State Bank. The competent authorities also decide on the form the contemplated agreement should take. Czechoslovak organizations may also form associations and consortia for the purpose of transfrontier cooperative undertakings.

An official permission to conclude a cooperation agreement does not automatically include permission to engage in foreign trade transactions, nor does it obviate the permission procedure required by the Law on Foreign Exchange Control [26, 27]. If the cooperation agreement is for goods deliveries to or from Czechoslovakia, the competent foreign trade organization, or a producer organization with equivalent powers, is responsible for its implementation. On petition the federal minister of foreign trade can grant a special arrangement to enable the Czechoslovak partner itself to effect the exports and imports provided for in the cooperation agreement. In certain cases the federal government may also permit simplification of the permission procedure.

The law as a whole is restrictive; in no place does it mention the need for the central authorities to promote cooperation agreements.

The federal Ministry for Finances has, however, issued an internal directive dealing with the principles governing the use of economic steering instruments in foreign trade for the period from 1973 to 1975, and in that directive it allows for certain tax concessions in cooperation agreements [28]. When in the course of especially effective exports — made under a cooperative agreement — favorable prices are obtained, which under generally applicable regulations are subject to special tax levies (see pp. 59-60 in this chapter), then the levies are reduced by 20%. In order to discourage cooperative exports at unfavorable prices, the same internal ministerial directive also limits subsidies to 25% for exports to socialist countries and to 20% for exports to capitalist countries. Czechoslovak organizations that achieve favorable export results as a part of cooperative undertakings receive additional bonuses for an increase in their export performance and for improving the reproduction cost ratio. These bonuses, when they are obtained with exports made as part of international cooperation agreements, are 50% higher than bonuses on normal export transactions.

Toward the end of 1975 Czechoslovakia showed signs of wanting to begin active promotion of cooperation with the West. In October 1975 the Czechoslovak government, in a resolution by the Council of Ministers, adopted a set of guidelines for the further development of economic cooperation with nonsocialist countries [29].

A study done prior to this government decision found that the unsatisfactory cooperative relations that had heretofore existed with Western firms were linked, in particular, to the existing planning and management system. It was pointed out that central planning and its methods created obstacles to the conclusion of cooperative agreements. The system of foreign exchange control is a further obstacle, while the mode of financing and taxing foreign trade activity makes the conclusion of cooperative contracts between firms unattractive. The permission procedure is also too complicated. It is understandable, therefore, that enterprises have not shown much interest in East-West cooperation. The steering bodies themselves have placed too little emphasis on East-West cooperation. The study then goes on to discuss the lack of a broad program for the development of East-West cooperation. The guidelines adopted in the government resolution are intended to eliminate these institutional obstacles.

In the resolution it is stated that East-West cooperation should serve primarily to step up technical progress and innovation. In particular the complex and long-term character of cooperative relations is stressed. Thus it is provided that for every cooperation agreement a special bank account is to be opened in the Czechoslovak Trade Bank (CSOB); its net balance is carried forward annually, and its foreign exchange funds are available for use throughout the entire duration of the cooperative agreement. Whereas exports and imports ensuing from the agreement should balance one another for the overall duration of the agreement, this need not be the case at any given time, in which case the bank must be prepared to provide the necessary stopgap credits. In special cases the stipulation requiring exports to balance imports may be waived.

The guidelines on cooperation adopted by the government also modify certain planning procedures in order to give domestic economic organizations a more flexible position in meeting the commitments of the agreement. The guidelines also specify other improvements in the use of financial steering instruments. The foreign trade organization Fincom and the Czechoslovak Chamber of Commerce have been given new responsibilities regarding the furnishing of information and services to promote cooperative undertakings. Industrial management board boards were given until the end of April 1976 to work out proposals setting forth concise concepts of cooperation for individual branches of industry (within the 1976-80 five-year plan). Through these measures the Czechoslovak government hopes to create the foundations for a long-term and active policy of cooperation with the West.

Bulgaria

Bulgarian legal measures governing agreements concerning trans-frontier economic, productive, and technical cooperation with foreign legal and physical persons are, in contrast to the Czechoslovak laws, geared primarily to the promotion of such agreements [30, 31]. A government resolution confirms the right of Bulgarian economic organizations to conclude contracts on economic cooperation in production and technology with firms in nonsocialist countries for the purpose of long-term joint activities of common interest and for mutual benefit [32]. As an incentive to economic organizations to enter into such agreements, favorable conditions are created through planning, financing and credits, and customs regulations.

Cooperation is permitted in the following areas (the list is not restrictive):

— utilization of licenses, technical data, know-how, exchange of technical information, etc.;
— delivery of factory equipment or complete assembly lines;
— agreements on specialization in the construction of particular types of machinery and equipment in accordance with specific plans and joint sale of these products in third countries;
— joint construction and sale of individual machines, equipment, and their components, as well as other types of industrial output in the chemical, foodstuffs, or light industries;
— subcontracting;
— joint delivery and installation of plant and equipment;
— joint construction and joint use of plant outside Bulgaria.

It is specified that payments between the cooperating countries be effected either wholly or in part through reciprocal deliveries of goods and services or with funds acquired in the process of fulfilling the terms of the contract. The legal regulations pertain to activities in industry, construction, agriculture, transport, tourism, trade, credits, and services associated with the cooperative undertaking.

Cooperation agreements are concluded from the Bulgarian side by the pertinent economic organization and the associated foreign trade organization after receipt of permission from the competent bodies appointed by the Council of Ministers.

Application for permission must be submitted together with a draft of the contract, a technical and economic analysis of the cooperative undertaking, and arguments demonstrating its efficiency and spelling out in detail the contractual commitments. The activities specified in the agreement are then incorporated into the plans of the economic organizations by the State Planning Committee and the competent branch ministries, and the required funds for investments, materials, salaries, and wages are allocated to the organization by the plan. If an agreement is concluded after the planning work for the current year has been terminated, the funds are furnished from the plan reserves or obtained through bank loans. Special credit terms may be granted within the limits of existing legislation.

Other Eastern Countries

The other Eastern countries have not established any special legal framework for East-West cooperation apart from certain regulations for joint ventures in Romania and Hungary (see Chapter 6).

The Hungarian law on foreign trade contains only the proviso that in cooperative undertakings in production or in specialization agreements, economic organizations without authorization to engage in foreign trade, as well as those enterprises with such authorization, may participate in the preparation and conclusion of such contracts [20].

The situation in the USSR is different from that in the other Eastern countries: as a rule no direct cooperation agreements between producing enterprises and Western firms are permitted. This role is fulfilled principally by the Soviet State Committee for Science and Technology of the Council of Ministers (Russian abbreviation GKNT); in the seventies this body became the official agency for foreign trade relations, especially East-West cooperation.

The committee's broad range of responsibilities is geared toward effecting a uniform state policy in scientific-technical progress, to which end it plans, organizes, and coordinates important scientific problems and seeks to establish foreign contacts for effecting scientific-technical cooperation. Given this dual set of responsibilities, the committee has a say in the development and introduction of new machinery, plant, procedures, and materials; it also acquires thereby an appreciable influence on the import decisions of the Soviet foreign trade associations.

If the Soviet Union desires closer cooperation in some particular area, the committee may conclude a cooperation agreement with a foreign firm. When necessary, the foreign firm is also accorded representative status in Moscow [33].

Notes

1. "In the USSR all foreign trade operations are concentrated in the hands of a specialized state agency . . . and are carried out in accordance with the state export and import plans, which are themselves an inseparable part of the national economic plan" [3].
2. Before the 1971 dollar devaluation, a ruble was worth 40 forints in Hungary, 18.60 Kčs in Czechoslovakia, while a dollar brought 60 forints and 31.39 Kčs [16]. The dollar devaluation led to a reduction of the rate to 43.5 forints in Hungary at the end of 1974 [17], and to 40.6 forints at the end of 1977.
3. Czechoslovakia is a federation consisting of the Czech and Slovak republics and is administered by a federal government and by the two republic governments and their agencies.

References

[1] D. P. St. Charles, "East-West Business Arrangements: A Typology," in C. H. McMillan ed., Changing Perspectives in East-West Commerce, Toronto-London, Lexington Books, 1974.

[2] R. Starr, "Evolving Patterns of East-West Business Transactions: Introductory Note on Cooperation Agreements," and "Introductory Note on Contracting with Enterprises in State-Planned Economies," in R. Starr ed., East-West Business Transactions, New York-London, Praeger Publishers, 1974.

[3] Politická ekonomie (Prague), 1955 (Czech translation from the Russian), p. 533.

[4] M. Selucká, "Erosion of Monopolistic Position of Eastern European Foreign Trade Enterprises: Legal Aspects," in C. H. McMillan ed., Changing Perspectives in East-West Commerce, Toronto-London, Lexington Books, 1974.

[5] T. Morva, "Planning in Hungary," in M. Bornstein ed., Economic Planning, East and West, Cambridge, Mass., 1975.

[6] K. Porvit, "Planning in Poland," in M. Bornstein ed., Economic Planning, East and West, Cambridge, Mass., 1975.

[7] V. Přibyl and J. Šťouračová, "Řízení vnějších ekonomických vztahů v zemích RVHP," Politická ekonomie (Prague), 1974, no. 1.

[8] Comprehensive Programme for the Further Extension and Improvement of Co-operation and the Development of Socialist Economic Integration by the CMEA Member Countries, Section 6, Moscow, CMEA Secretariat, 1971.

[9] ECE, "Recent Changes in the Organization of Foreign Trade in the Centrally Planned Economies," Economic Bulletin for Europe, vol. 24, no. 1, New York, United Nations, 1973.

[10] I. Apostolov and Y. Laskov, "The People's Republic of Bulgaria"; K. Herman, "The Czechoslovak Socialist Republic"; J. Varro, "The Hungarian People's Republic"; K. Grzybowski, "The Polish People's Republic"; J. A. Burgess, "The Socialist Republic of Romania," in R. Starr ed., East-West Business Transactions, New York-London, Praeger Publishers, 1974.

[11] ECE, "Institutional Changes," Economic Survey of Europe in 1968, chap. 11, 2, New York, United Nations, 1969.

[12] A. Zwass, Monetary Cooperation between East and West, White Plains, N.Y., International Arts and Sciences Press, 1975.

[13] J. M. Michal, "Price Structures and Implicit Dollar-Ruble Ratios in East-European Trade," Weltwirtschaftliches Archiv, vol. 107(1), 1971, pp. 159-80.

[14] M. Hrnčíř, "Devizový kurs při zdokonalování soustav plánovitého řízení," Politická ekonomie (Prague), 1973, no. 7, pp. 601-12.

[15] "K teorii vnějších ekonomických vztahů," Politická ekonomie (Prague), 1973, no. 11, pp. 981-1080.

[16] J. Stankovsky, "Bestimmungsgründe im Handel zwischen Ost und West," Forschungsberichte des Wiener Institutes für Internationale Wirtschaftsvergleiche, 1972, no. 7.

[17] Business International, Eastern Europe Report, June 27, 1975.

[18] F. Nemschak, "Perspektiven und Probleme des Ost-West-Handels unter besonderer Berücksichtigung Osterreichs," Der Donauraum, 1973, no. 4

[19] Decree of the Romanian Council of Ministers, on the Authorization and Regulation of Commercial Representatives of Foreign Firms and Economic Organization within Romania, no. 15, January 25, 1971, Offizielles Bulletin, 1971, no. 10.

[20] Hungarian Law on Foreign Trade, no. III, 1974; Resolution of the Council of Ministers on the Enactment of Law No. III, 1974, on Foreign Trade, no. 1053, October 17, 1974; Decree of the Minister of Foreign Trade, no. 7, 1974, October 17, 1974.

[21] Decree of the Federal Ministry of Foreign Trade of the CSSR, no. 125, November 19, 1975, on the Foreign Trade Activities for Foreign Enterprises within the CSSR, Gesetzblatt, no. 29.

[22] B. M. Pounds and M. F. Levine, "Legislative, Institutional, and Negotiating Aspects of United States-East European Trade and Economic Relations," in J. P. Hardt, ed., Reorientation and Commercial Relations of the Economies of Eastern Europe, Joint Economic Committee, Congress of the United States, Washington, U.S.G.P.O., 1974.

[23] "Bulgaria Okays Western Offices," Business International, Eastern Europe Report, 1976, no. 2.

[24] A. Kiralfy, "The Union of Soviet Socialist Republics," in R. Starr ed., East-West Business Transactions, New York-London, Praeger Publishers, 1974.

[25] CSSR Law no. 85, 1972, on Procedures in Concluding Agreements on Economic Cooperation with Foreign Countries, Gesetzblatt, no. 25.

[26] R. Kobza, "Hospodářská kooperace s kapitalistickými státy," Hospodářské noviny (Prague), October 12, 1973, no. 41, p. 5.

[27] Law on the Procurement of Foreign Exchange of the CSSR, no. 142, 1970, Gesetzblatt.

[28] R. Kobza, "Ekonomické zásady pro hospodářskou kooperaci," Hospodářské noviny (Prague), November 30, 1973, no. 48, p. 5.

[29] Decision of the Czechoslovak Federal Government no. 273, October 2, 1975, on the Approval of Guidelines for the Further Development of Economic Cooperation with Nonsocialist Countries, in O. Henyš and J. Krupka, "Hospodářská kooperace ČSSR s kapitalistickými státy — tendence k vyšším formám," Hospodářské noviny (Prague), January 30, 1976, no. 5, pp. 1 and 4.

[30] Decree No. 1196 of the Bulgarian State Council on Economic, Productive, and Technical Cooperation with Foreign Legal and Physical Persons,

Österreichisches Ost- und Südosteuropa Institut, Presseschau Ostwirt-schaft, 1974, no. 9, app. 8.

[31] Decree of the Bulgarian Council of Ministers, no. 85, 1974; Guidelines for the Application of Order No. 1196, Österreichisches Ost- und Südosteuropa Institut, Presseschau Ostwirtschaft, 1974, no. 11, app. 5.

[32] I. Davidov, "Rechtliche Regelung der Produktionskooperation mit nichtso-zialistischen Ländern," Bulgarischer Aussenhandel, 1975, no. 1.

[33] ZVO-Informationen, UdSSR I, II, information bulletin of Siemens AG (Red. v. Heyking), Munich, 1974.

6

The special case of joint ventures: their possibilities and limits

Definition of Joint Venture

A trend from simpler toward longer-term and more active ties is discernible in the development of economic relations at the enterprise level. There has been a movement from the short-term, traditional trading transactions, concluded by a purchasing agreement, deliveries of goods, and payment, through the various forms (described in Chapter 3) of functional interfirm East-West cooperative undertakings that bring the partners together on a contractual basis in long-term reciprocal activities, to the most developed form, the joint venture [1].

In all functional types of cooperation the particular activities performed are coordinated by the agreement, but they are not totally integrated with one another. Stipulated quantities of goods and services are, simultaneously or with some lapse of time (e.g., after the venture has begun operation), repaid wholly or partly by counterdeliveries of goods and services. In all these forms the partners are associated contractually with one another for a specified time interval without losing their own legal and economic identity. Apart from the mutual commitments specified in the contract, the partners remain independent of one another; each is liable only for its own firm, and the profits or losses of the other are not its concern.

Joint ventures have some properties in common with the simpler forms of cooperation, e.g., they are long-term and reciprocal; but in addition these relations are institutionalized. Individual reciprocal operations are not only coordinated with one another, they are fully integrated into a new legal entity, a joint undertaking. The contractual agreement between the partners entails:
— a pooling of assets in the form of money, plant, machinery, equipment, and other material inputs; intellectual property (trademarks, patent and license rights); and other facilities (technical, organizational, and management know-how);

69

— an evaluation of the assets required of the partners as capital participation;
— common enterprise objectives, such as joint production, joint purchasing, sales, joint maintenance, and such other services as consultation, financing, etc.;
— distribution of the risks entailed and profits accruing from the achievement of the venture's objectives, usually in proportion to capital participation;
— achievement of the objective through joint, contractually agreed management.

A joint venture invariably entails a set of reciprocal transactions whose scope depends on capital participation and which may involve a number of different activities in the area of production, sales, and services. For joint ventures situated in the Eastern countries, an element of technology transfer is usually included in addition to the procurement of money and fixed capital [2, 3].

These basic features of joint ventures illustrate that they are a close form of cooperation that requires a high degree of mutual trust. Such close ties are usually preceded by simpler forms of cooperation in which the joint venture partners get to know each other.

In principle the common undertaking may be located in either of the partner countries or in a third country. In practice establishment of the joint venture in the Western country (or in a third country, e.g., a developing country) has proven to be much simpler than in one of the Eastern countries.

Joint Ventures in a Western Partner Country and in a Third Country

The older and more common form of East-West joint venture, with its seat in the West, is usually established for the marketing and postsales service of the Eastern partner's product. Ordinarily the Eastern partner lacks sufficient sales experience to successfully combat experienced competition with its new product. By establishing a joint venture, access to the market is considerably improved. The joint undertaking in the West can also fulfill other functions: e.g., joint production, provision of services (in banking and insurance), providing technical and commercial consultation, and transport and shipping. Joint East-West undertakings in third countries, usually developing countries, entail, for example, the exploitation of natural resources, the construction and subsequent operation of industrial plants (the latter often also includes setting up training programs for the indigenous personnel) [1, 4].

In these projects it is often difficult to get the capital share of the Eastern partner in convertible currency. Ordinarily, Eastern European producers maintain no direct ties with foreign firms and only exceptionally have convertible currency at their disposal. For this reason the foreign trade organizations conclude the joint venture contracts, while the financial resources for capital participation are obtained from the state budget [5].

In Hungary a joint ordinance was issued in 1975 by the Ministry of Finance and the Ministry of Foreign Trade which authorized Hungarian producers to directly establish joint ventures abroad [16].[1] According to this ordinance any enterprise or cooperative can begin joint venture negotiations as soon as it receives authorization from the competent ministry or the competent branch administration. Before concluding any agreement a foreign exchange authorization must be obtained from the Ministry of Finance.

The firm can take the resources it needs for the foreign investment from its development fund (retained profits and sums set aside for depreciation), or it may obtain credit from the National Bank, which it then pays back from its development fund. Finally, the enterprise may obtain credit or a direct allocation from the state budget. That this possibility exists indicates that certain foreign investments may be included in the state economic plan. Profits from joint ventures are taxed at a rate of 10% for eight years and at 30% from the ninth to the twelfth year, or until the total capital is repaid; only then are normal (higher) tax rates applied. The new legal provisions thus give Hungarian enterprises considerable incentives for establishing joint ventures abroad.

Apart from the particular conditions mentioned above, such joint activities ordinarily cause no special institutional, legal, or organizational problem in a Western country; and in its essential aspects such a joint undertaking does not differ from analogous associations between partners in market economies. The venture is usually established in conformity with the legal system of the Western country. The legal systems in the Eastern countries, with their state monopoly on foreign trade, usually allow legal persons to operate abroad, who then function as owners of capital and partners in joint ventures. Profits are subject to the tax laws of the Western partner, and there is usually nothing to hinder a transfer of profits to the Eastern country.[2]

71

The absence of institutional or legal obstacles indicates that in principle nothing stands in the way of the further expansion of joint ventures in a Western partner country or in third countries and that the only limits to such further expansion lie with subjective factors. As far as the Eastern countries are concerned, especially the smaller ones, the lack of capital in convertible currency is a limiting factor. If the venture involves the sale of an Eastern product on Western markets, a potential Western partner might be annoyed by the occasional lack of flexibility of the Eastern supplier. If Eastern European capital acquired too strong an influence in important sectors of the economy, political resistance would probably be encountered in the Western country. In view of the marginal importance of Eastern European investments in Western industrial countries (see Table 15), however, this danger is not very great in the foreseeable future.

Joint Ventures in Eastern European Countries

The establishment of a joint venture in an Eastern socialist country is surrounded by much more difficult problems. Although both blocs (or at least some Eastern countries) publicly declare their interest in this form of cooperation and strong reasons seem to exist for establishing joint ventures, so far only a few projects have been realized and the practical results are not yet very impressive. There seem to be a number of serious political, ideological, and practical obstacles to establishing a close partnership based on capital participation between Eastern European state enterprises (in Yugoslavia self-managing labor associations) and Western firms on Eastern territory.

In most CMEA countries establishment of joint ventures domestically is currently prohibited, and in some countries joint ventures would probably contradict constitutional principles [4, 16].

Apart from Yugoslavia, where joint ventures have been allowed since 1967 and where the most experience has been accumulated with this form of East-West cooperation, joint ventures are permitted only in Romania and Hungary, and then by special legislation. Poland has recently given assurances that the present legal system, which dates back to the prewar period, allows joint ventures in the form of limited stock companies and "capital guests" even without special enabling laws [10, 11]. However, nowhere, not even in Yugoslavia, where there are currently ninety joint venture agreements, is the amount of invested Western capital significant, amounting, according to estimates, to only slightly more than $200 million. This is less than the capital participation in a single relatively large joint venture project between partners in the Western industrial nations [4].

In a decree issued in May 1976, foreign legal and physical persons were given the right to exercise certain economic activities in Poland, for example, in handicrafts, domestic trade, restaurants, and the hotel trade. Capital participation in such undertakings must be deposited in convertible currency in the Bank Polska Kasa Opieki S.A. in Warsaw. The size of a firm and its number of employees are set by the regional authority that issues the authorization. The licenses are usually for ten years and may be renewed [33].

Despite these restrictions there exists an extraordinary interest in this form of East-West cooperation, especially in the West. This is not surprising if one considers that capital participations are the form of cooperation most suited to market economies. According to Wilczynski [4] the initiative to establish East-West joint ventures usually comes from the Eastern partner. This may be true for joint ventures in the Western partner country (see the second section of this chapter), and perhaps also in Yugoslavia, but it is more often the Western firms that are interested in this form of cooperation when it concerns ventures in the Eastern countries.

Eastern and Western Motives for Establishing Joint Ventures in the East

The principal interest of the Eastern partner in a joint venture project lies in the possibility of obtaining better access to superior Western technology, Western markets, and Western management, manufacturing, and marketing know-how. Associated with these objectives is the desire to improve the foreign exchange situation and to expand and rationalize production by effecting a division of labor with Western firms, and in general to take advantage of economies of scale. The need to import capital is probably not a primary Eastern interest.

One may suppose that all these objectives could also be achieved through less complex forms of cooperation, i.e., without capital participation. Another reason for establishing joint ventures, then, according to many Eastern conceptions, is the fact that capital participation by the Western partner gives the latter a direct interest in the effective application of his technology and know-how, since he then also has a share in the profits and losses of the joint venture. This higher level of management, together with the joint, continuous day-to-day management of the enterprise, gives the Eastern partner the best guarantee that he will receive the latest, rather than obsolete, technology from his Western partner, in addition to the advantages accruing from the sales network and management experiences of the Western parent enterprise.

Even more than other forms of East-West cooperation, joint ventures have the advantage that they finance themselves. The foreign exchange proceeds from the joint venture pay for the import of foreign capital, technology, and the imported industrial input. In addition the Eastern country expects the superior Western management methods to be adopted at some point by other nonparticipating domestic enterprises and the overall level of industrial management to be increased in this way [3, 12].

Some motivations operative in the West are similar: e.g., access to protected markets and utilization of the technology and research potential of the Eastern partner. The special profit opportunities that generally exist in the industrially less-developed countries, such as the exploitation of raw materials and a cheaper, disciplined labor force, also play a role. In addition to these general advantages, the following particular aspects of joint ventures are especially valued in the West:

— Direct and continuous participation in the enterprise management. This considerably enhances the chances that the firm's objectives will really be achieved, compared with what would be the case if it were necessary to rely exclusively on the management abilities of the Eastern partner.

— Market access: Both the quantity and the stability of sales are secured, whether it is the products of the joint venture or the subcontracted products of the Western partner that are being sold. The sale of the joint venture product is not only guaranteed domestically (in Romania, for example, the production and sales plans of joint ventures are included in the state economic plan), but bilateral agreements of the host country with other CMEA countries or with the developing countries also often ensure third markets as well. The possibility of acquiring a monopoly covering the entire CMEA area is an especially attractive objective for the Western partner. His chances of initiating business contacts in the host country with other firms are also quite favorable.

— Technology transfer: Technology and know-how cannot always be transferred by the sale of equipment and licenses alone. Only in joint ventures can transfer take place continuously and in both directions. The profitability of Western technology capital can better be ensured by direct participation in profits than by license transactions.

— Another substantial advantage for the Western partner is the psychological factor of familiarity with this form of association, which is more comprehensible to him than the often unfamiliar forms of industrial cooperation without capital participation, which often entail compensation in goods.

The Principal Legal Regulations for Establishing Joint Ventures[3]

The legal principles for foreign capital participation vary in those Eastern countries where this form of economic cooperation with private Western firms is permitted. The differences lie in the form, the terminology, and the substance of the law.

Romania

The legal principles governing foreign capital participation in Romanian enterprises are set forth in the Foreign Trade Law of 1971 [13]. This document refers explicitly for the first time to the possibility of establishing "mixed companies." The formulations are couched only in general terms, with the exception of the provision that the foreign partner's share must not exceed 49% of the founding capital. Mixed companies may operate in industry, agriculture, construction, transportation, trade, and technical-scientific research and services. The state guarantees the transfer of depreciation and net profits abroad. Other provisions are left open, to be specified in the particular agreement [16].

In the autumn of 1972 two ordinances were issued by the Romanian Government Council [14, 15] dealing with provisions for implementation. These ordinances contained much more detailed regulations for establishing and operating mixed companies than the 1971 Foreign Trade Law, but numerous questions are still left open for the partners to settle in their agreement (for details, see pp. 77-85).

A Western partner will be able to look forward to satisfactory collaboration if he is able to settle all the relevant questions and cover all eventualities in the original charter agreement.

Hungary

In Hungary the possibility of establishing joint ventures on Hungarian territory is guaranteed by law in the "Law on Cooperation in the Economy" [17]. An executive ordinance by the Hungarian finance minister [18] issued two years later also enables economic associations with foreign participation to be established if they contribute to raising the technical-scientific level of the economy and promote trade relations. The area of activities is basically restricted to research and development, industrial consultation, trade, and other services; but the direct participation of economic associations in production is not completely prohibited by the executive ordinance, provided it is explicitly established, in the light of clear economic advantages it would bring, in an intergovernmental agreement after approval by the Council of Ministers. This, however, is an exceptional situation which has so far not taken place. Economic associations can be established in the form of stock companies, limited liability companies, or even as joint enterprises with no limitations in liability. Capital participation of the foreign partner is categorically limited to 49%.

Yugoslavia

In contrast to Romania and Hungary, in Yugoslavia the legal terms and conditions for the establishment of joint ventures are not spelled out in a few provisions derived from a higher legal norm. Rather there are a number of more or less mutually independent norms, such as constitutional provisions, federal laws, supplementary and amending laws, and dispositions and ordinances of the individual republics dealing with particular aspects of the subject [19]. Some of these provisions determine the legal forms and legal framework within which joint venture agreements with Yugoslav "organizations of associated labor" (i.e., the self-managing enterprises) may be concluded. Others deal with various financial, fiscal, and foreign exchange conditions of foreign capital participation. The most important of these laws are listed in the references [20].

In 1973 a number of the earlier regulations were consolidated into two new legal norms [21, 22]. The "Law on the Investment of Resources by Foreigners in Domestic Organizations of Associated Labor" [22] sets down the basic conditions for the establishment of joint ventures with domestic enterprises and is the most comprehensive legal document on foreign capital participation in Yugoslavia. Beyond it there are other legal norms, some cited in the foregoing, which cover other areas.

Comparative Description of Joint Venture [4]

As is evident from the brief description of the basic legal norms in the previous section, there is no uniformity even in the terminology used by the different law-making bodies. The Romanians refer to "mixed companies," the Hungarians to "economic associations with foreign participation," the Yugoslavs to "foreign investments in domestic organizations of associated labor." The content of the terms and conditions varies considerably too, as may be seen in the following comparative description.

Basic Terms and Conditions

1. Areas of activity of joint ventures

Romania: in industrial and agricultural production, construction, transportation, trade, research, development, services, and tourism.

Hungary: mainly in research and development, trade, and services; only exceptionally in production, and then only on the basis of a government resolution and an intergovernmental agreement. However, since in most cases the Hungarian partner of a joint venture is a Hungarian producer, with whom the joint venture enterprise can then contract for production, production activity is indirectly influenced in this way [23].

Yugoslavia: all branches of the economy, with the exception of those which serve mainly the domestic economy, such as banking, insurance, domestic communications, trade, and municipal services.

2. Objectives of joint ventures

Romania: development of the Romanian economy, promotion of exports, development of modern research and management facilities, training of specialists. Principal emphasis is placed on export promotion and procurement of foreign exchange.

Hungary: export promotion, foreign exchange procurement, import substitution, and activities covering the domestic and CMEA markets.

Yugoslavia: mainly production of export goods. Projects leading to import substitution are of no importance because of existing foreign exchange regulations.

3. Scope of capital participation

In Romania and Hungary no maximum is prescribed. In Yugoslavia the minimum is 1.5 million dinars. In all three countries the maximum foreign participation is 49%. In Yugoslavia the Federal Assembly (parliament) may grant an exception to this limit (although to date this has not taken place), and Hungarian legislation prescribes a maximum of 49% "as a rule"; in Romania the maximum allows of no exception. In all three countries both the foreign and the domestic partner may be a group of firms; the Romanian and Yugoslav legislation specify this explicitly, while the Hungarian contains no statement to the contrary.

4. Coordination with the state economic plan

In Romania joint ventures must work out one-year and five-year plans that may then be incorporated into the overall state economic plan. Yugoslavia does not even require domestic enterprises to submit plans to the government. Hungarian legislation contains nothing pertinent to this point.

5. Government permission

In all three countries the original contract document, and in Romania and Hungary the statutes of the joint venture as well, must be approved by government authorities. In Hungary and Yugoslavia permission is obtained from the Ministry of Finance or Economics, and in Romania from the State Planning Commission, the Ministries of Finance and Labor, and the Romanian Foreign Trade Bank. After being approved the documents must be submitted to the Council of Ministers and State Council for final decision and then deposited with the Ministry of Foreign Trade.

The Organization and Status of Joint Ventures

1. Legal person

In Romania the "mixed company" is a newly created legal person that takes the form of either a joint stock company or a limited company. The same is the case for the Hungarian "economic association with foreign participation," which may also be an unlimited company or a joint undertaking. In Yugoslavia a joint venture may not be an independent legal entity. Foreign capital participation is regarded as an investment in an existing (or specifically created for the purpose) Yugoslav firm, or in a separate section of such a firm whose relative independence must be defined in the partnership contract. In Yugoslavia, therefore, the joint venture remains a typically Yugoslav enterprise (with workers' self-management) subject to the general domestic enterprise laws. The foreign supplier of capital is neither a founder nor cofounder of such an enterprise, so that the formation of mixed companies is precluded.

2. Basic contract documents

In Romania the conditions and terms governing the founding, organization, and practical management are set forth in the association contract, the enterprise constitution, and the statutes. In Hungary the corresponding document is the "memorandum of association," which provides the groundwork for the joint economic activities. In Yugoslavia a contract on joint investments concluded in conformity with existing Yugoslav law (and also possible between Yugoslav partners) spells out the common objectives of the partnership, the joint risk, and other long-term arrangements.

3. Management bodies

Romanian legislation provides for the establishment of annual "general meetings" — a "board of directors" in the case of a joint stock company, and a "managing committee" in the case of a limited company. The Hungarian legislation does not go into the question, but such bodies in principle are possible within the framework of existing legislation on cooperations. In Yugoslavia a joint venture contract sets forth the terms and conditions for the establishment of a managerial body (operating committee). This joint operating committee divides its responsibilities with the workers' council of the Yugoslav enterprise of which the joint venture is a part. The workers' council may delegate some of its powers to the operating committee of the joint venture. In Romania representatives of the workers are also on the managerial board, but only as members of the Romanian representation in the mixed company.

Rights of the Partners

Although in all three countries the capital participation of the foreign partner is limited and usually (in Romania without exception) may not exceed 49%, this does not rule out equal representation on the bodies of the joint venture or preclude the stipulation that certain important decisions must have unanimous approval. The Romanian government guarantees the financial share of the Romanian partner. In Hungary the foreign capital investor may obtain a guarantee from the Hungarian Foreign Trade Bank or Hungarian National Bank which protects him from damages resulting from actions of the Hungarian government or the Hungarian partner, or guarantees compensation for such actions (such a guarantee must be contained in the original association memorandum and approved by the Ministry of Finance).

In Romania the capital share may be in the form of money, goods, or technology; a Romanian partner can also submit its capital share in the form of the right of use of the land on which the joint venture is built. The Yugoslav legislation does not deal with this point, nor does the Hungarian, although the delimitation of activities does provide some guidelines for the form the capital share can take. In Romania all capital values are expressed in convertible currency, and all operations of a joint enterprise, including domestic sales and purchases, are effected in convertible currency at the more favorable tourist rate, not the official foreign exchange rate. Only the wages of the Romanian workers and employees are paid in the domestic currency, although they too are calculated in convertible currency and paid into a separate account with a Romanian bank. Financial shares of both partners are deposited in a joint venture account with a Romanian bank. In Hungary the total sum of the participatory shares is expressed in monetary form (in forints at the current official Hungarian exchange rate). In Yugoslavia the financial resources of both partners are evaluated and expressed in shares; the foreign currency holdings of the foreign partner are expressed in Yugoslav currency at the official conversion rate in force at the time the final contract was concluded.

There is no obligation to reinvest profits in any of the three countries. In Romania the consent of both partners is required for a change of ownership of the foreign capital participation. In Yugoslavia the foreign shares may be sold to either a foreign or a Yugoslav enterprise; the Yugoslav partner has an option to buy. Hungarian legislation provides no possibilities for the transfer of the foreign part to other enterprises.

In Hungary an economic association cannot own a factory, although to a limited extent it may own industrial assets, such as machinery and patents. The economic association enters into contractual relations with Hungarian industrial firms, including those of the Hungarian partner. These contractual agreements may deal with industrial consultation, manufacture under contract, the purchase and marketing of components and final products, subcontracts, licensing agreements, etc. In this indirect way the foreign shareholder can protect his interests, e.g., industrial intellectual property, and oversee its proper use.

Accounting

In all three countries the bookkeeping and general accounting system are a matter decided in the partnership contract. In Yugoslavia the principle of free contractual agreement is most broadly applied, so that all the particulars must be stated in the joint venture contract. Such agreements include the bookkeeping system to be used, the currency in which all operations must be recorded, and methods for calculating current expenditures. The Yugoslav partner must present separate books for the joint venture operations and show the financial proceeds from joint venture operations in its own books. The foreign shareholder has the right to examine all accounts and books pertaining to joint venture activities. In Hungary the accounting system is also contractually agreed upon, but the finance minister must approve it. For transactions in foreign currencies the regulations governing Hungarian enterprises are applicable. Credits may also be taken out under the same conditions and terms applying to Hungarian enterprises. In all three countries financial resources deposited in domestic banks are paid interest on the same terms applying domestically. In Romania and Hungary a portion of profits must be set aside in a reserve and risk fund before taxes are deducted. In Romania this portion is 5% of the profits before taxes until the reserve fund reaches 25% of the total invested capital. In Hungary the reserve fund must be built up to total 10% of the capital of the economic association. The Hungarian regulations also provide for the possibility of creating a participation fund for employees (bonus fund) after the reserve fund has been deducted from the profits. The sum set aside for this purpose may not exceed 15% of the annual aggregate payroll.

Losses are covered by the reserve and risk fund in Romania and

Hungary. If this fund is not sufficient and the partners are unable to meet their commitments by other means, the state authorities must decide whether to continue the joint venture or liquidate it.

Taxation

In Hungary economic associations with foreign participation are exempt from the tax on capital (production fund levy) that domestic enterprises must pay. They are likewise free from the obligation to hand over a share of the amortization charges to the central administration. In Yugoslavia the foreign partner's share of the invested capital in a Yugoslav enterprise is also exempt from the imposts otherwise prescribed by law.

In all three countries recorded profits are subject to taxation. In Romania the profits tax is assessed on the net proceeds after deduction of all expenses (including depreciation) for the fiscal year. In Hungary a profits tax is levied on the annual profits of the economic association after deduction of the sums set aside for the risk fund and the bonus fund. In Yugoslavia only that share of the foreign investor's profits stipulated in the contract is subject to a profits tax. The domestic enterprise, however, must deduct and pay the tax. Since the value added rather than profit is the real criterion of efficiency in self-managing Yugoslav enterprises, the profit-calculating procedure must be stipulated in the partnership contract. For this purpose the following items are regarded as operating costs: costs of materials, producer and commercial services, travel and advertising expenses, depreciation, salaries and wages, and contractual and statutory commitments.

In Romania the profits tax is 30% of the recorded annual profits before their distribution to the partners. Profits transferred abroad are taxed an additional 10%. In Hungary taxable profits are taxed at a rate of 40% up to 20% of the net capital of the association and at 60% for any profits in excess of that figure. The tax on any profit reinvested in the association may be reimbursed on application to the Ministry of Finance. In Romania the tax on profits reinvested for at least five years in the same or another domestic joint venture may be reduced by 20%. In Yugoslavia the profits tax of the foreign investor is 35%, which is reduced to 29.75% if at least 25% of the profit is reinvested. For larger reinvestments the tax rate falls progressively to 17.5%. Lower tax rates apply for Yugoslavia's developing areas: Montenegro, Macedonia, Bosnia, and Herzegovina (Table 13).

Table 13

Tax Rates on Profits of Foreign Joint Venture Partners
in Yugoslavia, in %

	Republics			
	Macedonia	Montenegro	Bosnia, Herzegovina	Serbia, Croatia, Slovenia
Tax rates for disbursed profits	14	14	20	35
Tax rates for reinvested profits:				
up to 25%	11.2	11.9	17	29.75
25-50%	8.4	9.8	14	24.50
over 50%	5.6	7.0	10	17.50

Source: The International Investment Corporation for Yugoslavia Bulletin.
June 1973, cited in E.A.A.M. Lamers, Jugoslavia: A Labour Managed Market
Economy with Special Reference to Joint Ventures Between Jugoslav and Foreign
Enterprises, Tilburg, Universitaire Pers, 1975, p. 164.

Transfer of Profit and Capital

After the profits tax has been paid, the profits of the foreign
partner may be transferred abroad in all three countries. In Romania the Romanian Foreign Trade Bank, and in Hungary the National Bank, are authorized to transfer profits and other sums
due to the foreign shareholder abroad in the currency specified
in the memorandum, to a maximum equalling the amounts deposited
with the bank. The Hungarian legislative regulation is regarded as
somewhat ambiguous. Its literal formulation permits transfer of the
recorded profit to be denied when it exceeds the amount deposited
with the national bank. In Yugoslavia transfer of profits is dependent on whether the Yugoslav enterprise possesses foreign currency. All Yugoslav enterprises have the right to retain a part of
the foreign exchange proceeds accruing from export transactions
(40% for tourism proceeds and 20% for other sectors). Additionally,
33% of the foreign exchange proceeds joint ventures get from exports can be used to transfer the foreign investors' profits abroad.
Untransferred portions may be used in following years. Some authors feel that this prohibition on the transfer of the foreign investors' profits abroad if sufficient foreign exchange is not on hand
for that purpose constitutes an obstacle to import-substituting
projects.

In Hungary and Yugoslavia the capital share can be withdrawn under certain conditions and transferred abroad in foreign currency. In Romania the transfer of proceeds from the sale of company assets to the Romanian partner and liquidation proceeds is guaranteed by the Romanian government.

Wages and salaries of foreign personnel may be transferred abroad after payment of taxes and social security (wholly in Romania and 50% in Hungary).

Arbitration of Conflicts

In accordance with Romanian and Yugoslav legislation, conflicts between joint venture partners may be settled by contractual agreement, domestic courts, or foreign arbitration courts. In addition, in Yugoslavia a court of arbitration set up specially for this purpose may be invoked for special cases. The Hungarian legislation makes no specific provisions on this point; the provisions set forth in the memorandum of association are therefore decisive. According to [4] a foreign court of arbitration may also be called in in Hungary. All three countries recognize the 1958 New York Convention on the acceptance and execution of the decisions of foreign courts of arbitration and the 1961 European Convention on international arbitrage.

Duration of Agreements

Joint venture contracts are usually long-term agreements. In Romania this is stated explicitly in the pertinent legal statutes. In Hungary and Yugoslavia the partners themselves decide on the duration of the joint undertaking, but it must be for a period considered sufficient by the approving authorities to achieve the objectives of the venture.

In Romania a joint venture may not be dissolved before its stipulated time. In Hungary the finance minister will order its dissolution if the association becomes insolvent and its liabilities exceed its assets. Other grounds for premature termination must be specified in the memorandum of association, and the agreement terminated in accordance with the terms and conditions set forth in the statutes. If the enterprise is dissolved on account of insolvency, by mutual consent, or because of expiration of the agreements, it remains in Hungarian hands. In Yugoslavia the joint venture may be terminated prematurely, if results fall far below expectations for at least two consecutive years, or if one partner does not meet its commitments. Force majeure and fundamental changes in circumstances are also grounds for termination.

Assessment of the Possibilities and Limits of Joint Ventures

Despite efforts of the participating countries and partners to formulate as clearly as possible the terms and conditions for joint ventures and the real relationships to which they may give rise, and despite the existing reasons for preferring this closer form of interfirm cooperation, the results so far leave something to be desired.

The greatest progress has been made in Yugoslavia, especially since 1971, when the earlier terms, requiring that at least 20% of the profits of the foreign partner be reinvested in Yugoslavia, were abolished. The establishment of joint ventures proceeded at its fastest pace before 1973. For some time now the climate in Yugoslavia for more joint ventures has seemed less favorable, and critical voices in the press are more and more frequent. This has probably been partly due to the recession in the West, which has made foreign partners less ready to accept products manufactured in Yugoslavia and has forced them to evaluate the export potential of new projects more critically (see Chapter 9).

Almost all of the more than ninety joint ventures registered in Yugoslavia have been in the manufacturing industries, and almost one third of their total value was concentrated in the vehicle industry.[5] Up to the beginning of 1974 a total of $870 million had been invested in joint ventures, the foreign share representing $210 million, or 24% of this sum. The average foreign share of the investment per joint venture was $2.3 million.

The foreign share reached the legally permissible maximum in only about 30% of the contracts [30]:

Share of foreign capital, in %	Joint ventures in Yugoslavia, number in %
10.0 or less	11.1
10.1–20.0	14.4
20.1–30.0	14.4
30.1–40.0	20.0
40.1–48.9	8.9
49.0–49.9	31.1

The following major corporations have participated in joint ventures in Yugoslavia:

Vehicle industry: Citroen (France); Daimler-Benz (FRG); Fiat (Italy); Renault (France); Volkswagen (FRG); Volvo (Sweden).

Chemicals: Bayer (FRG); Ciba-Geigy (Switzerland); Dow Chemical (USA); Dunlop (Great Britain); Farbwerke Hoechst (FRG); Solvay (Belgium); Semperit (Austria); and Teijin (Japan).

Metal manufactures and other industries: Gilette (USA); Siemens (FRG); Klöckner-Humboldt-Deutz (FRG); Svenska Kugellagerfabriken (Sweden); Bell Telephone (Belgium); St. Gobain (France); Control Data (USA); Sumitomo Shoji Kaisha (Japan) [4].

Through 1976 Hungary and Romania have concluded about ten joint venture contracts with Western partners (see the third section of Chapter 10 on Hungary [pp. 195-97] and Romania [pp. 198-200] and Case Studies 5-8 in Appendix 1), and negotiations have been conducted on another ten and twenty-five ventures, respectively. The Western partners have been: Bowmar (Canada), British Petroleum (Great Britain), Control Data (USA), Cummings Engine (USA), Sumitomo Shoji Kaisha (Japan), Teijin (Japan), and Zahnräderfabrik Renk (FRG). Table 14 lists some of the major joint ventures in the Eastern countries.

To give some idea of the low level of Western capital participation in the Eastern European countries, and of the East in Western Europe, we have compiled a table contrasting total foreign investments of the Federal Republic of Germany, which is the principal trade partner of the Eastern countries, with its investments in the Eastern countries alone. Second, total foreign investments in the FRG are compared with investments stemming from the Eastern countries. Table 15 shows the marginal importance of FRG joint venture investments in the Eastern European countries. The figure does not even reach 0.01% of the total net capital foreign investments of the FRG. Eastern European joint venture investments in the FRG were thirty times greater than German investments in the Eastern countries in 1973. Even so, the Eastern countries account for only a very minute portion (0.17%) of foreign investments in the FRG [24]. It should be pointed out, however, that German investments in the Eastern countries and Eastern investments in the FRG are growing at a more vigorous pace than foreign investments on the whole.

Ideological factors are often made responsible for the slow progress in effecting joint ventures in the Eastern countries. The principal issue is to what extent a socialist country with state-owned or nationalized means of production can permit foreign capital

Table 14

Western Participations in East-West Joint Ventures in the East

Name, location, and year joint venture firm set up	Eastern partner	Western partner	Starting capital, in $1,000	Western share, in %	Branch
1. Yugoslavia					
Belinka, Ljubljana (1973)	Belinka	Solvay (Be)*	6,685	49	Chemicals
Fadip, Belgrade (1971)	Fadip*	Dunlop (GB)	2,490	43	Hydraulic hoses
Jugoslavija Commerce, Belgrade (1972)	Jugoslavija Commerce	Gilette (USA)	1,470	20	Razor blades
Iskra, Kranj (1972)	Iskra	Bell Telephone (Be)	44,120	6	Electric precision products
Kovaska Industrija, Zrece (1972)	Kovaska Industrija	Renault (Fr)	4,520	22	Forge products
Kromos, Umag (1970)	Kromos	Hempel (Dk)	7,300	38	Marine products
Lek, Ljubljana (1970)	Lek	Bayer (BRD)	3,150	49	Pharmaceuticals
Pliva, Zagreb (1972)	Pliva	Ciba-Geigy (CH)	880	49	Pharmaceuticals
Sava, Kranj (1971)	Sava	Semperit (A)	31,340	20	Radial tires
Tomos, Koper (1973)	Tomos*	Citroen (Fr)	11,910	49	Automobiles
Unioninvest, Sarajevo (1973)	Unioninvest	Marlo Italiana (I)	3,200	20	Air conditioners
2. Romania					
Rifil, Bucharest (1973)	Fibrex	Romalfa (I)	2,100	48	Acrylic fibers
Romcontrol Data, Bucharest (1973)	CIETV	Control Data (USA)	4,000	45	Peripheral equipment for computers
Resita Renk AG, Bucharest (1973)	Resita Uzinexport	Renk AG (BRD)	16,600	49	Ship motors

Roniprot (1974)	Industry-Central for Dyestuffs	Dainippon Inc. (J)	11,300	43	Dyestuffs
Elarom	Industry-Central for Electronics	L'Electronique appliqué (Fr)	2,030	49	Electronic equipment
Romelite (1975)	Industry-Central for Heavy Machinery	F. Kohmeier KG (A)	6,600	48	Heavy machinery
3. Hungary					
Sincontact, Budapest (1974)	Inter-Cooperation Csepel*	Siemens (BRD)	530	49	Technical advice and servicing
Volcom, Budapest (1974)		Volvo (Sw)	1,740	48	Assembly of motor vehicles
Hirbow, Budapest (1975)	Hiradás Technika*	Bowmar Canada Ltd.	1,000	49	Industrial advice and sales

Source: J. Wilczynski, "Joint East-West Ventures and Rights of Ownership," Institute of Soviet and East European Studies, Carleton University, Ottawa, Working Paper No. 6, 1975; various press reports.
*Also other partners.

The Special Case of Joint Ventures

Table 15

Foreign Capital Involvement of the FRG, Total and with Eastern Countries

	Net capital position of FRG in German investments abroad				
	1952 to			Change over previous year	
	end of 1971	end of 1972	end of 1973	1972	1973
Total, million DM	23,780	26,596	32,233	+2,816	+5,637
Eastern countries, million DM	0.3	0.8	2.4	+ 0.5	+ 1.6
Share of Eastern countries, in %	0.001	0.003	0.007	–	–
	Net capital position of foreign countries in FRG				
	1962 to			Change over previous year	
	end of 1971	end of 1972	end of 1973	1972	1973
Total, million DM	25,585	29,314	35,442	+3,729	+6,128
Eastern countries, million DM	6.0	21.4	61.4	+ 15.4	+40.0
Share of Eastern countries, in %	0.023	0.073	0.173	–	–

Source: Berlin Bank, Mitteilungen für den Aussenhandel, 1974, no. 5.

investment in its own economy. The hope is often expressed that a more pragmatic attitude might do away with these ideological reservations. It is pointed out that in the USSR's first years, its founder, Lenin, had explicitly acknowledged the feasibility of using foreign capital for building socialism. The Comprehensive Program of the CMEA also provides for the establishment of international economic organizations, including international enterprises with the participation of several CMEA countries, which in the final analysis is nothing else than the participation of "foreign capital" in a nation's productive system.

It seems, however, that the roots of the difficulties lie somewhat deeper. The comparison with the Soviet Union's earlier years is not too persuasive, since at that time the USSR had a multiple sector economy in which, along with state-owned means of production, some capital and means of production still remained in the hands of private individuals, while private petty producers predominated in the countryside and were quite common even in the cities. Moreover, the system of central directive economic planning had not yet been developed. The situation today is completely different both in the USSR and in most of the other CMEA countries. The state or cooperative sector (in the countryside) is preponderant, and in most countries the development of a system of hierarchically organized directive plan targets has been accompanied by the emergence of a bureaucracy to administer the plan. This bureaucracy guards its privileges zealously and will not tolerate decisions being made by persons or bodies outside the planning apparatus.

Some idea of how difficult it is to overcome this system, formed over a period of many years, may be gleaned from the problems experienced in the establishment of "international economic organizations," which, according to the Comprehensive Program, are to be formed between CMEA members. An international symposium in Prague in June 1973, and a later scientific conference in Sofia on December 6, 1973, took up the question of the establishment and activity of such organizations. Both meetings dealt with a number of difficult, long-unsolved problems and brought to light differences of opinion among experts from the various CMEA countries. The following questions were treated: the implications of the international character of these organizations; property rights (property of the state in which the organization has its seat, with the participating countries having the right of administration and use, or an international ownership proportional to each country's capital participation); supply of raw materials and sale of the product in connection with price formation; calculation of sale price; juridical status; applicability of national legislation or creation of new international legal principles; majority or unanimous decisions, etc. The mere listing of the problems touched on shows that the establishment of joint ventures is no simple matter even between CMEA partners and that many fundamental questions still remain unsolved [25].

In addition to the obstacles stemming from existing institutions and from the vested interests of the national planning, administrative, and party machinery, another serious obstacle also deserves mention. According to the original conceptions of scientific socialism, the nationalization of the means of production was not to be a goal in itself but merely a starting point for the socialization of relations between the cooperating producers and consumers. Nationalization as the point of departure for socialization was supposed to make possible the emancipation of labor and ultimately lead to a higher stage of democracy, which in brief had to be some form of synthesis of political and economic democracy. In reality the Eastern European countries carried out nationalization but go no further than the initial stages of socialization. For the working class and the citizen, freed from the capitalists, political and economic self-determination and democracy still remain out of reach. Yugoslavia has taken steps in the direction of economic democracy but has negated it to a large extent by restricting democratic development in the political sphere. In the economic domain self-management by the producers in Yugoslavia is also often merely of a formal nature. Objective factors, such as the low educational and cultural level of the common workers, the large majority of whom come from uneducated rural families, partially explain the discrepancy between theory and actual developments in Yugoslavia. Despite these limitations the Yugoslav factory system of associated labor seems to have better institutional prerequisites for the establishment of joint ventures with capitalist firms than the system prevailing in the other Eastern countries, since in Yugoslavia the workers' councils ratify the terms and conditions of a joint venture contract and are hence legally the real partner of the foreign investor [19, 26].

In the other Eastern European states the insufficient say of workers and employees in enterprise management is offset by propaganda about the achievements of socialism, in which the abolition of capitalist exploitation by nationalization of the means of production is stressed. Strikes are prohibited because the state-owned factories are considered to belong to society and hence to the workers; wages are set centrally and not through wage negotiations by the unions; and socialist discipline in fulfillment of plan targets is stressed. Undoubtedly the participation of foreign capital could upset these notions. If the workers were to become conscious of their real class position and proceed with their own demands against the capitalist shareholders, they would have no reason to stop with the joint venture, but could then go on to advance demands against the management of domestic firms. These worries are contained implicitly in the Hungarian legislation, which prohibits joint ventures with foreign capital participation in production, i.e., just the area where management would have to face the workers collectively. In research and development or in industrial and technical consultation, where it is the technical intelligentsia, traditionally little concerned with trade union matters, with whom one must deal, the risk of confronting a broad range of demands is patently smaller.

In view of all these obstacles, this form of East-West cooperation does not appear to have too many prospects for development.

On the other hand, the economic advantages for both partners that this form has over the mere functional forms of cooperation are obvious, and it is not surprising that the Eastern countries are increasingly turning to this form of interfirm cooperation whenever the joint venture is located in the West.

Considering the advantages an institutionalized merger of Western and Eastern partners would offer, it has also been considered whether some alternative solutions might not be found that would retain the advantages of joint ventures in the East without touching on the question of the ownership title to the joint resources [4]. Bulgarian legislation [27, 28] aims at such quasi participation when it enables a foreign firm to participate in the profits and risks of a domestically established Bulgarian enterprise to an extent corresponding to its own contribution, without that contribution giving it the right of title to a capital share. This Bulgarian model [16] is palpably somewhat unusual for Western firms. It is not known whether in Bulgaria or anywhere else in the East any joint venture contract has been concluded on this basis.

If however one takes the view that ownership is actually a set of rights, the exercise of some of these rights could be guaranteed in the joint venture contract. Some of them would be the setting of common enterprise objectives, profit and risk sharing in accordance with a preset schedule, and the institution of joint management. The lack of a property title for the material and intellectual contribution of the Western partner could be compensated by a larger share in the manufactured product or the accrued profits [4]. A time limitation on the Western capital share is also conceivable. After a certain period of use, the joint property could become the sole socialist property of the Eastern country, or the Western capital share could be gradually bought up by the Eastern partner [11]. Different forms of leasing of Western machinery and equipment are also possible; for example, instead of rental fees, contractually fixed shares in the output or in the profits could be paid to the Western partner, who could participate in the management. At present all these possibilities are only in the discussion or, at most, experimental stage; it still remains to be seen whether the aforementioned institutional obstacles can be eliminated.[6]

Notes

1. For new developments in the organizational forms in foreign trade in the Eastern countries, see the second section of Chapter 5.

The Special Case of Joint Ventures

2. For examples of operating joint ventures in the West, see [1, 4, 7, 8, 9] and Appendix 1, Case Study 2.

3. Yugoslavia will be omitted in other sections of this study, since its economic and foreign trade systems differ in many respects from their counterparts in the other Eastern countries. Since, however, Yugoslavia has had considerable experience with joint ventures and is also counted as a socialist (noncapitalist) economic system, we feel it is warranted to include Yugoslavia in this discussion of joint ventures.

4. This description is based in particular on [2, 3, 19, 29].

5. Until early 1974 the official register of joint ventures was open to public inspection. Since January 31, 1974, onward it has been classified as confidential, and since then there have been no official statistics on joint ventures concluded.

6. The various possibilities of joint venture projects without direct capital participation are now being examined in the Soviet Union, and it looks as if the previous totally negative attitude might now be giving way to more positive views. See [31, 32].

References

[1] D. P. St. Charles, "East-West Business Arrangements: A Typology," in C. H. McMillan ed., Changing Perspectives in East-West Commerce, Toronto-London, Lexington Books, 1974.

[2] C. H. McMillan and D. P. St. Charles, "Joint East-West Ventures in Production and Marketing — A Three Country Comparison," Institute of Soviet and East European Studies, Ottawa, Carleton University, Working Paper, August 1973, no. 1.

[3] C. H. McMillan and D. P. St. Charles, Joint Ventures in Eastern Europe: A Three Country Comparison, Montreal, Canadian Economic Policy Committee, 1974.

[4] J. Wilczynski, "Joint East-West Ventures and Rights of Ownership," Institute of Soviet and East European Studies, Ottawa, Carleton University, Working Paper, 1975, no. 6.

[5] J. C. Conner and J. R. Offutt, "Joint Venture in Eastern Europe," in R. Starr ed., East-West Business Transactions, New York-London, Praeger Publishers, 1974.

[6] Decree of the Hungarian Ministry of Finances and Ministry of Foreign Trade, no. 4, 1975, III, 27-KkM-PM.

[7] "Die gemischten Gesellschaften — wirksame Förderungsform der rumänischen Warenexporte und -importe," Mitteilungen des Österreichischen Büros für den Ost-West-Handel, Vienna, June 1975.

[8] "Rumänische Gesellschaften im Ausland," Österreichisches Ost- und Südosteuropa-Institut, Presseschau Ostwirtschaft, 1974, no. 12, app. 10.

[9] "Ausländische Tungsram-Unternehmen fördern ungarischen Export," Österreichisches Ost- und Südosteuropa-Institut, Presseschau Ostwirtschaft, 1974, no. 12, app. 8.

[10] L. Ciamaga, "Co-operation Between the East and the West (Introductory Comments)," in Collective Study of Foreign Trade Institute, East-West Economic Relations (Warsaw), 1973.

[11] L. Zurawicki, "Korporacje międzynarodowe a kraje socjalistyczne," Sprawy międzynarodowe (Warsaw), 1975, no. 1.

[12] I. Toldy-Ösz, "Joint Ventures mit ausländischer Beteiligung," Marketing in Ungarn, 1974, no. 3.

[13] Law on Foreign Trade and Economic and Technical-Scientific Cooperation in the Socialist Republic of Romania, March 1971.

[14] Decree on the Founding, Organization, and Activities of Mixed Enterprises in the Socialist Republic of Romania, no. 424, November 2, 1972.

[15] Decree on Taxing Profits of Mixed Enterprises in the Socialist Republic of Romania, no. 425 of November 2, 1972, in Österreichisches Ost-und Südosteuropa-Institut, Presseschau Ostwirtschaft, 1972, no. 2.

[16] J. Stankovsky, "Kapitalbeteiligungen — Neue Form der Kooperation im Ost-West-Handel?" Vienna, Creditanstalt-Bankverein, Wirtschaftsberichte, December 1973, no. 6.

[17] Law on Cooperation in the Hungarian Economy, Legislative Ordinance no. 19, 1970.

[18] Implementation Order of the Hungarian Minister of Finance on Economic Associations with Foreign Participation, no. 28, 1972.

[19] E. A. A. M. Lamers, Yugoslavia: A Labour-Managed Market Economy with Special Reference to Joint Ventures Between Yugoslav and Foreign Enterprises, Universitaire Pers Tilburg, 1975.

[20] — Basic Law on the SFRJ, 1965, republished in 1973 as the Law on the Founding and Registration of Organizations of Associated Labor, Službeni list SFRJ, 1973, no. 19.

— Law on the Assets of Organizations of Associated Labor, 1967, with Annual Supplements and Alterations.

— Basic Law on the Associated Chambers of Commerce and Economic Cooperation in the Economy.

— Law on Foreign Exchange Operations, with Annual Supplements and Alterations.

— Law on Profit Taxes for Foreign Investors in Domestic Economic Organizations with Respect to Joint Ventures — Promulgated in 1967, with Numerous Alterations and Supplements.

— Law on Credit Operations with Foreign Enterprises — Promulgated in 1966, with Alterations and Supplements in 1972 and 1973.

— Law on Banks and Credit and on Banking, 1971.

[21] Decree on Long-term Agreements on Cooperation in Production between Domestic Organizations of Associated Labor and Foreign Persons, no. 7, February 1973, Službeni list SFRJ.

[22] Law on the Investment of Resources of Foreign Persons in Domestic Organizations of Associated Labor, No. 22, April 1973, Službeni list SFRJ.

[23] "A Hungarian Interpretation of Joint Venture Questions," Business International, Eastern Europe Report, vol. 4, no. 5, 1975.

[24] "Bundesrepublik Deutschland: Deutsche Auslandsinvestitionen/Auslandsinvestitionen in Deutschland," Berliner Bank, Mitteilungen für den Aussenhandel, 1974, no. 5.

[25] "Economic Organizations with International Status in the CMEA," report on a symposium in Prague, June 1973 and a conference in Sofia, December 1973, in Ikonomičeski život, December 1973, no. 52, and Magyar Hirlap, March 1974, no. 84, cited in Österreichisches Ost- und Südosteuropa-Institut, Presseschau Ostwirtschaft, 1974, no. 9.

[26] M. Sukijasovic, "Investment of Foreign Capital in the Yugoslav Economy," Yugoslav Survey, vol. 14, no. 4, 1973.

[27] Decree No. 1196 of the Bulgarian State Council on Economic, Productive, and Technical Cooperation with Foreign Legal and Physical Persons, Durzaven vestnik, 1974, no. 46.

[28] Decree of the Bulgarian Council of Ministers, no. 85, 1974, on the Approval of the Guidelines for the Application of the Order on Economic, Productive, and Technical Cooperation with Foreign Juridical and Physical Persons, Durzaven vestnik, 1974, no. 73.

[29] UN Economic and Social Council, Commission on Transnational Corporations, "National Legislation and Regulations Relating to Transnational Corporations," E/C. 10/8/Add. 1, January 26, 1976.

[30] OECD, Foreign Investment in Yugoslavia, Paris, 1973.

[31] O. Bogomolov, "East-West Economic Relations: Economic Interests of the Socialist and Capitalist Countries of Europe," in World Economy and East-West Trade, Vienna, East-West European Economic Interactions, Workshop Papers, vol. 1, 1976.

[32] N. P. Shmelev, "Scope for Industrial, Scientific and Technical Co-operation Between East and West," IEA Conference on "Economic Relations Between East and West," Dresden, June 29 to July 3, 1976 (mimeographed).

[33] Decree of the Polish Council of Ministers, no. 123, May 14, 1976, on the Approval for Foreign Legal and Physical Persons to Engage in Certain Economic Activities, Dziennik Ustaw, 1976, no. 19.

7

Economic policy and industrial
East-West cooperation

In many respects there is a connection between East-West industrial cooperation and the economic policy of the participating countries. Specific problems arise from the interaction between the integrating tendencies in East and West and the efforts to increase East-West cooperation. In this section we shall deal with only a few aspects of economic policy that are especially relevant to East-West cooperation: the question of CMEA integration and East-West cooperation; the relationships between CMEA and the EEC; the economic relations of the United States and the Eastern countries; the implications for the developing countries; and the meaning of the Helsinki acts for East-West cooperation.

As experience shows, the East attaches much more importance to international cooperation agreements than the West (see Chapter 8). At the government level the initiative to conclude such agreements almost always comes from the East. The West, on the other hand, seems more reluctant and stresses rather the problems and contradictions that accompany any expansion of East-West industrial cooperation and East-West relations in general.

This difference in attitude, which is apparent in both the professional literature and the daily press, should not be overestimated. It may be partly explained by differences in the way the tasks and responsibilities of the press and of journalism in general are conceived in the East and West. In the West it is part of the professional ethic of experts and journalists to explore all sides of a problem, to point out possible internal contradictions, and to allow the reader a certain liberty in ultimately arriving at his own final views on the problem. In the East, on the other hand, it is customary to present a situation as unambiguously as possible in a written document meant for public consumption. If the basic attitude is positive, then all reservations, possible difficulties, and

risks are relegated to the background (or even left out of the picture completely), and the problems are often aired only in internal
discussions. On the other hand, if the basic attitude is negative,
all possible arguments are presented in support of this view, and
any positive aspects that may be present are excluded. Such practices, however, should not mislead one into believing that the experts in the Eastern European countries are not themselves per-
fectly aware of the problems and contradictions involved in East-
West cooperation.

CMEA Integration and East-West Cooperation: Contradictions or Two Means to One End?

Since the adoption of the "Comprehensive Program for the Further Expansion and Improvement of Cooperation and Development
of Socialist Economic Integration of the CMEA Member Nations"
in August 1971, the CMEA has stepped up its efforts to bring the
economies of the individual CMEA members into closer relation
to one another through various measures. This means in particular to integrate them with the vast economy of the USSR, which
carries most of the weight in the Eastern bloc. Common projections
and forecasts, coordination of five-year plans, joint planning of selected sectors and branches on a bilateral and multilateral basis, specialization agreements, establishment of joint economic organizations,
and monetary, financial, and credit measures are the various modes
the Comprehensive Program recommends [1]. The program is a
long-term one, covering fifteen to twenty years, and is still only in
its beginning stages.

Although the thought is not often stated explicitly, it is clear
from the substance of the Comprehensive Program that economic
integration of the CMEA nations is to be given top priority and that
ultimately an essential component of such an economic policy is
the achievement of an integrated economic area in the East comparable to the Western European economic area.

The Comprehensive Program was adopted at the end of a period
in which economic relations within the CMEA had grown, yet at the
same time goods exchange with the West had also risen considerably. From 1960 to 1970 East-West trade grew at a much more
rapid pace than trade within the CMEA area: intra-CMEA exports
grew at an 8.7% annual average rate, while CMEA exports to the West
grew by 9.9% annually. The difference in growth was even more evident
in imports, which increased within the CMEA area at an average annual

rate of 8.8% during this period, while imports from the West grew by 10.5% [2, 3]. Thus the share of the Western industrial countries in total CMEA imports increased from 21% in 1960 to 26% in 1970, while the share in total exports rose from 20% to 22% (Table 16). Since CMEA imports from the West increased more rapidly than CMEA exports to the West, it was reasonable that the Comprehensive Program should want to put an end to this trend. Indeed, the five-year plans for 1971-75, adopted roughly around the time of the Comprehensive Program, clearly show the intention to give the development of intra-CMEA trade priority and hence to give the mutual trade flows a more rapid growth rate than trade with third countries.

Table 16

Structure of CMEA* Foreign Trade by Groups of Countries

| | Share of group in import-export of CMEA in % | | | | | | |
	1960	1965	1970	1971	1972	1973	1974
Imports from:							
Western industrial countries	21.4	22.1	25.8	25.7	27.8	31.9	35.9
CMEA[†]	58.9	62.8	61.2	61.7	61.5	57.3	51.2
Other socialist countries[‡]	12.3	7.1	5.5	5.2	3.6	3.4	4.2
Developing countries	7.4	8.0	7.5	7.4	7.1	7.4	8.7
Total	100.0	100.0	100.0	100.0	100.0	100.0	100.0
Exports to:							
Western industrial countries	19.7	20.2	21.7	22.2	21.9	25.4	29.4
CMEA[†]	61.1	63.1	60.1	60.0	63.5	59.3	54.0
Other socialist countries[‡]	12.7	6.9	7.5	7.7	4.7	4.2	4.8
Developing countries	6.5	9.8	10.7	10.1	9.9	11.1	11.8
Total	100.0	100.0	100.0	100.0	100.0	100.0	100.0

Source: B. Askanas, H. Askanas, and F. Levcik, "Structural Developments in CMEA Foreign Trade over the Last Fifteen Years (1960-1974)," Forschungs-berichte des Wiener Institutes für Internationale Wirtschaftsvergleiche (Vienna), 1975, no. 23, and later calculations.
*Including Albania, the Mongolian Peoples Republic since 1962, and Cuba since 1972.
[†] Intra-CMEA trade.
[‡] Yugoslavia, socialist countries in Asia.

For the most part this is not stated explicitly in the plans, but the published planned growth rates for total foreign trade turnover and the planned growth in the turnover of intra-CMEA trade indicate the intention to expand trade with the West only moderately [4]

Table 17

Foreign Trade of CMEA Countries by Groups of Countries,
Actual Development 1966-70 and Plan Figures 1971-75

	Total foreign trade*		Intra-CMEA trade*		Trade with rest of world* †	
	1966-70	1971-75‡	1966-70	1971-75‡	1966-70	1971-75‡
	Average annual growth rate in %					
Bulgaria	10.3	10.5	10.7	11.3	9.0	8.1
CSSR	6.9	6.6	5.7	7.7	9.3	4.5
GDR	9.9	10.0	9.2	11.2	11.6	7.7
Hungary	9.7	8.5	8.6	8.2	11.7	8.9
Poland	9.4	9.4	10.4	11.5	7.9	5.5
Romania	11.8	11.5	7.3		17.7	
USSR	8.6	6.2	5.6	9.0	13.2	2.4
Total CMEA	9.0	8.2	8.3	10.4	10.9	4.4

Source: ECE, Economic Bulletin of Europe, vol. 23, no. 2, UN, New York,
1972; our own calculations.
*Foreign trade turnover (import and export).
†Implicit growth rates, taking into account growth of total foreign trade
and of intra-CMEA trade.
‡Plans.

Table 18

Patterns of CMEA* Foreign Trade by Groups of Countries

	Average annual growth rate in %				
	1961-70	1971	1972	1973	1974
Imports from:					
Western industrial countries	10.5	8.0	22.5	36.3	42.6
CMEA	8.8	9.2	13.2	10.5	15.5
of which, USSR	8.2	7.1	3.2	9.7	17.9
Developing countries	8.7	7.5	7.4	25.2	48.6
Total	8.5	8.2	12.9	18.7	26.9
Exports to:					
Western industrial countries	9.9	11.6	7.7	36.9	44.6
CMEA	8.7	8.8	15.4	10.5	13.5
of which, USSR	9.0	9.4	17.7	5.3	6.3
Developing countries	14.4	3.2	7.1	31.4	32.2
Total	8.9	9.1	9.0	18.2	24.6

Source: B. Askanas, H. Askanas, and F. Levcik, "Structural Developments in
CMEA Foreign Trade over the Last Fifteen Years (1960-1974)," Forschungsberichte des Wiener Institutes für Internationale Wirtschaftsvergleiche (Vienna),
1975, no. 23, and later calculations.
*Including Albania, Mongolian People's Republic since 1962, and Cuba since
1972.

(Table 17). In 1971 growth of imports from the West actually was slowed down, while in 1972 it was exports to the West which grew primarily at a reduced rate (Table 18).

When, however, it became evident that the Soviet Union would not reach its plan targets in either 1971 or 1972, and the fulfillment of the overall five-year plan was in jeopardy, the Soviet Union altered its foreign trade orientation in order to obtain additional resources for economic growth through stepped-up economic relations with the West. This shift in the Soviet position on foreign trade was a welcome opportunity for the other CMEA countries to abandon the foreign trade strategy implicit in the Comprehensive Program and at the same time to broaden their trade and cooperation ties with the West. The price increases in fuels and raw materials that have taken place since 1973 and the worldwide stockpiling that went on in 1974 have made it easier for the Eastern countries to obtain the foreign exchange they require for Western imports; in some cases imports from the West have been financed with credits (especially in 1975).

Economic Implications

It may be assumed that as East-West relations expand, the share of intra-CMEA trade will continue to decline, or at best remain stable.[1] The question thus arises whether such a development may be regarded as a failure of the CMEA integration program. The answer has both an economic and a political aspect. It would surely be a simplification to measure the level of integration within an economic area merely by the share that trade within that area has in total foreign trade.[2] At the peak of the cold war in the fifties, the share of intra-CMEA trade was highest, while the share of trade with the Western industrial countries was negligible. Yet one could hardly say that the CMEA area was economically integrated. The trade of the Eastern nations with one another was by far not commensurate with existing potential; it took place within the framework of basically autarkic national economic plans, it was settled only bilaterally, and payments were made within a rigorously controlled clearing system. While the USSR was able to make unrestricted use of its political and economic position of power in its trade with the other CMEA countries at that time (something which later induced Khrushchev, in a self-critical evaluation, to propose negotiations within the CMEA to establish more harmonious forms of cooperation on a basis of mutual advantage and with avoidance of the mistakes of the past), national egoism flourished in the reciprocal trade of the other CMEA nations.

The share of intra-CMEA trade in the total foreign trade of the CMEA nations thus cannot be the only, and also not the most important, criterion for the scope of economic integration. The CMEA countries have realized in various ways that intra-CMEA trade has often been marked by "mutual exchange of domestic inefficiency" [6]. Whatever was not good enough for sale in the West could always be traded to a CMEA partner. In particular, the vast market of the USSR was relatively easily satisfied with large lots. Thus differences between hard (convertible) and soft (nonconvertible) currencies were compounded by differences between hard and soft goods. Hard goods can be sold anywhere in the West for convertible currencies, while soft goods could only be used in intra-CMEA trade.

As a result, in the seventies a new form of intra-area trade developed: In addition to trade with hard goods on a quota basis that was set contractually in long-term trade agreements between CMEA member countries and paid for or settled at the contract prices in transferable rubles, a new form of trade emerged with hard goods that were sold at world market prices and paid for in convertible Western currency. The share of intra-CMEA trade settled in convertible currency[3] has been increasing steadily, in Hungary, for example, from 2.5% in 1971 to 10-15% at present. In 1974, 9% of Hungarian foreign trade with the CMEA countries and the socialist countries of Asia was settled in hard currency. Hungarian exports brought in $340 million, and imports from these countries came to $260 million in hard currency. According to Hungary's new ten-year treaty with the USSR, deliveries in excess of the agreed on plan quotas for, as an example, Soviet crude oil, gasoline, cotton, lumber, wood pulp, and Hungarian wheat, corn, and beef are to be considered hard goods [7].

This development, which has also taken place in the trade relations between other CMEA countries, can however only be considered an emergency solution, since it runs counter to integration efforts, which should come about mainly through the coordination of the five-year plans. If intra-CMEA trade is to be conducted on a par with trade with the West, the technical level of the traded goods must be raised to Western standards. The CMEA countries have set themselves the goal, as part of their integration efforts, to create modern and specialized economic structures. Only then will the greater volume of intra-CMEA trade reach the same technical and qualitative level as trade with the West, and only then will it be possible to bring the economic level of the integration partners up to the level of the industrially most developed CMEA nations, whereas development to date has rather seen a decline to the level of the less developed countries.

Defects inherent in a directive planning and steering system hold back swift improvements of the technical and qualitative standards for products, since they inspire a speedy and efficient incorporation of the results of research and development into production. This is also the major reason why the CMEA nations are promoting East-West industrial cooperation, which, it is presumed, will raise the overall level of the CMEA economy to the world standard by giving enterprises access to the most up-to-date know-how of Western science, technology, and business management. It is certain that these objectives are easier for a country to achieve if it is able to cooperate with Western firms than if it is relatively cut off from the West. From an economic viewpoint one can only conclude that the expansion of East-West cooperation not only will not impede the implementation of the CMEA integration program but is even indispensable for this goal.

Political Implications

The problem takes on a somewhat different hue if political implications are also taken into consideration. An integrated, efficient economic area is not the only objective of the integration program. The CMEA is also intended to serve as a countervailing force to Western economic integration, particularly the European Economic Community. Integration is to be promoted with other instruments and for other reasons than in the West. These distinctive features (e.g., renunciation of the formation of supranational bodies), which are intended to focus on the specific advantages of the Eastern system over the Western market economies, will of course largely be lost if cooperative relations with the West are further expanded. On the contrary, it cannot be ruled out that some market aspects of the Western economies might even be adopted in the process of CMEA integration. Presumably the political leadership of the CMEA countries are aware of this possibility.

To combat the sociopolitical hazards that might arise from close industrial cooperation with Western firms, representatives from CMEA countries several years ago expressed their desire to develop a joint strategy for developing economic relations with the West. A scientific conference of economists from all CMEA countries (with the exception of Romania), Yugoslavia, and representatives of the CMEA Economics Institute was called in Budapest in the summer of 1973 to discuss the problems of economic cooperation between countries with different economic systems. The development of a joint strategy vis-à-vis the West was held to be a necessity [8]. The possibilities of further development of East-West economic relations and cooperation were estimated in general as positive; principles were spelled out to delineate the political context within which these possibilities should be developed; it was unanimously agreed that East-West economic relations should strengthen the unity of the socialist countries, buttress socialist integration, and augment the economic power of the CMEA.

To secure these goals East-West trade would still constitute the smaller portion of total foreign trade volume. In developing strategy attention would be paid to the political implications, the increased uncertainty, and the increased risk that were characteristic of a capitalist market system, and to repercussions on relations with the developing countries. The greater uncertainty factor would also necessarily influence the working out of long-term and middle-term economic plans, since expanded scientific, technical, and economic relations with the market economies and the consequences of such relations would become an integral component of the national economic plans.

In view of these uncertainty factors and the actual situation, it has also been recommended that variants and alternative strategies for the further development of East-West economic relations be worked out.

With regard to interfirm cooperation the responsibilities of the higher state institutions to protect the nation's economic interests was pointed out. It should be kept in mind that technology is supposed to improve competitiveness on Western markets and that the Eastern enterprises should not fall into a situation of dependence on the Western partner. Since cooperation was usually restricted to some specific area of activity of the Eastern enterprise, this risk was not considered too great.

In order to make adequate use of modern Western technology, the modern organization and management methods of the Western partner should be assimilated. A positive evolution of interfirm cooperation also requires an improvement in business methods and a streamlining of the legal framework. A large number of international financial experts, experts in marketing, and experts in international commerce law should be trained. Since multinational corporations play a major role in the development of interfirm East-West cooperation, the establishment of international socialist enterprises should, in the opinion of some of the conference participants, be encouraged, inasmuch as their economic potential would make possible an equal partnership and could yield advantages for the CMEA in price policy and marketing. The qualfication was added, however, that the establishment of joint socialist enterprises is not just a question of organization but would also require mobilization of the resources necessary to ensure efficient management.[4]

In developing a joint strategy account should also be taken of the varying size of the different countries, their different economic potentials and levels, their specific economic structures, and their specific planning and management systems. For this reason a joint long-term strategy should only serve as a general guideline, enabling joint coordinated actions to be undertaken in the pursuit of basic objectives. On the other hand, every country should be able to develop its own conceptions and action programs within the framework of these guidelines [8].

The developments of the past few years have shown that the various Eastern countries do indeed proceed roughly[5] according to common principles in their economic relations with the West, although at the more specific level of their cooperative relations with Western firms they have developed their own independent conceptions and programs. Lately this independence of the smaller CMEA nations has been subject to admonitory criticism from the Soviet Union for being too great. In particular, in Voprosy ekonomiki (Problems of Economics) "inadequate coordination of the cooperative relations of CMEA countries with the capitalist world" was criticized for "weakening the effectiveness of the integrative relations among fraternal countries" and "introducing disorganizing elements, e.g., in making provisions for standardized types of machinery and equipment, in the development of uniform standards, and the purchase of licenses" [9]. It would seem the Brezhnev doctrine, which restricts the sovereignty of the CMEA nations in matters of national security in the interests of a socialist community of nations, is now being applied to foreign trade relations as well. To be sure, the Soviet authors affirm that "foreign trade relations are a sovereign domain of the policy of socialist countries"; yet "at the same time, the international interests of the socialist community and the objectives of socialist economic integration require a certain coordination of the foreign trade relations of the individual CMEA countries." Specifically, this coordination should be effected "within the basic guidelines and priorities, the legal and organizational mechanisms, and within the basic attitudes taken in cooperation with nonsocialist partners, especially in monetary, price, financing, and credit questions." In the view of Soviet authors, "there exists an objective need to shape cooperative relations in conformity with an agreed on model that takes into consideration the specialized and cooperative structure of production within the CMEA." To work out such a scheme, "bilateral and multilateral consultations between governments, within the CMEA and its agencies, as well as between the competent ministries and offices, foreign trade associations, and other organizations are necessary." The socialist countries are pointedly warned against "permitting the establishment of foreign control over the development of the economy and of science and technology, or the formation of technological or financial dependence." To preclude this danger, "which would ultimately threaten the security of the individual socialist countries and of the entire community" ... "the socialist countries must always be guided by the general and economic criterion that economic and scientific-technical cooperation with other countries must always be undertaken on a rational scale and in rational forms."

It is of course possible that these statements reflect only the personal views of two Soviet authors. However, the authoritative and didactic tone of the article in Voprosy ekonomiki gives the impression that it is inspired by official Soviet circles and reflects the official view.[6] The Soviet criticism is not directed against East-West cooperation as such. Rather, admonitions and warnings are used to curb the individual initiative of CMEA countries in developing cooperative relations with Western firms so as to bring them under the control of the CMEA and hence the USSR.

The CMEA proposal to the European communities in February 1976 that an agreement be concluded between the CMEA and the EEC is also to be understood in the light of these objectives (see pp. 111-18). It is still too early to determine to what extent the efforts of the USSR and the CMEA to regulate East-West cooperative relations could seriously hamper the expansion of reciprocal economic relations or cause a change in the basic attitude toward East-West cooperation. That will depend on whether, on the scale of preferences of the CMEA strategists, the impulse toward dynamic and effective economic development or the desire to acquire political and ideological advantages vis-à-vis the West gains the upper hand.

In the near future, however, it is not likely that an essential change will occur, and the negotiations between Western firms and enterprises in the smaller Eastern countries on more cooperation agreements will continue; but in these negotiations it will be the mutual advantages expected rather than the economic and political objectives of the EEC or CMEA that will be decisive [10].

Relations between the European Communities and the CMEA

The EEC is the most important partner of the Eastern countries in foreign trade and cooperative relations. Over half of trade with the West and over 20% of the total imports of the CMEA are with the nine members of the expanded EEC.[7] The East is also an attractive market for the EEC countries, and it is growing in importance as a source of raw materials and fuels [16, 17].[8]

Relations between the EEC and the CMEA

Trade relations between the EEC countries and the Eastern countries have been burdened by unsolved problems of economic policy: in particular, whether (and in what form) questions of trade policy and cooperation should be settled bilaterally between the individual EEC and CMEA countries, between the EEC and the individual Eastern countries, or between the two groupings (EEC and CMEA). Most of the difficulties arise from the fact that up to now the EEC and CMEA have used different instruments to effect integration: in the EEC the supranational "Common Commercial Policy," made binding in the founding document of the EEC (the Treaty of Rome), is an essential element in the process of integration.[9] In contrast, coordination of trade policy with third countries has not played an important role in CMEA integration [17].[10]

The differences between EEC and CMEA integration are partly the result of differences in the respective economic systems, which of course necessarily will require divergent forms of integration [5]; but they also derive partly from the fact that integration in the West involves countries at about the same level of development, whereas in the East the countries concerned vary in

106

this respect. Moreover, in the EEC there is no country that has an absolute economic and political predominance, whereas in the CMEA and the USSR's economic weight surpasses by far that of all other member nations taken together.

An agreed regulation of matters of trade policy between the EEC and the CMEA or the CMEA member countries is made difficult by the following circumstances:

— For both integration groups there is a fundamental question involved in which prestige and political and ideological considerations play a decisive role. In the EEC the obvious problem is that the substance of the Common Commercial Policy has so far not been precisely defined,[11] nor has it been very successful in important questions. The exclusive competence of the commission to determine trade policy toward Eastern countries, called for in the Treaty of Rome, is to a certain extent a "touchstone" for the willingness of the nations involved to integrate.

— In the East relations with the EEC have been tainted by long years of a negative attitude deriving from economic, political, and military-strategic considerations;[12] for years the East refused to acknowledge the EEC or establish contact with it. A gradual change in official policy in the Eastern nations toward the EEC first[13] became noticeable early in 1972.[14]

— Within both groupings there are considerable differences of interests from nation to nation on the question of how to deal with East-West relations. This point will be discussed in more detail below.

Development of the EEC Common Commercial Policy toward the Eastern Countries [15]

The EEC treaty provides that after the termination of the transitional period, trade agreements with third countries will be concluded only by the Community. According to Article 113 the EEC Commission is responsible for negotiations and is specifically empowered in this by the Council of Ministers, whose guidelines it must follow. Since 1960 an EEC clause should be contained in all agreements of EEC countries with third countries. This clause provides for expeditious commencement of negotiations to amend an agreement if that should prove necessary as a consequence of the institution of the common commercial policy. However, the consistent refusal of the Eastern countries has made it impossible to include this EEC clause in agreements with them. Nor have the

EEC countries been interested in shifting to a common commercial policy vis-à-vis the East too rapidly, for a variety of reasons. Thus at different times in the first half of the sixties the FRG stressed the bilateral nature of its trade relations with the East, since the trade agreements partly made up for the absence of diplomatic relations. Later it was France which rejected a closer coordination of trade policy toward the State Trading Countries.[16]

To avoid undesired conflicts, but also in deference to the interests of the member nations, the transfer of treaty-making power in trade relations with the East to Community agencies has been postponed beyond the transitional period. The member nations were authorized by an EEC decision of December 1969 [4] to conclude bilateral trade agreements until the end of 1972 if Community negotiations were not possible. Before such negotiations should begin obligatory consultations were specified, and the range of the negotiations was narrowed by guidelines set down by the Community. In line with this procedure the EEC nations concluded bilateral trade agreements with most Eastern nations, with a maximum validity, however, of no later than the end of 1974. After January 1, 1973, the individual EEC countries could conclude no new trade agreements with the Eastern countries nor extend those already existing.

Great Britain, Denmark, and Ireland (which entered the EEC in 1973) have accepted the commitments of the common commercial policy, with the exception of a few transitional conditions. However, as of the end of 1974 it has been impossible to put into effect the common commercial policy toward the Eastern countries. Since the beginning of 1975 no treaty has existed between the EEC countries and the Eastern nations, a situation which has been bridged by an autonomous commercial policy, i.e., one free of contractual commitments; in practice this means extending the terms of earlier contracts. The most important point in the terminated contracts, that is, the setting of quotas for the import of nonliberalized goods from the Eastern countries, is stipulated annually by the central agencies of the EEC with reference to earlier valid lists [25].

In addition to the traditional trade policy, measures to actively promote international economic cooperation and the international division of labor have been turned to increasingly in the past few years, especially in relations with the Eastern countries. The corresponding intergovernment agreements were initially spelled out in cooperation clauses in the trade agreements, but now this is done mainly in separate agreements on scientific and technical cooperation (agreements promoting cooperation) (see Chapter 8). Since agreements of this sort were almost unknown at the time the EEC was founded, the question was not taken up in the EEC treaty, so that intergovernmental cooperation agreements remained a matter for the individual governments of the EEC nations to decide. In recent years the EEC countries have concluded bilateral intergovernmental agreements with most of the Eastern countries, and some of these have a validity of up to ten years (see Table 23 in Chapter 8); they also deal directly or indirectly with questions of trade policy. The cooperation agreements have thus undermined the common commercial policy in major questions. It has been variously commented that the common commercial policy of the EEC actually bypasses essential features of economic relations with Eastern Europe. The EEC countries have also so far not been politically willing to make cooperation agreements a community matter; moreover it is clear that such a decision would make negotiations with the Eastern countries even more difficult.

A compromise solution was for a consultation procedure that had already proved itself in commercial agreements to be employed before the conclusion of new cooperation agreements with state trading countries and oil-producing nations. In the autumn of 1973 the EEC commission submitted such a proposal to the EEC Council of Ministers [26, 27] which approved it in the summer of 1974 [28]. In this procedure the EEC nations are required to inform the Commission and the other EEC nations of their intent to conclude or prolong cooperation agreements. Information must be submitted on any measures that might affect trade relations. A consultation procedure may be instituted on the proposal of the Commission or a member nation with regard to any cooperation agreement in the negotiating stage.

The future commercial policy of the EEC, as well as the regulation of cooperation relations, might be influenced by an opinion handed down by the EEC court in November of 1975 on the interpretation of the terms and conditions of the EEC treaty on the common commercial policy.[17] In the specific case the matter in question was a norm for local expenditures in export transactions; this norm had been agreed upon in the OECD in connection with credit guarantees. The court ruled that in this matter the Community had sole jurisdiction; the substance of the court's ruling, however, went beyond the given case. The court ruled that the Community alone had jurisdiction in negotiations on export credits; further, that the common commercial policy "was designed to protect the functioning of the Common Market and the common interests of the Community; that the particular interests of the member nations must accommodate one another within the framework of that common interest"; and that it is, in particular, incompatible with this intention for member nations "to continue to tend to their own separate interests in the area of foreign relations" [29].

In view of the EEC Commission, commercial relations with the East can best be dealt with by the conclusion of long-term trade agreements by the Community with individual Eastern countries.[18] The EEC Council of Ministers accordingly approved a draft "prototype agreement" between the EEC and one Eastern country and brought it to the attention of the Eastern nations.[19] However, from the very outset it was not likely that the Eastern nations would be able to accept negotiations between the Community and themselves individually.

Content of the Common Commercial Policy of the EEC toward the Eastern Countries

The common commercial policy of the EEC consists of a contractually based trade policy that is agreed upon in negotiations with third countries and an autonomous trade policy that is unilaterally applied, in accordance with EEC resolutions, in the communities' relations with their trading partners. In particular it deals with customs arrangements; liberalization of imports; export aids; measures against dumping; credit, agriculture, and energy policy; the iron and steel industry; and the regulation of relations with the developing nations. The EEC common commercial policy stipulates special conditions for state trading countries only in some of the cited areas [13].

The EEC realizes that its notion of a common commercial policy can only be made acceptable if it grants broad concessions to the individual Eastern nations. No great regrets were felt, therefore, in the EEC, that no serious negotiations on long-term trade agreements with CMEA nations had gotten started during the recent recession years. As the recession is gradually overcome, the EEC might be more willing to grant concessions if the basic principles of the common commercial policy are accepted.

One of the most important concessions the EEC could offer in a trade agreement with the Eastern countries would be a broad liberalization of quota restrictions on imports. At present the liberalization lists governing Eastern imports vary from one EEC country to another. In addition, since 1969 the EEC has had a common import policy with regard to Eastern partners. This policy, which provides for a common liberalization list along with various protective and supervisory measures, is much smaller than the schedules of the particular EEC nations [30]. Since 1969 this common liberalization list has been broadened several times.

There is room for major concessions to Eastern countries in agriculture policy; less so in the iron and steel sector (ECSC). The readiness to grant concessions of easier credit terms or a reduction in the common customs duties of the EEC is probably much smaller. At the most the EEC might be willing to reduce or suspend the duties on a few tariff items that are especially important for the Eastern countries. In the light of GATT such tariff reductions would of course have to take place on a worldwide basis. The only possible special customs measures that might benefit a few Eastern countries would be the customs preferences accorded to developing countries (general preference system). In December 1974 these concessions were granted to Romania, which had decided to make a formal application to the EEC [31]. Of the other Eastern countries only Bulgaria[20] seems to have prospects for being granted preferential treatment.

Relations of CMEA Countries with the EEC

Behind the outwardly uniform policy of the CMEA countries toward the EEC may be discerned quite varied economic, commercial, and political interests among the CMEA countries. In view of their export structure, the smaller CMEA countries are very interested in the abolition of the existing import restrictions and in concessions in agricultural policy.[21] Some of the smaller Eastern countries (Bulgaria, Poland, Romania, and Hungary) had already established contact with EEC agencies on "technical agricultural agreements." For the USSR, however, which delivers mainly fuels and raw materials (but no agricultural products) to the EEC, a contract with the Community is much less important.[22] The GDR is a special case, in that through intra-German trade[23] it has almost unrestricted access to FRG markets and hence to the entire EEC, and is therefore more interested in maintaining the status quo [6].

The USSR was extremely skillful in taking advantage of this situation. It made the recognition of the EEC as a trading partner of the East contingent on the recognition of the CMEA as an equal partner, and thereby confronted the EEC countries and the smaller Eastern countries with a dilemma: either bilateral negotiations between the individual EEC and CMEA countries (which would mean a serious setback for EEC integration) or a bloc-to-bloc agreement. The second alternative would require the conferral of some form of supranational jurisdiction on the CMEA, which would be in contradiction to the CMEA statutes and the basic interests of the smaller Eastern nations, but thoroughly in accord with the interests of the Soviet Union, which could then consolidate its control over the foreign relations of the other CMEA countries. The smaller Eastern nations would have to decide whether the concessions expected from the EEC were worth the partial loss of sovereignty to the CMEA — for which the EEC would ultimately be responsible.

It is often asked in this connection whether the CMEA statutes give it any mandate at all to conduct and conclude international agreements, but such a question has a more formal and legal than de facto importance. [24] Even from the strictly juridical standpoint, the 1959 statutes (revised in 1962) do not in any event wholly preclude CMEA jurisdiction over external affairs [35]. [25]

The Twenty-eighth Meeting of the CMEA approved an amendment of the Council Statutes (Sofia Protocol, June 21, 1974) providing for the extension of the Council's jurisdiction to include the conclusion of international agreements and the establishment of relations with nonmember nations and with international organizations [36]. Statute amendments enter into force only when they are ratified by all the members. It seems that this has not yet occurred.

Possible Solutions

The dialogue between the EEC and the CMEA first began in 1975. The first official talks were held in February 1975 in Moscow and were more of an exploratory character. [26] In February 1976 the vice prime minister of the GDR submitted a draft agreement between the EEC and the CMEA to the acting president of the EEC Council [19]. So far there is only an unofficial English translation of the draft treaty, which was originally in Russian [37]. [27]

At the time the present study was being completed, neither the EEC Commission nor the EEC Council of Ministers had taken any official position on this proposal. The sparse comments that have been made are rather restrictive and pessimistic. This may be due partly to tactical considerations, in order not to give too much hope at the outset to the opponents in the negotiations, which will surely be long and drawn out. Undoubtedly the CMEA draft agreement, too, meant only as a negotiating proposal, in which the cards are not put on the table from the outset, and in which not too great a willingness to make concessions will be shown before the parties come to the negotiating table. The CMEA seems, however, for the first time to be ready to admit bloc-to-bloc agreements between the EEC and the CMEA and between individual CMEA countries and the EEC, in addition to the bilateral agreements with individual EEC countries still preferred by the CMEA nations.

From the draft agreement it is not clear which topics would be the subject of bloc-to-bloc agreements and which would be decided between the EEC and the individual CMEA countries. The more restrictively these two points are defined, the more room there is for bilateral agreements between the members of the two groupings, and hence for a partial reversion to the situation prevailing before 1975. It may be supposed that such a solution is preferred by the CMEA for reasons of prestige (minimal recognition of the EEC and its agencies) and by the individual countries out of considerations of national economic policy (as little loss of sovereignty to the CMEA agencies as possible and maximum freedom of action in relations with individual Western countries). The draft agreement now authorizes negotiations on the competence (as small as possible) for bloc-to-bloc agreements and for agreements of individual CMEA countries with the EEC.

On the other hand, the EEC would like to acquire for itself as broad a competence as possible for agreements between EEC agencies and individual Eastern countries and to allow bloc-to-bloc agreements only for a few less important questions. In the view of the EEC Commission, bilateral agreements should be reduced to a minimum. The individual EEC countries would probably like to retain their freedom of action not only in respect of intergovernmental agreements but also in some other areas as well, e.g., credits.

The particular provisions of the CMEA draft agreement have to be examined in more detail in the light of these initial differences in interests. Too much importance should probably not be attached to the fact that the draft agreement mentions only the EEC and not the EEC bodies (Council, Commission), which according to the Treaty of Rome are empowered to carry out negotiations on commercial policy and conclude agreements. The CMEA bodies and their range of powers and responsibilities are also not men-

tioned. Where powers are given to the CMEA and EEC in the draft agreement, it remains for the legal statutes of each to determine which bodies shall exercise these powers. The powers and responsibilities of the CMEA and EEC are described in Article 3 of the CMEA proposal as follows:
— improvement of conditions for trade and economic cooperation between CMEA member countries and EEC member countries;
— standardization;
— protection of the environment;
— statistics;
— economic forecasting in the sphere of production and consumption under the agreed headings.

By mutual agreement other areas of reciprocal relations may also be specified when necessary. In accordance with their mandates the EEC and CMEA will promote and support the development of direct cooperation between CMEA and EEC members in the above-specified areas.

The view, expressed in many commentaries, that the powers and responsibilities of the two economic communities should be reduced to subsidiary areas [37] does not follow clearly from the text of Article 3. True, the draft speaks of the member countries and not of the EEC and CMEA with regard to "improving the conditions for trade and economic cooperation"; but it must be borne in mind that even in the EEC conception, which envisages agreements between EEC agencies and the Eastern nations, a contract would indeed be undersigned by the Commission, but trade and cooperation would, within the framework of these agreements, be pursued and implemented between the EEC and CMEA member countries or their firms. The last paragraph of Article 3 of the CMEA proposal, which additionally mentions the promotion and support of direct cooperation between member countries of both communities in the areas indicated, does at least suggest that the community bodies themselves should be given some powers in the area of commerce and economic cooperation.

The text of Article 4 of the CMEA proposal could cause greater reservations; it cites the forms in which relations should be developed under the jurisdiction of the CMEA and EEC. The draft agreement speaks only of studies, preparation of problems, exchange of information, regular contacts between representatives of both communities, and the organization of conferences, seminars, and symposia. Nothing is said about negotiations or the conclusion of agreements. The CMEA jurists have obviously not yet thought

114

this question out thoroughly. If, namely, the EEC and CMEA agencies have no way to negotiate with one another and to come to an agreement, then there can be no negotiations over the proposed CMEA draft agreement, not to speak of the possibility of concluding such an agreement.

Article 5 contains a nonbinding list of desirable points pertaining to the assistance given by the CMEA and EEC for a constant and balanced growth of East-West trade, diversification of the commodity structure, and the assurance of favorable conditions for commercial and economic cooperation.

Articles 6 through 10 require most-favored-nation status, the abolition of all import and export restrictions insofar as they are not applied to all third countries, the prohibition of measures that would disrupt markets, the elimination of all protectionist policies on agricultural products that do not apply equally to all third countries, and the granting of favorable credit terms. Clearly the CMEA draft agreement is demanding here unilateral concessions to the CMEA countries without offering any concessions in return. It cannot be expected, however, that the CMEA would offer concessions in return on its own initiative before serious negotiations on these questions have even begun, without knowing which of the concessions it wants the EEC is ready to grant. The EEC must obviously take a stand on these points and spell out what it wants in terms of concessions from the CMEA.

Article 11, which is technically the most important but most ambiguously formulated article, permits, for the first time in an official CMEA document on relations to the EEC collectively and to its members, multilateral as well as bilateral arrangements between EEC and CMEA countries. Furthermore in Paragraph 2 of Article 15 direct contacts, understandings, and agreements between individual CMEA countries and agencies of the EEC are provided for. These contacts, understandings, and agreements may also be established between individual EEC countries and CMEA bodies as well as between "competent economic organizations."[28]

One positive feature of Article 11 — in addition to its permitting agreements between the EEC and individual CMEA countries — is that agencies of the EEC which could conclude such agreements and understandings are mentioned for the first time. But it is extremely unclear what sort of questions could be negotiated and what sort of contractual arrangement could be reached. The first paragraph speaks of "individual questions of commercial-economic relations," while the second paragraph mentions "individual concrete questions." In the second paragraph it is stated that contractual agreements between the agencies of the EEC and individual CMEA countries may be undertaken "on the basis of the accepted principles of the Agreement." The accepted principles of the agreement are not set forth unambiguously; it is nevertheless clear from the document as a whole that the countries individually, not the community as a whole, should be the principal party to reciprocal relations. Nevertheless, as we have indicated above, both the EEC and the CMEA shall have certain areas of responsibility (see Articles 3 and 4) with regard to developing mutual relations.

The various areas listed in Articles 6 through 10 belong under the jurisdiction of the EEC agencies, as indeed the Treaty of Rome makes explicit; but the formulation in the CMEA draft agreement gives the impression that these matters shall be the responsibility primarily of the individual CMEA and EEC countries. This is especially clear from Article 6, which provides for reciprocation of most-favored-nation status. Agreements between the particular countries are mentioned explicitly. Negotiations on the abolition of import and export restrictions in accordance with Article 7 are to be carried out by the member countries, while the EEC and CMEA should cooperate "as much as possible" in implementing the appropriate measures. Article 8 states that the EEC and CMEA and their members individually may act to prevent conduct that might damage the market, while according to Article 9, the EEC and CMEA themselves should intervene directly to promote trade in agricultural products. With regard to credits both organizations should study the relevant questions in order to find ways to achieve balanced growth of trade, while the member countries should grant credits to one another on the most favorable terms possible.

The principles of the Treaty of Rome concerning the common commercial policy are but inadequately taken into account, as witness the relevant clauses, some of them quoted verbatim, of the CMEA draft. On the other hand, it emerges from Article 3, read with Paragraph 2 of Article 11, that the competent bodies of the EEC (and of CMEA) should also be given an official standing in the matter of improving conditions for trade and economic cooperation between the member states of the two groupings. If we assume that this does not refer to the spheres dealt with in Articles 6 to 10, the question arises whether there are other spheres left where an improvement of conditions for trade and economic cooperation might possibly be achieved.

116

Although nowhere clearly stated, a feasible solution does seem to take shape on which, after protracted preliminary preparations and without prematurely disclosing its designs, the CMEA seems to be setting its sights. The EEC and CMEA might negotiate the principles underlying Articles 6 through 10 and enter into frame agreements, while concrete provisions would be worked out in bilateral negotiations between individual member states of the two groupings on the basis of those principles. This, then, is visualized on the CMEA side. But the EEC side wants the EEC Commission brought in under such circumstances to ensure adherence to its common commercial policy. In terms of Article 11, Paragraph 2, CMEA member countries would then be permitted to come to understandings and enter into agreements directly with the appropriate EEC organs "concerning individual concrete questions."[29] But CMEA wants to maintain and enforce "bloc discipline" and wishes to reserve to itself at least a say in decisions whether individual CMEA member countries should in any particular case be permitted to negotiate, in terms of Article 11, Paragraph 2, with the EEC organs. It is with this end in view that the CMEA draft agreement demands, under Article 14, the institution of a mixed commission of representatives of the CMEA, EEC, and member states concerned. The mixed commission is to assist, among other things, in solving the "individual concrete questions" referred to in Article 11, Paragraph 2, thereby effectively reserving to itself the ultimate decision whether the individual CMEA member country is to be allowed to negotiate with the EEC Commission. The EEC must now think about whether such a solution, which from an institutional viewpoint is probably the most extreme possible for the CMEA, is acceptable. The conditions would be that it recognize the CMEA's authority to negotiate, which it had long refused to do, since according to the official EEC view, the CMEA agencies do not have this authority. Furthermore, the counterconsiderations for concessions in the areas listed in Articles 6 through 10 would have to be stipulated precisely. So far the EEC has insisted on the principle of mutual concessions but has usually not been able to define concretely the required counterconsiderations. The draft agreement contains a number of other controversial terms, whose analysis however would go beyond the bounds of this study. Given the complexity of the matter one can understand that the EEC has not hastened to come up with an official reply to the CMEA draft agreement.

Despite EEC hesitation recent developments indicate that relations between the two integration groupings probably will ultimately be negotiated on a modified bloc-to-bloc basis. Whether, or to what extent, such negotiations will curb the freedom of action of the smaller Eastern countries will depend essentially on the EEC side's negotiating skill and flexibility, but also on numerous political and economic background factors.

Economic Relations and Cooperation between the United States and the Soviet Union

For two decades economic relations between the United States and the Soviet Union were almost nonexistent. After President Nixon's visit to Moscow in May 1972, however, a change occurred whose significance went beyond the basic accord on numerous American-Soviet agreements. After this Soviet-American rapprochement at the government level, Soviet officials in economic matters and a number of leading American corporations displayed great interest in expanding mutual economic relations.

The aftermath of the basic accord of May 1972 between the Soviet Union and the United States provided a basis for a number of specific contracts and agreements [39]: e.g., a trade agreement (November 18, 1972);[30] an agreement to liquidate old Soviet lend-lease debts from World War II; an agreement on scientific-technical cooperation (May 24, 1972); further agreements on wheat deliveries on credit to the Soviet Union (July 8, 1972), on certain maritime questions (October 14, 1972, and May 25, 1973), on cooperation in agriculture (June 9, 1973), on health (May 23, 1973), on space exploration (January 21, 1973), on the peaceful use of atomic energy (June 22, 1973), on environmental protection (May 23, 1972); and a dual taxation agreement (June 20, 1973).

In June 1973 (during Brezhnev's visit to the United States) the two countries agreed to establish a USSR-USA chamber of commerce, and the US-USSR Trade and Economic Council Inc. was founded in October 1973. To date, 120 American firms and about 80 Soviet organizations have established ties with the Council. In late 1973 the Council opened an office in New York, and in October 1974, one in Moscow.

In December 1974 the U.S. Congress approved a new trade act that made most-favored-nation status for the Soviet Union contingent on a liberal Soviet emigration policy. In response the Soviet

Table 19

U.S. Exports of Industrial and Agricultural Goods to the USSR and other Eastern Countries

U.S. exports to	Mill. $				Change over previous year in %		
	1972	1973	1974	1975	1973	1974	1975
USSR							
all goods	546.6	1,187.1	611.9	1,832.6	117.2	−48.5	199.5
of which, industrial goods	102.4	264.9	292.5	670.1	158.7	10.4	129.1
agricultural products	444.2	922.2	319.4	1,162.5	107.6	−65.4	264.0
Eastern Europe*							
all goods	270.1	605.2	819.8	945.5	124.1	35.5	15.3
of which, industrial goods	71.9	105.7	283.1	303.8	47.0	167.8	7.3
agricultural products	198.2	499.5	536.7	641.7	152.0	7.4	19.6
CMEA							
all goods	816.7	1,792.3	1,431.7	2,778.1	119.5	−20.1	94.0
of which, industrial goods	174.2	370.6	575.7	973.9	112.7	55.3	69.2
agricultural products	642.5	1,421.7	856.0	1,804.2	121.3	−39.8	110.8

Source: Business International, Eastern Europe Report, 1975, no. 7, and 1976, no. 12.
*Without USSR.

119

Union terminated the Soviet-American trade agreement in January 1975. At the same time, the agreement for the liquidation of old Soviet debts was also canceled. The U.S. Export-Import Bank's credit restrictions also probably contributed to the Soviet withdrawal from the trade agreement.

The effects of this move on Soviet-American relations were variously assessed, to some extent contradictorily. No immediate slackening of American deliveries to the Soviet market was noticeable in export development. U.S. exports on industrial goods to the Soviet Union rose by 159% in 1973, by only 10% in 1974, but again by 129% in 1975, after cancellation of the agreement (Table 19). The United States was thus more successful than Western Europe in both 1973 and 1975; Western European exports to the Soviet Union increased by 45% in 1973, 55% in 1974, and 50% in 1975. On the other hand, U.S. Treasury Secretary Simon called attention to Soviet figures according to which Soviet orders to the sum of $1.6 billion were given to Japanese and West German firms, rather than American firms, in the first ten months of 1975 [40]. In a number of cases the Soviet Union's orders were probably placed with Western European subsidiaries or licensees of American firms that gave them access to more favorable Western European (government) credits as well as to the desired technology.[31] Some specific examples are the orders placed with the Kellog Co. in France (subsidiary of Pullman Inc.), the German subsidiary of KATY Industries Inc., and the British subsidiary of General Motors (for an order from Poland) [41].

Despite the cancellation of the trade agreement, economic contacts between the United States and the Soviet Union continued in 1975, and numerous proposals concerning the expansion of trade, the exchange of information, etc., have been put forth. For example, the Soviet Union gave the United States confidential information on priorities in the 1976-80 five-year plan [42]. According to reports in 1976 the United States postponed negotiations of several Soviet-American commissions as a reaction to the Soviet role in Angola [43]; the effect of such a move on mutual trade, however, will probably not be very significant.

The Soviet-American agreement on scientific-technical cooperation, regarded as the most central, was not canceled by the USSR. The obvious implication is that the Soviet Union is interested in expanding economic relations with the United States, with emphasis on technology transfer and the exchange of knowledge and know-how.

Article 3 of the Soviet-American cooperation agreement provides for the following forms of cooperation between the two countries:
— exchange of scientists and specialists;
— exchange of scientific and technical information and source material;
— common development and execution of projects and programs in basic and applied research;
— common research, development, and experiments and exchange of research results and experience between scientific institutions and organizations;
— organization of joint conferences and symposia;
— promotion of contacts between U.S. firms and Soviet enterprises, insofar as this seems desirable to interests on both sides; and
— other forms of scientific and technical cooperation by agreement.

Cooperation shall start in six principal areas (with a total of twenty-five working groups): energy technology; use and management of computer technology; agricultural research; microbiological synthetic processes; chemical catalysis; water regulation and supply. Six other areas were selected for possible cooperation: forestry; norms and standards; oceanography; transportation; physics and metallurgy; deep-sea drilling projects.

As a result of this agreement forty-four U.S. firms had concluded agreements on scientific and technological cooperation by mid-1975, and six other agreements were being negotiated. In almost all cases the Soviet partner in these agreements was the State Committee for Science and Technology,[32] while the Americans were mostly multinationals or major corporations.[33] Another ninety-two cooperation agreements between American and Soviet firms, including thirty-three license and know-how agreements[34] and fifty-four agreements on the delivery of complete plants, were in force by mid-1975 [44].

East-West Cooperation and the Developing Countries

Trade and Cooperation of the Eastern Countries with the Developing Countries

While in their policy statements the Eastern countries stress the importance of expanding economic relations with the developing countries (see the Comprehensive Program [1]), trade between the two groups has not been very extensive; indeed, over the past decade it has grown at a below-average rate. Of total world exports, deliveries from the Eastern countries (including the communist countries of Asia) to the developing countries were 1.7% in 1965 and only 1.3% in 1974; exports from these countries to the East were 1.3% and 1.0%, respectively, of the world exports [3, 14].

In the sixties exports from the East to the developing countries increased at a much faster rate than imports from them [14]. In 1968-72 exports and imports increased by an average of 8% annually [15]. Since 1973 Eastern trade with the developing countries has in general grown more rapidly than the total trade of the Eastern countries, whereby in addition to price hikes a growing willingness to receive products from the developing countries was also discernible [3].

Of total CMEA exports and imports, 12-14% and 8-11%, respectively, go to or come from the developing countries. Trade between the Eastern countries and the developing countries is typically complementary, with foodstuffs and raw materials being exchanged for finished products (particularly machinery and chemicals) [46]. The foreign trade of the Eastern bloc is concentrated on a few developing countries: 83% of all Soviet imports from the developing countries in 1974 came from ten principal nations which seemed important because of political considerations [46]. Of the total imports of the oil-producing countries, 6.2% and 4.8% came from the Eastern countries in 1972 and 1974; for the other developing countries these figures were 8.6% and 6.9%, respectively. Of the total exports of the oil-exporting countries, 1.7% went to Eastern Europe in both 1972 and 1974, while 6.4% of the exports of the other developing countries went to the East in these years [3].

For some years now the Eastern countries have been encouraging the expansion of cooperation relations with the developing countries, just as they have been doing with the Western industrial countries; political reasons are, of course, also involved in addition to the economic ones. By the end of 1970 the number of cooperation agreements between the Eastern countries and the developing countries seems to have been about 200; at the end of 1974 there were as many as 600, with 180 being concluded in that year [15, 47]. There are, however, few statistics available on the actual scope of cooperation agreements between the developing countries and the Eastern nations.

Table 20 reviews 167 agreements on industrial cooperation concluded from 1970 through 1974 between the Eastern countries and the developing nations; the breakdown is by industrial branch and shows the Eastern countries and the major developing countries

Table 20

Agreements on Industrial Cooperation between Eastern Countries and Developing Countries by Industrial Branch, 1970-74

					Number of Agreements						
	Mining	Metallurgy	Oil, gas	Power plants	Agriculture	Machinery	Transportation facilities	Foodstuffs	Textiles, leather	Other	All branches
Total	32	8	20	14	8	27	8	19	21	10	167
Participating Eastern countries											
CSSR	3	2	5	5	1	7	1	6	7	4	41
USSR	9	3	3	5	1	4	1	2	4	2	34
Hungary	7	–	1	2	–	6	2	2	3	2	25
Romania	4	1	5	1	2	5	2	1	2	–	23
Bulgaria	4	–	3	–	1	3	–	2	3	1	17
Poland	3	1	1	1	1	2	2	3	1	–	15
GDR	2	1	2	–	2	–	–	3	1	1	12
Main developing countries											
India	4	2	2	5	1	6	2	2	3	–	27
Egypt	1	4	1	1	1	2	1	2	2	–	15
Iran	2	–	3	2	–	1	–	1	3	1	13
Algeria	3	–	3	1	–	2	1	–	2	–	12
Iraq	2	–	1	–	–	1	1	1	3	–	9
Chile	1	–	–	2	–	3	1	–	–	–	7
Others	19	2	10	3	6	12	2	13	8	9	84

Source: UN, World Economic Survey, 1974, part one, New York, 1975, table 64 (agreements of Eastern European planned economies with developing countries, without Cuba).

123

involved. The breakdown is very uneven: there is a concentration in mining (32 agreements), energy resources (crude oil 20, power station construction 14 agreements), and foodstuffs and light industry. There are 27 agreements in the machine-building industry. Most of the agreements have been made with developing countries with which the Eastern countries have or had good political relations: 27 with India, 15 with Egypt, 12 with Algeria, 9 with Iraq, and 7 with Chile. Czechoslovakia was involved in almost a quarter of the agreements, followed by the USSR and Hungary. It is noteworthy that the GDR has concluded only 12 agreements (including 5 in the foodstuffs industry and agriculture) with developing countries.

There is no more detailed information on the forms of cooperation practiced between the Eastern countries and the developing countries, yet a good portion of them seem to involve deliveries of plant by the Eastern countries to the developing countries or similar such projects, in which payment is effected at least in part in products manufactured or procured with the delivered plant. Agreements on subcontracting and coproduction and on joint ventures seem also to have increased. Most of the joint ventures have involved projects for tapping raw materials in the developing countries.

Agreements concluded by the CMEA with Iraq and Mexico provide for the expansion of cooperation to financing, science and technology, trade, industry, mining, and maritime transport. Quite recently cooperation between the Eastern countries and the OPEC countries has intensified. Several projects provide for capital imports to the Eastern countries and cover both simple credit (e.g., from Kuwait to Romania and Hungary) and closer forms of cooperation. For example, Kuwait will supply half the costs of a petrochemical plant in Romania designed to process crude oil from Kuwait. Iran intends to invest $350 million in the paper and foodstuffs industries in Poland, with payment to be made in products manufactured in the new plant. Iran and Romania have concluded agreements on joint ventures for the construction of cement and tool factories, mechanized bakeries, petrochemical plants, and refineries. A pulp and paper combine is being constructed in the USSR with the help of Iranian credits ($100 million), with payment to ensue in pulp and paper products. A 740-km-long crude oil pipeline through Yugoslavia, Hungary, and Czechoslovakia will be financed largely by Kuwait and Libya. In November 1974 Iran granted Bulgaria a $185 million credit for joint ventures, including a $50 million project for foodstuff packaging. Iran's share in these projects is 25%[35] [15, 48].

Some cooperation projects between Eastern nations and developing countries are still in the negotiation stage. It is questionable whether in view of the diminishing foreign exchange incomes of the OPEC countries in the last years all these projects will actually be realized.

Tripartite Cooperation[36]

Industrial cooperation in third countries, particularly in developing countries, is an especially interesting and promising form of East-West cooperation. Where the participants in such projects are enterprises and organizations from the Western industrial countries, the Eastern countries, and the developing countries, it is called "industrial tripartite cooperation."[37]

Tripartite cooperation has reached a significant level only in the last few years. Statistics from UNCTAD [50] show 132 cases of tripartite cooperation in mid-1975, in which thirty-three developing countries, thirteen Western industrial countries, and seven Eastern countries participated. Since 1971 alone 92 agreements (69.5%) have been concluded, and 55 of them (41.7%) were in 1973-74. Table 21 shows a breakdown of tripartite cooperation by country.[38]

Although the number of participations in joint projects provides only a very inexact picture, it still has a number of interesting features. The FRG and France lead the field in the West; these countries maintain close relations with both the developing countries and the Eastern countries. In third place, before Italy, the United States, and Great Britain, is Austria, whose trade with the developing countries is very modest. Austria's high ranking on the list of nations involved in tripartite cooperation evidently derives from its many years of close cooperation with the East. UNCTAD has also called express attention to the fact that only a very loose connection exists between participation in tripartite cooperation and trade among the respective countries. Among the Eastern nations most agreements have involved Poland and Hungary, countries which also lead the way in East-West cooperation. Czechoslovakia and the USSR, which usually have bilateral agreements with the developing countries (see Table 20), are in third and fourth place. Among the thirty-three "developing countries" Yugoslavia is involved in 23 agreements out of 132; the OPEC countries participate in another 43 (Iraq alone participates in 12). The developing

125

Table 21

Tripartite Cooperation* between East, West, and Developing Countries, 1975

Number

Developing countries†

	Number			Number
OPEC countries	43	Other developing countries		66
of which:		of which:		
Iraq	12	India		12
Iran	7	Morocco		9
Algeria	6	Egypt		6
Libya	5	Syria		5
Nigeria	5	Brazil		4
Kuwait	5	Lebanon		4
Other OPEC	3	Cameroon		3
		Others		23‡
Yugoslavia	23			
Developing countries, total	132			

Western industrial countries†

	Number
FRG	36
France	33
Austria	20
Italy	18
USA	15
Great Britain	9
Belgium	8
Sweden	6
Switzerland	6
Others	17§
Total	168

Eastern countries†

	Number
Poland	40
Hungary	39
USSR	21
CSSR	19
Romania	16
GDR	11
Bulgaria	6
Total	153‖

Source: UNCTAD, Tripartite Industrial Co-operation, UNCTAD/secretariat, November 25, 1975.

*Concluded projects and projects in progress.

†The total of cooperative undertakings is not the same in all the groups because several countries are participating in several projects.

‡Including three projects in which the participating developing country is not known.

§Including five projects in which the participating Western industrial country is not known.

‖Including one project in which the participating Eastern country is not known.

countries of the "fourth world" are involved in only 66 projects.

The total cost of tripartite cooperation projects was $21 billion (at the prevailing prices) according to UNCTAD estimates; this is one eighth of the capital goods imports of the developing countries from 1964 to 1973. The figure, however, would seem to exaggerate the importance of tripartite cooperation, since obviously counterdeliveries as well as projects that are still in the negotiating stage are also included in the figure cited.

The majority (83%) of tripartite cooperation agreements involved the manufacturing industries, above all iron and steel, chemicals, vehicles, and crude oil. Another 10% were in power plant construction, and 3.5% each in mining and transport. The UNCTAD statistics indicate that most of the technology involved in tripartite cooperation agreements came from Western industrial nations; in several instances the Eastern countries were willing to enter into compensation agreements.

In many instances the financial problem can be solved more easily by distributing the financing among suppliers in the East and West. In the Western countries the subcontracts of the Eastern partner are frequently cofinanced. In some financing agreements between West European countries and developing countries, the possibility of tripartite cooperation is explicitly provided for [50]. Occasionally, however, further problems arise in tripartite cooperation: in projects financed by the World Bank no credits may be granted by the bank for the Eastern European share of the delivery since no Eastern European country, with the exception of Romania, is a member of the World Bank. This problem arose, for example, in a joint project of the FRG with Poland and Morocco [51].

Payments between many developing countries and the Eastern nations are settled by bilateral clearing. The developing countries, which have scant foreign exchange reserves, do not need hard currency to pay for the Eastern European portion of the delivery; sometimes it is even possible to clear the entire tripartite cooperation project between the developing country and the Eastern nation, the latter then paying the Western European partner in foreign exchange (or by compensation with Eastern European products). This procedure was used at the beginning of the sixties in a joint project between the Austrian firm Simmering-Graz-Pauker and Hungarian enterprises to build two power plants in India.

German firms cooperate with Eastern firms on projects in developing countries because of cheaper subcontracting, the payments agreements existing between the Eastern countries and the developing countries, the willingness of the Eastern nations to take over counterdeliveries, and finally even to facilitate exports to the Eastern countries [51]. In the West tripartite cooperation is often evaluated with caution, both with regard to its present significance and the possibilities of its expansion [51]. In the FRG this form of cooperation has been utilized in only a few cases, mainly in deliveries of whole plants to developing countries.

The advantage of tripartite cooperation to developing countries is that they receive tried and proven Western technology while saving foreign exchange, and they are better able to invest in counterdeliveries; the sale of the product of the cooperation venture is less vulnerable to business cycle fluctuations, and the financing of the project is shared among several countries. For the Western partner tripartite cooperation often means that the offer may be made cheaper. Finally, the Eastern partner can sometimes be spared costly and risky new developments. East-West cooperation may of course entail disadvantages for the developing country when possible competitors from East and West form a sellers' cartel to the detriment of the developing country before offers are tendered.

Effects of East-West Cooperation on the Developing Countries

Aside from the mixed advantages of tripartite cooperation, any enhancement of cooperative relations between East and West would probably have indirect disadvantages for the developing countries if suitable countervailing measures are not adopted.

The most serious problem of the oil-importing developing countries is at present their negative balance of payments. At the end of 1973 the foreign debt of eighty-six developing countries ran to $118.9 billion; the debt service alone on outstanding commitments will be $10-13 billion annually [52] during the seventies. The total debt of the oil-importing nations rose further in 1974 and 1975. The promotion of exports from developing countries by giving them easier access to the markets of the industrial countries in East and West is one of the most important measures of development aid.

The Eastern countries can promote imports from the developing countries by giving them greater consideration in their five-year plans. Also, if they were to reduce retail prices, which are sometimes quite exorbitant, for southern fruits and other foodstuffs and semiluxuries from the developing countries,[39] they could raise

128

consumption of these goods, now rather low, and thereby increase the sales potential of the developing countries. Although Eastern European nations (except for the USSR) are typically coffee-consuming countries, their coffee imports per capita for 1972-73 were only 1.35 kg (0.15 kg in the Soviet Union) compared with 5.04 kg for the EEC. Imports of cocoa were 0.97 kg per capita (0.51 kg in the Soviet Union and 1.90 kg in the EEC countries). The differences for southern fruits are sometimes even greater [47]. The developing countries' (Group of 77) demands in this respect on the Eastern countries were set forth in the Manila Platform in early 1976 [53].

Western import barriers against the developing countries consist of duties, import quotas, and nontariff trade obstacles. Protectionism is strong in agriculture, the foodstuffs industry, and the textile and garment industries, sectors which are important for the developing countries. Although most of the Western industrial nations have given the developing nations customs preferences (even total freedom from duties), the expansion of economic relations between West and East (particularly the expansion of cooperation) creates special problems for the developing countries.

For many products, especially simple and wage-intensive industrial products (textiles, garments, chemicals, metal goods, toys, and wooden articles), the developing countries and the Eastern nations compete in their offers; and this problem will be further aggravated as the developing countries become increasingly industrialized. East-West industrial cooperation is also intended to promote the sale of Eastern products in the West, and the Eastern nations have their sights set on duty reductions, at least for the products of cooperative undertakings. A reduction of customs duties for the Eastern countries would to a large extent neutralize the customs advantages the developing countries have already obtained. Most of the Western industrial nations anyway give the same preferential customs treatment to the more backward Eastern nations as to the developing nations.

A reasonable solution to this problem can only be reached through a gradual streamlining of the commodity structure of East-West trade, eliminating products the developing countries could produce at lower costs now or in the near future. In practice this means an increase in the proportion of high-grade finished products in Eastern deliveries to the West. Moves of this sort would require extensive structural changes in East and West.

The CSCE and East-West Industrial Cooperation

The final act of the Conference on Security and Cooperation in Europe (CSCE)[40] contains in "Basket II"[41] general guidelines for an expansion of cooperation among the participating nations in the economy, science and technology, and environmental questions. The question of economic cooperation was taken up in the CSCE negotiations at the request of the Soviet Union.[42]

Industrial cooperation plays a major role in "Basket II."[43] In the agreement the multiplicity of forms and objectives of cooperation is commented on, and it is acknowledged that new forms can even be developed to meet specific needs. The improvement in the reciprocal flow of information, especially on laws and regulations, (e.g., on foreign exchange) is especially stressed. Information on the general features of state economic plans and programs, priorities, and economic market conditions is also vital. Business contacts could stand substantial improvement, and trained personnel to work on cooperative projects should be ensured suitable working conditions. Protection of the interests of the partners in a cooperative venture, including legal protection of all assets, should be guaranteed. Economic policy and state economic plans and programs should meet the requirements and conform to the possibilities of industrial cooperation in a way compatible with both economic systems. Greater participation by smaller and medium-sized enterprises in industrial cooperation should be encouraged.

Interestingly, a distinction is made between industrial cooperation in the strict sense and projects of common interest. The latter term refers to long-term cooperation on large-scale ventures involving the harnessing of energy sources and the tapping of other raw material sources, as well as transport and communication; for projects of common interest the terms and conditions regulating industrial cooperation ought to apply. This distinction has obviously been made in an effort to embrace all definitions of industrial cooperation that vary from country to country.

The agreements of the CSCE on industrial cooperation can be seen as a basis for the conclusion of bilateral cooperation agreements (see Chapter 8), or even as the first step toward a multilateral agreement on cooperation.[44]

Notes

1. Since prices in intra-CMEA trade are currently rising more slowly than

prices in East-West trade, a fall-off in the share of intra-CMEA trade in the total foreign trade of the CMEA does not necessarily imply a decrease in the volume of intra-CMEA trade.

2. Although this approach is often found in the literature; see [5].

3. The transferable ruble is meant only for clearing outstanding balances in intra-CMEA trade and cannot be used as a convertible currency outside the CMEA.

4. On the difficulties and unresolved problems of international socialist enterprises, see the last section of Chapter 6.

5. E. g., in their relations with the EEC; see the next section of this chapter.

6. The opposite view has been expressed by M. M. Maksimova: "As distinct from the capitalist-type economic relations, industrial cooperation between countries with different social systems contains no possibility for one partner to become unilaterally dependent, economically or technologically, on the other; neither can it ever lead to subordination or absorption of, let us say, a smaller partner, whether socialist or capitalist, by the larger one." See [9a].

7. In Poland and Romania, even more than 30% of total imports come from the EEC. For the importance of the EEC in East-West trade see [11, 12, 13] and statistical material in [14, 15].

8. From 3% to 5% of total EEC trade is with the Eastern countries. In the recession year of 1975 the share of Eastern exports rose considerably in all EEC countries, e.g., in the FRG 7.2%, as compared with 5.5% in 1973.

9. The Western European EFTA countries, which are associated with the EEC through free trade agreements (leading to complete elimination of customs duty), retained their full sovereignty in trade matters.

10. On the other hand, see the most recent trends and proposals of the CMEA and the USSR (pp. 97-106 and 111-18).

11. "The CCP (common commercial policy) is still a rather nebulous affair" [11].

12. "The EEC was and is a reactionary and aggressive supranational state monopoly alliance with one goal: to transform the small capitalist Europe into an imperialistic superstate, to work as long as possible against a change in power relations in favor of the world socialist system, and to counter national liberation movements with a special form of neocolonialism" [20]. Also see [19, 21, 22].

13. Brezhnev's statement in March 1972 marked a turning point: "The Soviet Union by no means ignores the real situation in Western Europe nor an economic grouping such as the Common Market.... Our relations with the grouping will, of course, depend on the extent to which the realities of socialist Europe, which includes the CMEA alliance, are acknowledged."

14. In the question of recognition and of economic policy there are no problems between the People's Republic of China and the EEC. In September 1975 an ambassador from the People's Republic of China was accredited with the EEC in Brussels.

15. See [11, 23].

16. In official EEC usage "a state trading country" refers to the Eastern European countries, the People's Republic of China, and the communist countries of Asia (but not Yugoslavia).

17. According to the provisions of the EEC treaty, the court may be petitioned by the Commission, the Council, and a member nation for an opinion on the compatibility of a contemplated international agreement with the treaty. This opinion was the first of its kind.

131

18. "With respect to state trading nations, in the view of the Commission the best way to ensure a harmonious and continuous expansion of trade and the solution of particular problems is through the conclusion of long-term trade agreements between the Community and these nations" [34].

19. This draft takes the trade agreement of the EEC with Yugoslavia, which provided for no reciprocal customs preferences, as its reference point.

20. As well as the non-European CMEA members, Cuba and Mongolia.

21. On the effects of a liberalization of Eastern imports by the FRG and Austria, see [32, 33].

22. This aspect is persuasively commented on by P. Hanson [11].

23. Exchange of goods between the GDR and the FRG for which special terms are laid out in the Treaty of Rome (e.g., no duty).

24. In informal conversations influential Soviet CMEA officials have pointed out that there is nothing in the valid CMEA statutes that would stand in the way of authorizing the CMEA to negotiate and conclude international agreements if the member nations declare their desire to do so.

25. For example, it was possible for the CMEA and Finland to conclude an agreement on cooperation in May 1973 that provided for the formation of a mixed CMEA-Finnish commission.

26. The request of the EEC delegation for a copy of the new CMEA statutes was rejected with the excuse that they were not yet in force, since not all the member nations had yet ratified them. Nonetheless the statutes were published in the CMEA information bulletin in January 1975 [35].

27. The English text of the draft agreement is presented in Appendix 3.

28. The English translation is extremely vague on this point. It is impossible to determine whether the EEC and the CMEA are the "competent economic organizations" referred to, or whether separate international economic organizations, as stipulated in the Comprehensive Program, chapter II, section 8 [1], are what is meant.

29. The CMEA draft agreement might be interpreted in this way by the smaller Eastern countries [38].

30. The major points of the agreement are: most-favored-nation clause (made contingent on the approval of the U.S. Congress); prevention of damage to U.S. markets; reciprocal trade credits; establishment of trade missions; establishment of a trade center in Moscow; arbitrage agreements.

31. Placing an order with the foreign subsidiary of an American parent company might have negative effects on American employment policy if no diversion of other orders to the parent company takes place.

32. According to Soviet statistics, fifty-five agreements between the State Committee for Science and Technology and the United States were in force in spring 1976 [45].

33. Firms on Fortune's 1975 list of the 500 largest American firms participated in thirty-eight of the forty-four agreements on scientific-technical cooperation.

34. Interestingly, thirteen of these agreements have dealt with the transfer of Soviet licenses and know-how to U.S. firms (see Tables 7, 8, and 9).

35. This information is not quite in accord with Bulgaria's refusal, to date, to enter into domestic joint ventures.

36. A recent study by Adler-Karlsson [49] deals with relations between developing countries, the Eastern nations, and the West.

37. This form of economic relations between the industrial nations of the East and West and the developing countries is a matter of special interest to UNCTAD. Tripartite cooperation was the subject of an UNCTAD seminar in December 1975, "Industrial Specialization through Various Forms of Multilateral Cooperation"[50].

38. Since firms from a number of Western and Eastern countries participate in numerous projects, the number of participations is higher for this group of countries than for the developing countries.

39. The retail prices of these products carry an extremely high turnover tax.

40. The CSCE opened on June 3, 1973, and closed in the session of July 29-August 1, 1975, in Helsinki. The Final Act was signed by thirty-five partici-pating nations (all the European countries, except Albania, and the United States and Canada) [54].

41. Basket II, "Cooperation in the Field of Economics, of Science and Tech-nology, and of the Environment," is broken down into a preamble and six sec-tions: 1. commercial exchanges; 2. industrial cooperation and projects of com-mon interest; 3. provisions concerning trade and industrial cooperation; 4. sci-ence and technology; 5. environment; 6. cooperation in other areas.

42. For the goals of the USSR in negotiations on "Basket II" and on the views of the EEC, see [55, 56].

43. The agreements of the CSCE on industrial cooperation are given in Ap-pendix 4.

44. In reference to this point the official bulletin of the EEC says: "The chap-ter (of the final document of the CSCE) on industrial cooperation is of special interest, since it is the first multilateral document on this question" [57].

References

[1] Comprehensive Programme for the Further Extension and Improvement of Co-operation and the Development of Socialist Economic Integration by the CMEA Member-Countries, Moscow, CMEA Secretariat, 1971.

[2] B. Askanas, H. Askanas, and F. Levcik, "Structural Developments in CMEA Foreign Trade over the Last Fifteen Years (1960-1974)," Forschungsberichte des Wiener Institutes für Internationale Wirtschaftsvergleiche, 1975, no. 23.

[3] GATT, International Trade 1974/75, Geneva, 1975.

[4] ECE, Economic Bulletin for Europe, vol. 23, no. 2, New York, United Na-tions, 1972.

[5] B. Balassa, "Types of Economic Integration," paper presented at 4th World Congress of the International Economic Association, Budapest, August 19-24, 1975.

[6] R. Selucky, "East-West Economic Relations: The Eastern European Policy Perspective," in C. H. McMillan ed., Changing Perspectives in East-West Commerce, Toronto-London, Lexington Books, 1974.

[7] Chase World Information Corporation, East-West Markets, April 19, 1976.

[8] G. Varga, "Közös Stratégia Kidolgozása," Figyelő (Budapest), June 1973, no. 26.

[9] Iu. Kormnov and I. Petrov, "Razriadka napriazhennosti i khoziaistvennoe sotrudnichestvo," Voprosy ekonomiki, 1972, no. 2.

[9a] M. M. Maksimova, "Industrial Co-operation Between Socialist and Capital-

ist Countries: Forms, Trends and Problems," in East-West Cooperation in Business. Inter-firm Studies, Vienna, East-West European Economic Interaction, Workshop Papers, vol. 2, 1977, p. 18.

[10] "East European Co-operation with the West Draws Soviet Criticism," Business International, Eastern Europe Report, April 1976, no. 15.

[11] Ph. Hanson, "The European Community's Commercial Relations with the CMEA Countries: Problems and Prospects," in C. H. McMillan ed., Changing Perspectives in East-West Commerce, Toronto-London, Lexington Books, 1974.

[12] C. Ransom, The European Community and Eastern Europe, London, 1973.

[13] J. Stankovsky, "Osthandel der EG und der EFTA," Vienna, Creditanstalt-Bankverein, Wirtschaftsberichte, 1972, no. 6.

[14] GATT, International Trade 1973/74, Geneva, 1974, p. 146.

[15] ECE, Economic Bulletin for Europe, vol. 27, Geneva, United Nations, 1975, table 2.6.

[16] Kommission der EG, Information — Auswärtige Beziehungen, 91/75: Die Europäische Gemeinschaft und die osteuropäischen Länder.

[17] M. Baummer and H. Jacobsen, Internationale Wirtschaftsorganisationen und Ost-West-Kooperation, Stiftung Wissenschaft und Politik, Ebenhausen, 1975, pp. 42 ff.

[18] F. Franzmayer and H. Machowski, "Willensbildung und Entscheidungsprozesse in der Europäischen Gemeinschaft und im Rat für gegenseitige Wirtschaftshilfe," Europa-Archiv., 1975, issue 2.

[19] "Initiative des RGW bei der Gemeinschaft," EG-Bulletin, 1976, no. 2.

[20] K. H. Domdey and J. L. Schmidt, eds., "Europäische Sicherheit und internationale Wirtschaftsbeziehungen," Berlin (DDR), cited in H. Machowski, "Länder des Rates für gegenseitige Wirtschaftshilfe," in Aussenpolitische Perspektiven des westdeutschen Staates, Munich, 1972.

[21] H. Mayrzedt and H. Romé, eds., Die westeuropäische Integration aus osteuropäischer Sicht, Vienna, 1968.

[22] H. Schaefer, "Kommunistische Westpolitik und die EWG," Osteuropäische Rundschau, February 1971, March 1971; "Osteuropa revidiert Einstellung zum Gemeinsamen Markt," Osteuropäische Rundschau, June 1972.

[23] J. Stankovsky, "Die Handelspolitik der Europäischen Gemeinschaften gegenüber den Oststaaten," Quartalshefte der Girozentrale, Vienna, 1973, no. 1-2.

[24] Entscheidung des Rates der EG über die schrittweise Vereinheitlichung der Abkommen über die Handelsbeziehungen zwischen den Mitgliedsstaaten und dritten Ländern und über die Aushandlung der gemeinschaftlichen Abkommen vom 16. Dezember 1969.

[25] Entscheidung des Rates vom 27. März über die autonomen Einfuhrregelungen aus den Oststaaten, Abl. der EG, Nr. L 99, April 21, 1975; see also EG-Bulletin, 1974, no. 12, Ziffer 2336.

[26] Kommissionsvorschläge zur Miteinbeziehung der "Kooperationsabkommen" der Mitgliedsstaaten mit den Ostblockländern in die Gemeinschaftlichen Verfahren, Europe-Dokumente, Brüssel, Nr. 766, September 23, 1973 (this also contains detailed explanations); also Abl. der EG, Nr. C 106/22, December 6, 1973.

[27] Ch. Sasse, "Kooperationsabkommen und EG-Handelspolitik. Parallelität oder Konflikt?" Europa-Archiv, 1974, no. 20.

[28] Entscheidung des Rates vom 22. Juli 1974 über die Einführung eines Konsultationsverfahrens für Kooperationsabkommen der Mitgliedsstaaten mit

dritten Ländern. Abl. der EG, Nr. L 208/23, July 30, 1974.

[29] EGKS, EWG, EAG-Kommission, Neunter Gesamtbericht über die Tätigkeit der Europäischen Gemeinschaften — 1975, Brussels-Luxembourg, 1976, p. 315.

[30] Verordnung zur Festlegung einer gemeinsamen Regelung für die Einfuhren aus Staatshandelsländern, VO 109/70, December 19, 1969.

[31] Verordnung Nr. 3054/74 des Rates für bestimmte Erzeugnisse mit Ursprung in Entwicklungsländern (Rumänien), Abl. der EG, Nr. L 329/70, December 9, 1974.

[32] T. A. Wolf, "The Impact of Elimination of West German Quantitative Restrictions on Imports from Centrally Planned Economies," Weltwirtschaftliches Archiv (Kiel), vol. 2, 1976.

[33] T. A. Wolf, "The Effects of Liberalization of Austrian Quantitative Restrictions on Imports from CMEA Countries," Empirica (Vienna), 1976, no. 2.

[34] EGKS, EWG, EAG-Kommission, Achter Gesamtbericht über die Tätigkeit der Europäischen Gemeinschaften — 1974, Brussels-Luxembourg, 1975, p. XXXIX.

[35] A. Lebahn, "Die Position des Rates für Gegenseitige Wirtschaftshilfe (RGW) gegenüber den Europäischen Gemeinschaften (EG)," Archiv des öffentlichen Rechtes, 1975, no. 4.

[36] Status des Rates für Gegenseitige Wirtschaftshilfe vom 14. Dezember 1974 in der Fassung vom 21. Juni 1974; also Konvention über die Rechtsfähigkeit, Privilegien und Immunitäten des Rates für Gegenseitige Wirtschaftshilfe vom 14. Dezember 1974 in der Fassung vom 21. Juni 1974, Informationsbulletin des RGW, 1975, no. 1, German translation (with commentary): Europa-Archiv, 1975, no. 11.

[37] East-West, Brussels, April 8, 1976, no. 151; also February 26, 1976, no. 148.

[38] M. Perczynski, "Economic Co-operation in Europe in the Context of Relations between EEC and CMEA," in Mario Guttieres, ed., New Aspects of Economic Relations Between the Two Integration Groups in Europe, Vienna, Gazzetta Publishing House, 1977.

[39] "U.S.-Soviet Commercial Relations," in The Soviet Economic Prospects for the Seventies, Washington, U.S.G.P.O., 1973.

[40] The Times, January 30, 1976.

[41] Business Week, February 23, 1976, in Moscow Narodny Bank, Press Bulletin, February 25, 1976.

[42] Chase World Information Corporation, East-West-Markets, March 10, 1976.

[43] Chase World Information Corporation, East-West-Markets, March 22, 1976.

[44] The U.S. Perspective on East-West Industrial Co-operation (preliminary), Bloomington, International Development Research Center of Indiana University, Team of Researchers, June 1975.

[45] Chase World Information Corporation, East-West-Markets, May 3, 1976.

[46] S. Schultz, "Osthandel der Entwicklungsländer," DIW-Wochenbericht, 1976, no. 10.

[47] UN, World Economic Survey 1974, part one, New York, 1975.

[48] W. Hendricks, "Banking and Financial Aspects of Tripartite Industrial Co-operation," Discussion Paper, UNCTAD, TAD/SEM, 1/4, Geneva, 1975.

[49] G. Adler-Karlsson, The Political Economy of East-West-South Co-operation, Vienna, Studien über Wirtschafts- und Systemvergleiche, vol. 7, 1976.

[50] UNCTAD, Tripartite Industrial Co-operation, UNCTAD Secretariat, TAD/SEM, 1/2, Geneva, November 25, 1975.

[51] K. Bolz and P. Plötz, "Participation in Tripartite Co-operation," Inter-economics, 1975, no. 9; K. Bolz and P. Plötz, Bericht über die industriellen Kooperationsbeziehungen zwischen der BRD, den sozialistischen Ländern Osteuropas und den Entwicklungsländern, Hamburg, HWWA-Institut für Wirtschaftsforschung, 1975.

[52] The World Bank Annual Report, 1975, tables 5 and 7.

[53] Chase World Information Corporation, East-West-Markets, May 17, 1976; UNCTAD, Manila Declaration and Programme of Action, GE 76-62076, February 12, 1976.

[54] "Conference on Security and Cooperation in Europe: Final Act," Department of State Bulletin, September 1, 1925, pp. 323-50.

[55] P. Hermes, "Die wirtschaftlichen Implikationen der KSZE," Wirtschafts-dienst, 1975, no. 8.

[56] G. Wettig, "Zum Ergebnis der KSZE," Berichte des Bundesinstitutes für Ostwissenschaftliche und Internationale Studien (Cologne), 1975, no. 42.

[57] EG-Bulletin, 1975, no. 7-8, pp. 10f.

8

Objectives and significance of intergovernmental cooperation agreements

Since the second half of the sixties, and particularly in the seventies, the establishment of cooperative relations between Western firms and Eastern European economic organizations and enterprises has been reinforced by more and more intergovernmental agreements concluded to promote economic, industrial, and scientific-technical cooperation. To understand the role and significance of these agreements it is useful to briefly discuss the development of trade relations between the market economies of Western Europe and the centrally planned economies of Eastern Europe.

International Agreements for the Regulation of East-West Trade during the Postwar Period

During the cold war East-West trade was minimal, since neither the autarkically oriented economic plans of the East nor the restrictive, quasi-blockade policies of the West permitted any positive development [1, 2]. The development of East-West economic relations did not get under way seriously until the late fifties, when long-term (usually five-year) trade agreements gradually entered the picture [3]. By 1960 there were over twenty long-term bilateral trade agreements in effect between Eastern and Western nations. Since then their number has quadrupled (Table 22).

The development of a payments system between Eastern and Western partners had a great deal to do with this rapid increase in the number of long-term intergovernment agreements. Whereas a system of bilateral clearing dominated through the fifties, the sixties were marked by a shift to payments in freely convertible currencies in East-West trade. Now Eastern trade with almost all Western industrial countries is settled in convertible curren-

Table 22

Long-term Bilateral Trade Agreements between
Eastern Countries and Western European Industrial Countries

	Number of agreements		
	1960	1966	1974
Eastern European countries			
Bulgaria	1	9	14
CSSR	5	8	15
GDR	—	3	6
Hungary	2	8	13
Poland	2	10	14
Romania	2	7	15
USSR	11	10	13
Total	23	55	90
Western European industrial countries			
Austria	4	5	7
Benelux	—	2	6
Denmark	2	6	6
Finland	1	6	7
France	2	6	6
FRG	2	3	6
Great Britain	5	5	6
Greece	2	6	4
Iceland	2	2	6
Ireland	—	—	4
Italy	1	7	6
Norway	1	4	7
Spain	—	—	7
Sweden	1	3	7
Switzerland	—	—	5
Total	23	55	90

Source: ECE Documents, TRADE/202, supp. 1, September 9, 1968, and
TRADE/R. 302, October 10, 1974.

cies. Only trade between the FRG and the GDR is still cleared
bilaterally.[1] Multilateral payments in freely convertible currencies involve a number of specific problems, however, since the

Eastern currencies are still nonconvertible.[2] Since the CMEA nations can now settle their trade with any Western country in its convertible currency, it is no longer necessary to settle accounts annually with each trading partner.[3] The Eastern nation has only to see to it that its overall balance of trade in convertible currencies is kept in equilibrium, with the aid of credits when necessary. In this way the burden of maintaining a balance between the goods flows between two trading partners is shifted to the Western partner [7].

One consequence of this development is that since the late sixties, economic relations between Eastern and Western countries have grown beyond simple commercial ties, and new forms of cooperation in economic matters, science and technology, and production itself have begun to emerge. Both sides are interested in agreements that will cover not merely trade but also more general economic questions, science and technology, and even credit and financing, and will in this way expand economic relations across a wide front.

New factors have emerged in this new phase: long-term trade agreements now cover broader areas and deal with different problems than in the past; initially they had served as merely a framework for setting annual quotas for products. Now broad intergovernmental agreements to promote economic, industrial, and scientific-technical cooperation are being concluded; and quite recently skeleton agreements have been arrived at covering trade and cooperation over the long term (at least ten years, or even with no specified time limit). Table 23 gives some idea how the number of these cooperative agreements has increased over the years. The result is a veritable net of intergovernmental agreements, often overlapping in content, to regulate economic relations between the respective partners.

Content and Aims of Intergovernmental
Commercial and Cooperation Agreements

In all long-term intergovernmental agreements one can discern the following new features:

The content and range of applicability of contractual arrangements are continuously expanding. It is not just nations already versed in the practice of formalizing their relations in international agreements that are entering into such accords; now nations that previously had had no or only informal relations are entering

Table 23

Long-term Bilateral Cooperation Agreements
between Eastern Countries and Western European
Industrial Countries

	Number of cooperation agreements	
	1966-67	1975
Eastern European countries		
Bulgaria	3	13
CSSR	1	11
GDR	—	11
Hungary	2	13
Poland	5	13
Romania	6	13
USSR	—	11
Total	17	85
Western European industrial countries		
Austria	—	7
Belgium-Luxembourg	4	7
Denmark	3	7
Finland	—	7
France	1	7
FRG	1	6
Great Britain	2	7
Italy	4	7
Netherlands	2	7
Norway	—	6
Spain	—	5
Sweden	—	6
Switzerland	—	6
Total	17	85

Source: ECE Documents, TRADE/202, Supp. 1, September 9, 1968, and
TRADE/R. 317/Add. 1/Corr. 1/20, November 1975.

the picture (e.g., Switzerland, the GDR). Whereas previously arrangements concerned mainly trade, now agreements on cooperation are becoming more frequent. All agreements anticipate the
establishment of joint commissions to prepare in detail and super-

vise the implementation of the agreement. In the more recent agreements the powers of these commissions are defined more precisely than had formerly been the practice. Thus a body whose functions had originally been limited primarily to handling grievances is being transformed into an instrument empowered to take positive action to promote trade and cooperation [8].

Commercial Agreements

The commercial agreements concluded at the end of the sixties and in the seventies usually covered the following points, in addition to provisions for the establishment of joint commissions:

1. Declarations of intent to expand mutual trade. Many agreements also contain general programs for the expansion of trade, e.g., to double it within the period covered by the agreement, with special stress on expanding trade volume through the exchange of machinery, equipment, and other finished products.

2. Stipulation of terms and conditions regulating the exchange of goods. In some agreements, especially with Eastern nations that are members of GATT, the most-favored-nation status is stipulated explicitly. Generally even Eastern nations that are not members of GATT are granted most-favored-nation treatment. For EEC member nations this means granting to the Eastern countries the lower conventional tariff given to all other third countries that are GATT members, but not exemption from the Community's common custom tariff on all goods coming from outside it. To date, the United States has accorded most-favored-nation treatment to Poland and Romania, but not to the other Eastern countries; for them this means much higher customs duties.

3. Declarations of intent from the Western partner to gradually eliminate quantitative restrictions, or at least to get rid of some of them during the period covered by the agreement, and to ease other nontariff trade restrictions (administrative formalities, standards, norms).

4. Mutual settlement procedures.

5. World market quotations are referred to in price-forming matters.

6. Usually procedures for conflict arbitration are specified in the agreement.

7. Ordinarily an agreement will extend over five years.

8. General measures to promote industrial cooperation, especially if no separate agreements on such matters had been made when the trade agreement is concluded.

Table 24

Long-term East-West Trade Agreements in Force at the End of July 1977
(period of validity and, in parentheses, date of signing)

	Bulgaria	CSSR	GDR	Hungary	Poland	Romania	USSR
Austria	—	1973-77** (11/7/72)	1973-78 (8/30/73)	1973-77 (11/11/72)	1977-81** (9/22/76)	1976-85 (5/20/76)	1976-85** (5/30/75)
Belgium-Luxembourg	—	—					
Canada	—	—	—	—	—	—	1971-76‡ (1/27/71) 1972-74** (4/7/72)
Cyprus	1970-74** (2/24/70)	1973-78 (6/6/73)	1969-73** (12/6/68)	1962-63** (3/6/62)	1974-75** (6/28/74)	1962-63** (6/19/62)	1977-81 (11/24/76)
Denmark							
Finland	1973-77 (12/21/72) indefinite# (4/26/74)	1975-80** (9/19/74) indefinite# (9/19/74)	1973-78 (6/20/73) indefinite# (3/4/75)	1969-73* (10/22/68) indefinite# (5/2/74)	1971-75** (12/4/70) indefinite# (9/29/76)	1971-75** (9/28/70)	1976-80 (9/12/74)
France	—	—	—	—	—	—	—
FRG		—	—	—			
Greece	1975-79** (2/28/75)	1964-67** (7/22/64)		—	1976-80** (11/4/75)	1976-81** (3/29/76)	1977-81** (4/29/77)
Iceland	—	1971-76** (10/12/72)	1973-77 (2/6/73)		1975-80** (4/30/75)	1972-77 (6/16/72)	1976-80 (10/31/75)
Ireland		—	—	—	—	—	—
Italy		—	—	—	—	—	—
Malta		indefinite (7/16/76)		1977-81** (1/19/77)			—
Netherlands	—	—					—

Country							
Norway	1975-79 (10/4/75)	1974-78** (11/29/73)	1974-78 (1/30/74)	—	1976-80 (3/29/76)	1976-80 (5/5/76)	1971-75 (6/18/71) extended for 1976-80 (10/15/75)
Portugal	1975-80** (2/11/75)	1975-79 (3/1/75)	1975-79 (1/25/75)	1975-80** (1/23/75)	—	1975-80** (6/14/75)	—
Spain	1971-75† (6/2/71)	1972-76** (10/5/71)	1974-75† (4/4/74)	1976-86‡ (4/8/76)	1974-84‡ (6/3/74)	1971-75‡** (3/5/71)	1972-75** (9/15/72)
Sweden	1972-76 extended for 1977 (9/14/72)	1973-77 (3/30/73)	1974-78 (7/26/73)	1973-78 (12/5/73)	1973-77 (10/25/72)	1973-77 (5/10/73)	1977-81** (4/7/76)
Switzerland	1973-77** (11/23/72)	1971-75** (5/7/71)	1976-80** (6/27/75)	1974-78** (10/30/73)	1973-78** (6/25/73)	1973-78** (12/13/72)	—
Turkey	1975-76† (8/29/75)	1975-76† (8/29/75)	†	1974-75† (11/12/74)	†	—	†
United Kingdom	—		—	—	—		
United States	—		—	—	§	1975-78** (4/2/75)	1973-75§‖ (10/18/72)
Yugoslavia	—	1976-80 (12/10/75)	—	—	—	—	—

Source: ECE Documents, TRADE/R.334/Rev. 2, Annex 1.

*Long-term agreement extended in current annual protocols.

†Annually extended trade agreements or protocols.

‡Agreements on trade, shipping, transport, economic, industrial, and technical cooperation.

§Protocols on different aspects of trade relations exist.

‖Agreement not yet in force.

#Agreement on reciprocal removal of trade barriers.

**Thereafter the validity is automatically extended unless notice of termination is given.

Table 24 reviews East-West trade agreements in force at the end of 1974.[4]

In general it is evident from these characteristics of long-term trade agreements between East and West that the aims of such agreements have changed with time. At the time of the first agreements, when bilateral clearing procedures were in general use, long-term trade agreements served mainly as a basis for the conclusion of an annual trade protocol that set goods quotas for individual commodities and groups of goods in both directions. This function diminished in importance as the shift was made to payments in convertible currency and the quantitative restrictions of the Western partners were gradually liberalized. In the process, however, the traditional type of trade agreement lost some of its raison d'être and was increasingly replaced by bilateral intergovernmental agreements on economic, industrial, and scientific-technical cooperation.

Cooperation Agreements

Since the late sixties promotion of cooperative relations has been included as a clause in trade agreements. Later, cooperation became the subject of special promotional agreements.

Intergovernmental cooperation agreements usually cover the following points, aside from the establishment of joint commissions and other working groups:

1. The specification of a mutual interest in stable and lasting cooperation and a declaration of intention to facilitate and promote the harmonious and dynamic development of cooperative relations between organizations and enterprises of both parties.

2. Definition of the form of cooperation in which the partners are especially interested. In particular, existing promotional agreements have preferred forms of cooperation such as:
— joint construction of industrial plant and modernization of existing plant;
— various forms of coproduction and specialization and cooperation in sales and marketing;
— cooperation in the field of licensing and patents, the transfer of know-how, and cooperation in industrial research and development;
— establishment of joint ventures in third countries.

3. Specification of economic sectors and areas of research in which cooperation is to be especially promoted.

4. Declaration of intention to promote cooperative ventures,

Table 25

Economic, Industrial, and Technical Cooperation Agreements in Force at the End of July 1977
(period of validity and, in parentheses, date of signing)

	Bulgaria	CSSR	GDR	Hungary	Poland	Romania	USSR
Austria	—	indefinite* (9/12/71)	1975-85†† (12/7/74)	indefinite (11/15/68)	1974-84 (9/6/73)	1975-85†† (7/14/75)	indefinite (5/24/68) 1973-83 (2/1/73)
Belgium-Luxembourg	indefinite** (6/14/66) 1975-84†† (3/26/74)	1975-85†† (9/10/75)	1974-84 (8/31/74)	1975-85†† (10/6/75)	1973-83 (11/22/73) 1975-80† (4/10/75)	indefinite (5/27/76)	1974-84 (11/19/74)
Canada	—	—	—	—	—	—	1971-76‖ (1/27/71)
Cyprus	—	—	—	—	—	—	indefinite (10/1/75)
Denmark	indefinite (4/22/75)	indefinite (11/9/70)	1974-83 (2/21/74)	1976-86†† (2/18/76)	indefinite (11/20/74) 1976-86†† (5/17/76)	indefinite (8/29/67)	indefinite (7/17/70) 1975-85†† (8/28/75)
Finland	1975-84 (8/12/74)	1971-75† (3/1/71)	1973-83 (6/20/73)	1975-84†† (9/2/74)	1974-84 (1/30/74)	indefinite (9/3/76)	1971-81 (4/20/71) 1977-90# (5/18/77)
France	indefinite* (7/10/68) 1974-84 (11/-/74) 1976-81† (3/19/76)	indefinite† (2/23/70) 1975-85 (11/14/75)	1973-83 (7/19/73) 1975-80† (7/11/75)	1974-84 (11/25/74)	1972-82 (10/5/72) 1975-80# (6/20/75)	indefinite (2/2/67) indefinite (1/17/69) 1975-85 (8/28/75)	1971-81 (10/27/71) 1973-83# (7/10/73)

Country							
FRG	1975-84 (5/14/75)	indefinite (1/22/75)	—	1974-84 (11/11/74)	1974-84 (11/1/74); 1976-81† (6/11/76)	1973-83 (6/29/73)	1973-83 (5/19/73); 1973-83† (10/30/74); 1973-83# (1/18/74)
Greece	indefinite (11/25/72)	—	—	—	1976-80†† (11/4/75)	1976-81†† (2/21/76)	—
Iceland	—	—	—	—	—	—	—
Ireland	—	—	—	—	1977-87†† (6/13/77)	—	1976-85†† (12/16/76)
Italy	indefinite* (9/20/66); 1974-84 (5/27/74); 1975-79† (6/23/75)	indefinite (4/30/70)	1973-83 (4/18/73)	indefinite* (12/1/65); 1974-84 (5/25/74)	indefinite (7/14/65); 1974-84 (1/17/74); 1975-79† (10/28/75)	indefinite (9/6/65); 1973-83 (5/22/73)	1974-84 (7/25/74); 1975-84†† (7/27/75); 1975-79†† (11/20/75)
Malta	—	—	—	—	—	—	—
Netherlands	1976-86 (12/11/74)	indefinite (11/19/75)	1975-85 (6/12/74)	1975-85†† (7/18/75)	1975-85 (7/2/74); 1977-82† (11/26/76)	1976-86 (5/14/75)	1976-86†† (7/15/75)
Norway	indefinite (9/22/70)	—	1975-85 (7/9/75)	indefinite (1/17/70)	1973-82 (11/28/72)	indefinite (11/29/68); 1975-80† (1/28/75)	indefinite (5/19/72); 1975-80† (10/3/75)
Portugal	1976-80 (11/23/75)	—	1976-80†† (6/29/76)	1975-80†† (1/23/75)	1975-80 (5/14/75)	1975-80†† (6/14/75)	1975-80 (10/3/75)
Spain	1971-75‖†† (6/2/71)	—	—	1976-86‖ (4/8/76)	1974-84‖ (6/3/74)	1971-75†† (3/5/71); 1977-... (1/19/77)	—

	1	2	3	4	5	6	7
Sweden	indefinite (5/26/70) 1975-85# (2/19/75)	indefinite† (10/13/71)	1976-86†† (1/15/76)	indefinite (5/12/69)	1974-84# (4/3/74) 1975-85†† (6/5/75)	indefinite (4/9/68)	indefinite (1/12/70) 1975-85# (4/25/75)
Switzerland	1973-77††† (11/23/72) 1975-80†† (9/13/75)	1971-75‡†† (5/7/71)	1975-80††† (6/27/75)	1974-78†† (10/30/73) 1977-81†† (1/11/77)	1973-78††† (6/25/73)	1973-78††† (12/13/72) 1975-82†† (8/29/75)	1973-78††† (12/13/72) —
Turkey		1976-80 (1/6/76)	—	indefinite (3/24/72)			—
United Kingdom	1974-84 (5/6/74)	1968-72‡†† (3/26/63) 1972-77 (9/8/72)	1973-83†† (12/18/73)		1973-82 (3/20/73) 1977-82††† (12/16/76)	1972-77† (6/15/72) 1975-85 (9/18/75) indefinite# (1/28/77)	1974-84 (5/6/74)
United States	—	—	—	—	—	1977-87†† (11/21/76)	1972-..‡§ (-.-.) extended for five years (7/8/77) 1974-84 (6/29/74)
Yugoslavia	indefinite (7/16/64)	indefinite (12/13/68)	—	indefinite (3/27/63)	indefinite (2/2/58)	indefinite (1/13/67)	indefinite (2/27/69)

Source: ECE Documents, TRADE/R.334/Rev. 2, Annex II/III.

*Agreements on economic and industrial cooperation.
†Agreements on economic/cooperation relations.
‡Agreements on scientific and technical cooperation
§Five-year agreement (renewable) in the field of applied science and technology.

‖Agreement on trade, shipping, transport, economic, industrial, and technical cooperation.
#Comprehensive program on economic, industrial, and technical cooperation.
**Agreement on economic and technical cooperation.
††Automatically extended.

147

particularly through the granting of special trade concessions which constitute exemptions from general rules. In some agreements most-favored-nation status, the abolition of quantitative restrictions, credits on especially favorable terms, and exceptional tariff concessions for goods specified in the cooperation agreement are mentioned.

5. Often the period of validity of the particular arrangements or of the basic cooperation agreement is unspecified; it will then be supplemented by other, more specific ten-year agreements and programs. The intended durability of the agreement is also in some cases indirectly alluded to by specifying a long-term period for giving notice.

Table 25 reviews current agreements promoting cooperation between Western and Eastern European countries. Special attention is paid to the establishment of institutions guaranteeing the fulfillment of the agreements. In addition to the joint commissions already mentioned, joint working groups for particular branches of industry or areas of cooperation may be established [9].

The executive machinery of an agreement can be illustrated by the example of an accord between France and the Soviet Union. A permanent joint commission ("Grande Commission") meets semiannually. This commission is supposed to supervise the implementation of all trade, economic, and cooperation agreements that have been concluded between the two countries. Another joint commission ("Petite Commission"), below the rank of minister, deals with concrete questions concerning the implementation of the agreement on economic, technical, and scientific cooperation. Below the "Petite Commission" joint working groups deal with individual branches and areas. Working groups have been set up for the basic industries (mining, forestry, and timber), branches of the manufacturing industry (e.g., automobiles and tractors), and research-intensive branches (precision instruments, electronics industry). Special working groups were set up for the exchange of information, licenses and patents, and the development of joint norms and standards. Still other working groups are responsible for the development of color television technology and the technology of space research. A French-Soviet Chamber of Commerce was set up along with the intergovernmental institutions [10].

Similar, if perhaps less differentiated institutions have been set up in long-term cooperation agreements between other Eastern and Western countries. Table 26 gives a review of all Austrian cooperation agreements with Eastern European countries and

Table 26

Intergovernmental Cooperation Agreements between Austria and the Eastern Nations

Country	Type of agreement	Focus of cooperation	from	to	Term for giving notice	Commission meetings	Comments
Bulgaria	cooperation agreement	expansion of production, utilization of capacities, manufacturing, production of raw materials, planning and implementation of projects	5/6/68	no time limit	6 months at any time	at least once a year, alternately in Vienna and Sofia	areas: machinery and ship construction, metallurgy, electronics and electrical equipment, petrochemicals, Danube tourism
	ten-year program	expansion and improvement of cooperation, especially in foreign trade, industrial projects, and scientific-technical cooperation	10/10/73	10/9/83	—		consultative
CSSR	cooperation agreement	production and expansion of production, planning of projects, utilization of capacity	12/14/71	no time limit	6 months at any time	at least once a year, alternately in Vienna and Prague	bank agreements to promote joint export to third countries; working groups for metallurgy and heavy machinery, general machinery building, electrical equipment and electronics; other areas: chemicals, lumber, glass, foodstuffs, construction
GDR	ten-year cooperation agreement	production and marketing, project planning, licensing and know-how, exchange of experience, technical research, standards and quality control	2/5/75	2/4/84	6 months before expiration	at partner's request, alternately in Austria and GDR	possible 5-year extension; area: machinery and turn-key plant, chemicals, metallurgy, and electrical equipment

Country	Agreement	Content	Start	End	Notice	Review	Area
Poland	cooperation protocol (added to long-term agreement, 9/9/71)	raw material deliveries, etc., and marketing of products manufactured from them, delivery of materials for current production and expansion of manufacturing program, expansion of production for subcontracting, cooperation on third markets	1/1/72	12/31/76	3 months before expiration	at partner's desire, at least once annually, alternately in Austria and Poland	possible 5-year extension; permanent working groups for heavy industry (especially metallurgy), machinery industry (especially cars), chemicals, and energy
	ten-year cooperation agreement	development and intensification of long-term cooperation with specific goals; common planning and implementation of projects, research, cultivation of contacts	11/5/73	11/4/83 or 88	6 months before expiration		area: machine building, electrical equipment, heavy industry, mining and energy sources, car industry, chemicals, lumber and paper, agriculture
Romania	cooperation agreement	utilization of capacity, planning and implementation of projects, expansion of manufacturing program, production of commodities	4/1/68	no time limit	6 months at any time	any time at partner's desire	area: heavy industry (metallurgy), cylinders and drive chains, textile products
	ten-year cooperation agreement	deepening and facilitating long-term cooperation, joint industrial projects, setting up mixed companies	5/75	5/85	6 months		
USSR	cooperation agreement	production and planning, research and exchange of experience, rationalization and technical development, exchange of information and experts	5/24/68	no time limit	6 months at any time		permanent contact office in Moscow; working groups for: machinery and equipment, and standardization and metrology; area of activity: electrical equipment; chemicals, car manufacturing; varnishes and paints, fertilizers, ferrous metallurgy, natural gas, and Danube shipping

		Start	End	Termination notice	Meetings	Committees/working groups
	development agreement	long-term expansion of cooperation with specific goals, promotion of exchange of goods, collaboration on building industrial complexes	4/2/73	4/1/83	6 months at any time	at least once a year, alternately in Vienna and Moscow	possible 5-year extension
	ten-year program	investing in areas for ten-year cooperation, especially trade, industrial and technical cooperation, industrial planning, transit trade	7/3/73	6/30/83	—		consultative, contact committee of chambers of commerce
Hungary	cooperation agreement	as in CSSR, also raw materials production and processing, joint exports	1/1/69	no time limit	6 months at any time	at least once a year, alternately in Vienna and Budapest	mutual contact committees; working groups: chemicals, machinery, light industry
Yugoslavia	cooperation agreement	raw materials production, and processing, production, specialization, marketing, project planning, patents and licenses, research, capital investments, co-operation on third markets	2/18/73	no time limit	6 months at any time	at partner's request, alternately in Austria and Yugoslavia	area: iron and steel, coal mining, nonferrous metals, permanent working groups for: energy, raw materials, and agriculture. Contact committee of chambers of commerce

Source: West-Ost Journal (Vienna), May 1975, no. 2.
As of: May 1975.

151

presents information on their legal form, the main point of cooperation, the period of validity and ways to give notice, commission meetings, relevant areas covered, and appropriate bank agreements [11].

Although the first experiences with long-term cooperation agreements were accumulated mainly between the nations of Eastern and Western Europe, this form of cooperation is by no means limited to the European nations. The Eastern European nations have also concluded such agreements with non-European partners; in particular, the USSR has agreements with Japan, Canada, and the United States that are of major importance for the expansion of economic relations between these countries.[5]

Assessment of the Significance of
Intergovernmental Cooperation Agreements

In attempting an assessment of the significance of cooperation agreements at the government level, it must first and foremost be borne in mind that the East in general ascribes far more importance to agreements of this sort, and indeed, the initiative to conclude such agreements usually comes from the East. Ordinarily the West responds to this initiative only with hesitation and accepts it often only under the pressure not to be left too far behind other Western countries that have already concluded such agreements.

Assessment by the West

The hesitation of Western governments is in part derived from theoretical and ideological conceptions of the role of the state in the economy. The textbook view, which still enjoys credence in many countries, that economic matters are exclusively the affair of autonomous economic units, and the state's role is only to create favorable general conditions for such activities, is extended to economic relations with the countries with a state foreign trade monopoly. Even in negotiations on traditional trade agreements, the Western representatives have had continually to stress that they could not assume commitments for private enterprises to deliver specified quantities of goods, much less commitments to purchase specified quantities of goods from the Eastern partner. However, cooperation agreements oblige Western governments to abandon the position of the arbiter who only sees to it that the rules are observed, and instead to perform positive acts to promote mutual economic relations.

Thus it is usually only the aim of promoting exports in a still relatively less developed market that induces Western governments to conclude cooperation agreements with Eastern nations. Since the possibility of direct contact between Western firms and Eastern European enterprises is extremely limited in most Eastern countries, Western governments hope through these agreements to obtain important information and contacts for Western firms or to create better conditions for their activities. Multinational corporations interested in trade with the East also exert their influence on Western governments to get them to conclude such agreements. They can point to their own experience that the mistrust, even fear, of Western contacts on the part of representatives of Eastern enterprises and agencies can be overcome if the cooperative ventures sought have prior official sanction in intergovernmental agreements.

In assessing all the numerous cooperation agreements that have been concluded, the close connection between political and economic factors should be borne in mind. Top-level meetings between politicians and statesmen of both blocs are becoming more and more frequent. It seems to have become almost a requirement in official state visits that a new agreement be signed to demonstrate the will to develop good relations. This partly explains why new agreements are concluded even though the formal arrangements already in force are still sufficient. This fact also makes it extremely difficult to maintain a clear distinction in an analysis between commercial agreements and cooperation agreements, since a mixed type with elements of both is becoming more frequent.

Assessment in the East

The Eastern assessment of cooperation agreements is basically positive, to a large extent because of the relationship between agreements promoting cooperation and trade agreements. According to the terms of the EEC common commercial policy (see the second section of Chapter 7), after the transitional period has elapsed, trade agreements with any third nations shall be concluded only by the Community and not by the individual nations as before. The Treaty of Rome, however, says nothing explicit about cooperation agreements. Since the Eastern European countries were so far unwilling to recognize the authority of the EEC Commission, they hoped to make the conclusion of "pure" trade agreements with the Community superfluous by entering into long-term cooperation agreements covering broader and broader areas. Although they have been partially successful in this aim, the CMEA countries seem to place some value on concluding additional commercial agreements with the EEC, judging from their most recent initiatives (see pp. 111-18).

The Eastern countries have even weightier grounds for positively assessing long-term intergovernmental agreements. Their entire planning mechanism, which must rely on long-term deliveries of final products, long-term supply of energy and materials, and long-term investment ventures, also prefers foreign trade mechanisms that help coordinate export and import flows and enter long-term, continuous connections, defined as specifically as possible, in production as well as in the stages preceding and following production (research and development, marketing).

The Eastern countries proceed from the assumption that a trend toward long-term planning and programming is also emerging in the West, at least at the enterprise level. In particular, most large and multinational firms program their production and trade activities several years in advance. Intergovernmental cooperation agreements setting down the main lines and contours of economic relations between two countries over the long term are taken into consideration by large corporations and indeed are often even shaped to conform to the wishes of the latter. Thus Eastern partners have found, in Western firms interested in Eastern trade, willing allies able to prod Western governments into concluding cooperation agreements. If intergovernmental agreements contain better customs and credit terms for products delivered under the terms of industrial cooperation, the private firms involved obtain advantages at the expense of state revenue, eventually the taxpayers.

The Eastern partners, particularly the USSR, have lately been trying, with increasing success, to promote compensation and payback deals, generally only reluctantly entered into in the West, in intergovernmental cooperation agreements. The reason given is that a material connection exists between the reciprocal deliveries. In 1975 the Soviet minister of foreign trade commented on the importance of such compensation transactions:

In accordance with such agreements (i.e., compensation agreements) the Western European partner supplies us on credit with equipment and material for developing specific types of goods and in return receives a portion of the output in repayment of the credit. The Soviet Union is very interested in expanding this form of cooperation, since it helps to speed up the exploitation of natural resources, the development of certain branches of the economy, and the expansion of our exports. In return the Western countries acquire an opportunity to expand their sale of machinery and equipment in the Soviet Union and hence of raising employment, which just at this time, when the Western economy is in serious difficulties, is hardly of minor importance [12].[6]

The minister goes on to praise cooperation with Finland and France and stresses the positive results of the cooperation agreements concluded with these countries at the government level over the past five years. However, statistics on the development of Soviet trade with Western European countries, which the minister evokes to support his position, do not fully accord with his assertions (Table 27).

Table 27

USSR Foreign Trade with Western European Countries

| | 1970 | 1974 | Average annual |
| | volume in mill. | | growth rate |
	rubles		1970-74, in %
Western Europe, total	3,674	9,623	27.2
FRG	544	2,209	42.0
Finland	531	1,540	30.5
Italy	472	1,137	24.6
France	413	941	22.9
Great Britain	641	990	8.6
Belgium	149	603	41.8
Netherlands	223	571	26.5
Sweden	235	436	16.7
Austria	155	340	21.7

Source: N. Patolichev, "The Current Stage of Trade and Economic Relations between the USSR and the West," Pravda, April 4, 1975.

The annual growth rates of trade on both sides show the FRG and Belgium leading the field in the last four years over Finland,

Holland, Italy, and France. The FRG has also had the greatest absolute increase in trade turnover, although it did not conclude a commercial agreement with the USSR until mid-1972, nor a co-operation agreement until mid-1973 (see Tables 24 and 25), whereas France was the first (as early as 1966) Western European country to enter into large-scale intergovernmental economic and cooperation agreements with the USSR.

The statistics also demonstrate the importance of normal and friendly political relations. Although already in the late sixties Great Britain had concluded long-term trade and cooperation agreements with the Soviet Union for the seventies, its trade with the Soviet Union has increased much more slowly over the past four years than has that of the other Western European countries. The cooling of political relations after a large number of Soviet diplomats and citizens were expelled from Great Britain was of course a setback for the development of economic relations. On the other hand, abrupt cooling of political relations between the USSR and the USA noticeable since early 1975 has had no immediate and direct negative effect on American exports to the Soviet Union, inasmuch as the latter is obviously interested in American technology.

It seems to be extremely difficult, then, to give a clear-cut evaluation of intergovernmental cooperation agreements without going into other aspects of them, such as, for example, the degree of interest of Western firms in expanding economic relations with the East, Eastern interest in Western technology, and smooth, untroubled political relations. If these factors are present, however, cooperation agreements can help create generally favorable conditions for the development of economic, technical, and industrial cooperation and may themselves develop into a useful instrument of trade policy.

Notes

1. Payments between Yugoslavia and some Eastern countries are now being made in freely convertible currency.

2. Although the CMEA Comprehensive Program provides for convertible Eastern currencies by 1980, no progress has been achieved so far in this area [4].

3. Swing agreements, which of course in most cases were equivalent to an interest-free credit from Western to Eastern nations, made bilateral settlements somewhat easier. EEC efforts to institute multilateral settlement of outstanding balances in bilateral clearing were not very successful. In Austria's clearing

settlements with the Eastern countries, which were not dissolved until the early seventies, some flexibility was achieved by means of transit and switch transactions [5, 6].

4. When this book went to press, no newer information was available.

5. Economic and cooperative relations between the USA and USSR are dealt with in the third section of Chapter 7.

6. The Soviet preference for this form of economic cooperation with the West was stressed at the Twenty-fifth Congress of the CPSU by both Brezhnev and Kosygin [13, 14].

References

[1] G. Adler-Karlsson, Western Economic Warfare 1947-1967, Stockholm, 1968.

[2] F. L. Pryor, The Communist Foreign Trade System, London, 1963.

[3] K. Owtschinnikow, "Europa: Langfristige Abkommen in den Wirtschafts- und Handelsbeziehungen zwischen Ost- und Westeuropa," Aussenhandel UdSSR (Moscow), 1974, no. 6.

[4] Comprehensive Programme for the Further Extension and Improvement of Co-operation and the Development of Socialist Economic Integration by the CMEA Member-Countries, Moscow, CMEA Secretariat, 1971.

[5] J. Stankovsky, "Der mittelbare Aussenhandel Österreichs mit den Oststaaten," Österreichisches Institut für Wirtschaftsforschung, Monatsberichte, 1967, no. 5.

[6] J. Stankovsky, "Der österreichische Transithandel," Quartalshefte der Girozentrale (Vienna), 1972, no. 3.

[7] F. Nemschak, "Perspektiven und Probleme des Ost-West-Handels unter besonderer Berücksichtigung Österreichs," Der Donauraum, 1973, vol. 4.

[8] ECE, Practical Measures to Remove Obstacles to Intra-Regional Trade and to Promote and Diversify Trade. Addendum: Long-term Agreements on Economic Co-operation and Trade, TRADE/R. 302/25. October 1974, and TRADE/R. 317/Add. 1/Corr. 1, 20. November 1975.

[9] L. A. Litvak and C. H. McMillan, "Intergovernmental Co-operation Agreements as a Framework for East-West Trade and Technology Transfer," in C. H. McMillan ed., Changing Perspectives in East-West Commerce, Toronto-London, Lexington Books, 1974.

[10] "Die französich-sowjetische Kooperation vor neuen Aufgaben. Neue Möglichkeiten der industriellen Zusammenarbeit," Neue Zürcher Zeitung, July 16, 1974.

[11] H. Boller, "Die Kooperationsabkommen Österreichs," West-Ost-Journal (Vienna), 1973, no. 6.

[12] N. Patolichev, "The Current Stage of Trade and Economic Relations between the USSR and the West," Pravda (Moscow), April 9, 1975.

[13] L. I. Brezhnev, "Report of the CPSU Central Committee to the 25th Congress of the CPSU, held in Moscow, Feb. 24, 1976," in Our Course: Peace and Socialism, Moscow: "Novosti" Publishers, 1977, pp. 126-28.

[14] A. N. Kosygin, "Hauptrichtungen der Entwicklung der Volkswirtschaft der UdSSR in den Jahren 1976-1980," XXV. Parteitag der KPdSU (Moscow), 1976, p. 56.

9

Industrial East-West cooperation
and the business cycle

An important, but somewhat neglected, aspect of the driving forces behind cooperation is its connection with the business cycle, e.g., the sensitivity of cooperation agreements to economic fluctuations.[1]

Effects of Western Business Cycles
on Foreign Trade and East-West Trade

There is a close relationship between economic growth and foreign trade which, however, may be obfuscated at times by other factors. In particular, a positive causal relationship exists between the business cycle and imports: fluctuations in domestic demand are disproportionately reflected in the demand for imported goods; this effect is usually compounded by price fluctuations, firm behavior, and government economic policy.[2]

A nation's exports are determined by its competitiveness, by the regional trade structure, and by the range of goods it exports. There is, if anything, a negative relationship between a nation's domestic economic activity and its exports because of "export push" (increased concentration on exports when the utilization of production capacity is low) [2].

The effect of Western business cycles on East-West trade is evident and may in part be demonstrated empirically [3]. During a boom the Eastern countries find a receptive market for their goods, even industrial finished products, in the West. There is a greater readiness to liberalize imports. During a recession, on the other hand, the Eastern countries are usually hit hard, since the demand, in terms of price and quantity, for their major export items (raw materials, primary products) is especially sensitive to business fluctuations; and for numerous finished products they are

158

marginal suppliers, so that they fall completely out of the picture during a recession.[3] On the other hand, the Western industrial nations step up their sales drive in the East during recessions and slacken it during booms.[4] A decline in foreign exchange proceeds forces the Eastern countries to make import cutbacks (usually after some delay). Lately, however, the relationship between the two commodity flows in East-West trade has been made somewhat slacker by an increased utilization of Western credit.

Connection between Western Business Trends and East-West Industrial Cooperation

East-West industrial cooperation is likewise affected by business trends. The conclusion of new agreements is especially sensitive in this respect. Usually, existing agreements cannot be adapted to business conditions easily because of formal contractual arrangements, but the partners may utilize those means they have at their disposal.

To assess the sensitivity of cooperation to business trends, a classification of cooperation agreements by the effects they are intended to have on production capacity is useful:
— expansion of capacity (creation of capacity reserves);
— better utilization of capacity;
— no effect on capacity.

The effects of cooperation on production capacity may be of short- (middle-), or long-term interest to the parties involved. In the first case cooperation is usually effected through a conjunction of complementary interests (i.e., expansion of capacity on one side, better utilization of capacity on the other) of the Eastern and Western partners; in the second case (long term) the two partners often pursue the same aims. Job processing and subcontracts are usually consonant with short-term capacity expansion in the West and with a better utilization of capacity in the East. In joint ventures long-term expansion of capacity is the primary interest of both partners. Coproduction and specialization agreements are also concluded to promote middle- and long-term expansion of capacity on both sides. In the case of long-term agreements, however, the partners usually reserve the right to adapt production to needs. In licensing agreements the better utilization of capacity (if the agreement is the only way to conclude a transaction)[5] or the expansion of capacity (if the Eastern partner has to make counterdeliveries) plays the more important role for the Western partner. Only where know-how is sold without any additional agreements on the sale of commodities is the effect on production capacity irrelevant.

The following hypotheses may be advanced to describe the sensitivity of cooperation agreements to business trends:

— During a boom Western firms will be interested in cooperative undertakings that promote short-term expansion of their delivery capacity (subcontracts and, more rarely, coproduction and specialization), while the interest in cooperative undertakings with only a long-term effect on capacity will be relatively less pronounced (also because of the credit restrictions and high interest rates that usually prevail during such periods).

— During downswings or recessions Western firms will not have too great an interest in forms of cooperation aimed at expanding capacity (or will try to reduce their commitments to such agreements). On the other hand, they will be very interested in long-term cooperation agreements without equivalent or with postponed material counterdeliveries (joint ventures, delivery of complete plants, most licensing agreements, cooperation on third markets).

— Cooperation agreements without an effect on capacity (agreements on scientific-technical cooperation and licensing agreements without additional sales objectives) are probably little effected by business trends.

These considerations are based on the reactions of Western firms; they may be modified by the long-term economic policies and programming of Western countries (this is especially important in connection with securing a durable source of fuels).

In Eastern Europe business trends evoke indirect reactions: in a recession foreign exchange restrictions could make it difficult or even impossible to conclude or implement a cooperation agreement; poor sales prospects for the product of a cooperative venture will diminish the Eastern partner's interest in cooperation. In general, Eastern enterprises are interested more in long-term cooperation agreements.

Empirical Evidence

The available material is not sufficient to analyze these hypotheses empirically: first, no method exists to arrive at even a rough idea of the scope of cooperative undertakings in quantitative terms;

and second, the period they cover is too short for adequate experience to have been accumulated. Still the following evidence may be adduced in support of our hypotheses.

In FRG statistics on cooperation with the East, a certain correlation with German business trends is discernible. FRG firms were eager for long-term cooperation agreements with the East in 1967, 1968, and 1972 (about 50% of the agreements during these years had a validity of ten years; in the other years long-term agreements made up only a small part of all those concluded). In 1967 and 1972 the number of cooperation agreements concluded was also far above average. In 1966, 1967, and 1971 the FRG economy recorded the lowest growth rate for the period studied. In periods of a business downswing and underutilization of capacity, German firms were especially interested in Eastern European markets and, moreover, were ready to make extensive concessions.

Table 28

Relationship between the Business Cycle and East-West
Industrial Cooperation in the FRG

Year	GNP, real change over previous year, in %	Share of cooperative undertakings over 10 years* in %[‡]	Frequency of cooperation[†]
1966	2.9	50	14
1967	0.0	50	ca. 10
1968	7.3	few	20
1969	8.0	few	under 10
1970	5.4	few	under 10
1971	2.8	50	40

Source: K. Bolz and P. Plötz, Erfahrungen aus der Ost-West-Kooperation, Hamburg, HWWA-Institut für Wirtschaftforschung, 1974, pp. 42 ff.
*Share of cooperative undertakings with a ten-year period of validity in total number of cooperative undertakings.
[†]Share of cooperation agreements concluded in respective year in total number of FRG cooperation agreements from 1967 through 1972.
[‡]One year behind the growth rate of GNP.

The Eastern European nations used this situation to conclude long-term cooperation agreements. Since negotiations usually ex-

tend over a long period, the effects of business trends on cooperation statistics show up only after about one year, which equals the
average length of cooperation negotiation. In good business years
the duration as well as the number of FRG cooperative undertakings with the East decreased (Table 28).

Three of the case studies in Appendix 1 illustrate the sensitivity
of East-West cooperation agreements to business trends. Study 2
shows that the success of the project was dependent on auspicious
timing with respect to the business cycle, in addition of course to
other factors (excess demand of Canadian farmers for tractors).
Study 1 shows how the Eastern partner lost interest in cooperation
during a recession in the West and hence placed the success of the
cooperative undertaking in jeopardy. Case study 11 describes a
cooperation agreement concluded during a recession: the agreement provided for extensive counterdeliveries from the East European partner at a later date, but with an escape clause for the next
downswing. All these examples, however, have only a testimonial
value and are not conclusive proof.

Potential Influence of Fluctuations in Eastern European
Growth on East-West Cooperation

The existence of middle-term growth fluctuations in the Eastern
nations has been demonstrated in numerous studies [6]. A number
of theories have been put forward to explain them. Some possible
factors causing fluctuations in Eastern European growth are investment cycles, long construction times, negative foreign trade balances, harvest failures, etc. It is also conceivable that Western
business trends have some repercussions eastward. In general
these fluctuations are set into motion by excessive strain on the
economic potential and are hence determined by supply and capacity (which is not the case in the West, where business ups and
downs are demand determined). Whereas excessive strain on resources is precipitated by subjective factors, such as unwarranted
optimism in constructing the plan, the subsequent fall-off in growth
must be ascribed to objective factors, such as the need to adapt to
the existing production capacity of basic industry and the capital
goods industry.

A correlation between Eastern European growth fluctuations
and East-West trade can be demonstrated by regression equa-
tions [3, 7]. A correlation with East-West cooperation also seems

likely: investment barriers arising in the East due to excessive strain on domestic capacities are reflected in the degree of interest shown in importing complete industrial plants from the West (to be paid off later in goods deliveries). Soviet interest in large-scale cooperative undertakings with the West picked up notably after the results of the first two years of the five-year plan (1971-75) showed longer and longer delays in the completion of planned investment projects. Numerous East-West cooperative projects have been built on the basis of long-term Western financing. The readiness of the Eastern countries to increase their indebtedness might be rooted in efforts to avoid an imminent slowdown in growth. The period of our experience is still too brief, however, to draw any definitive conclusions.

Final Comments

In addition to its long-term character, stability is also a major consideration in the development of industrial cooperation. It may therefore seem to be a contradiction to postulate that growth fluctuations have an influence on cooperation. Cooperation does not guarantee stable economic relations, but it can help to maintain ties between two enterprises (this could also be called reduced flexibility). To stabilize economic growth from the Western point of view, cooperative undertakings would have to function as a countervailing force to fluctuations in the business cycle. This, of course, may be possible with a deliberate economic policy, but it can hardly be achieved at the firm level [4]. In view of the still marginal importance of East-West cooperations, even such governmental policy measures may not have the desired effect. To date, the Eastern nations seem to have been more adept at using East-West trade and cooperation to get out of bottlenecks than the Western countries, even considering that trade with the West is more important for the East than trade with the East is for the West.

Notes

1. This section is an extensively reworked version of a talk given at a DIW symposium in Berlin, September 1975 [1]. The author thanks the DIW for its kind permission to republish it here.
2. During a recession import restrictions are demanded of the government (domestic producers with idle capacity will try to drive foreign competition from

their own market); suppliers from countries enjoying a boom will prefer the easier domestic market over export transactions.

3. This is not only because of the often poorer quality of Eastern European goods; such a "fate" often awaits "newcomers" in general.

4. This correlation is especially evident in the case of capital goods [3]. See also the statements of the vice-chairman of the Polish Planning Commission, J. Pajestka, in his April 1976 talk given in New York [4].

5. About two thirds of FRG licensing projects with the East were concluded to open up a new market or to safeguard an existing market from competition. Machinery was also delivered in about 40% of the agreements [5].

References

[1] J. Stankovsky, "Ost-West-Kooperation im Konjunkturverlauf," in D. Cornelsen, H. Machowski, and K.-E. Schenk, eds., Perspektiven und Probleme wirtschaftlicher Zusammenarbeit zwischen Ost- und Westeuropa, Berlin, DIW-Deutsches Institut für Wirtschaftsforschung, 1976, no. 114.

[2] K. Rothschild, "'Push' und 'Pull' im Export," Weltwirtschaftliches Archiv, 1966, no. 2.

[3] J. Stankovsky, "Bestimmungsgründe im Handel zwischen Ost und West," Forschungsberichte des Wiener Institutes für Internationale Wirtschaftsvergleiche, 1972, no. 7.

[4] Chase World Information Corporation, East-West Markets, April 19, 1976.

[5] K. Bolz and P. Plötz, Erfahrungen aus der Ost-West-Kooperation, Hamburg, HWWA-Institut für Wirtschaftsforschung, 1974, pp. 52, 98.

[6] J. H. G. Olivera, "Cyclical Growth under Collectivism," Kyklos, vol. XIII, 1960, pp. 229 ff.; G. J. Staller, "Fluctuations in Economic Activity: Planned and Free-Market Economies 1950-1960," American Economic Review, June 1964, pp. 385 ff.; ECE, "Some Factors in the Fluctuation of the Industrial Growth Rate," Economic Survey of Europe in 1968, pp. 130 ff.; A. Bajt, "Fluctuations and Trends in Growth Rates in Socialist Countries," Ekonomska analiza, 1969, no. 3-4; A. Bajt, "Investment Cycles in European Socialist Economies: A Review Article," Journal of Economic Literature, March 1971; J. Goldmann, "Tempo růstu a opakující se výkyvy v ekonomice některých socialistických zemí," Plánované hospodářství (Prague), 1964, no. 9, and "Tempo růstu v některých socialistických zemích a model řízení národního hospodářství," Plánované hospodářství (Prague), 1964, no. 11; J. Goldmann and K. Kouba, Economic Growth in Czechoslovakia, chaps. 3 and 4, Prague, 1969; also see J. Goldmann, "Fluctuation and Trend in the Rate of Economic Growth in Some Socialist Countries," Economics of Planning, 1966, no. 2; J. Goldmann, "Fluctuations in the Growth Rate in a Socialist Economy and the Inventory Cycle," in M. Bronfenbrenner ed., Is the Business Cycle Obsolete, New York, 1969, pp. 332 ff.; Julia Zala, "1958-1967: The Economic Trends of Decade," Acta Oeconomica, 1968, no. 2, pp. 133 ff.; A. Bródy, "Cycles and Equilibrium," European Economic Review, 1969, no. 2, pp. 307 ff.; A. Bródy, "The Rate of Economic Growth in Hungary, 1924-1965," in Is the Business Cycle Obsolete, op. cit., pp. 312 ff.; L. Brainard, "A Model of Cyclical Fluctuations under Socialism," Journal

of Economic Issues, March 1974; O. Kyn, W. Schrettel, and J. Sláma, "Growth
Cycles in Centrally Planned Economies. An Empirical Test," Munich, Osteuropa-Institut, Workshop Paper, August 1975, no. 7.

[7] K. P. Prodromidis, "Greek Disaggregated Import and Export Demand Functions," Weltwirtschaftliches Archiv, 1975, no. 2, p. 373 and table 2.

10

Interim evaluation of East-West
industrial cooperation

After ten years of practical experience it is now possible to draw up an interim balance sheet on industrial cooperation between East and West. In this section we shall try to summarize the available information on the scope and concentration of cooperation and on the differences among the CMEA countries in their approach to cooperation.[1]

Number and Scope of Registered Cooperation Agreements

There are no legal provisions for keeping statistics on cooperation agreements in Western countries, so any census depends on the voluntary cooperation of the participating firms.[2] In the Eastern countries all cooperative undertakings are registered, but the documents are not accessible (for example, the cooperation registry in Hungary for undertakings with the West, kept by the Intercooperation Co., is not open to everyone).[3] In addition, estimates of East-West industrial cooperation are made even more difficult by the fact that there are no generally accepted guidelines for compiling, classifying, and assessing the statistical data. Single or continuous statistics compiled by various official and private institutions therefore yield widely divergent findings.

Great differences arise from the fact that the definition of which undertakings are to be considered cooperation varies widely. Without any qualification only agreements on coproduction have consistently been considered cooperative undertakings and hence may be regarded as the "core" of East-West industrial cooperation [2]. Differences of viewpoint exist with regard to licensing agreements, complete plant deliveries, and the tapping of raw material deposits. In the view of some countries (especially the USSR), these are without qualification to be regarded as cooperative undertakings; but in the view of others they are so only when there exists some "material connection" between deliveries and counterdeliveries.[4] Compensation transactions, promoted for some time now by the Eastern countries (especially the USSR [3, 4]), are generally not counted as cooperative undertakings.

Other differences arise from the fact that although normally only the number of agreements is counted, there are some instances where the number of cooperating firms is counted as well. Numerous surveys cover not only cooperation agreements but also those that are still in the negotiating stages or have already expired.

Almost all existing cooperation statistics count only the number of agreements. How to assess the cooperative undertaking in monetary terms is an unsolved problem, and indeed it has only rarely been attempted, although a reasonable notion of the importance of cooperative undertakings will be possible only when statistics are available on the worth of these transactions. Obviously, the cooperative venture of the Austrian firm Steyr-Daimler-Puch with the Polish auto industry (see Case Study 11, Appendix 1), which provides for deliveries and counterdeliveries to a sum of 8.4 billion Austrian schillings (over $560 million), carries much more weight than ten simple licensing transactions. Estimates of the share of deliveries from cooperative undertakings in total foreign trade volume vary widely and are only rarely based on verified statistical material.[5] C. H. McMillian [5] correctly points out, however, that the trade volume deriving from cooperation is a poor parameter for evaluating cooperation (even if it were possible to determine it and differentiate it from the total trade of the partner).

Partners may, for example, cooperate in research and development and put to use their findings on their domestic markets or in exports with third countries. This cooperation would produce no increment in the total trade volume of the cooperation partners. In fact, it would even supplant trade to the extent that the cooperative undertaking replaced direct investments. McMillan even says that there is no particular reason why cooperation should increase trade volume. Indeed, this is probably true theoretically, but it probably partly misses the point as regards present practices in East-West cooperation.

According to McMillan the value of the funds invested in cooperative undertakings is a conceptually interesting notion, although not a very practical one for evaluating the importance of cooperation.

Number of East-West Cooperative Undertakings

Tables 29 through 36 present available, relatively reliable statistics on industrial East-West cooperation (also see Tables 4 through 9 in Chapter 3).

According to ECE surveys, a total of 134 agreements on East-West industrial cooperation were concluded between 1965 and 1967; of these Hungary participated in 43, Poland in 41, and Czechoslovakia in 20, and in the West, the FRG in 31, followed by Great Britain, France, and Austria (Table 29).

Table 29

Agreements on East-West Industrial Cooperation, 1965-67

Western countries	Eastern countries								
	Hungary	Poland	CSSR	Romania	Bulgaria	GDR	USSR	Total	In %
	Number of cooperation agreements								
FRG	17	7	2	2	2	–	1	31	23.1
Great Britain	7	15	3	1	–	–	–	26	19.4
France	4	6	7	1	1	2	2	23	17.2
Austria	5	2	3	–	2	2	–	14	10.4
Sweden	4	7	2	–	1	–	–	14	10.4
Italy	–	2	2	2	2	–	–	8	6.0
Switzerland	3	1	–	–	–	2	–	6	4.5
USA	1	–	1	1	1	–	–	4	3.0
Other countries	2	1	–	2	–	1	2	8	6.0
Total	43	41	20	9	9	7	5	134	100.0
In %	32.1	30.6	14.9	6.7	6.7	5.2	3.7	100.0	

Source: E. Sárosi, "Zur industriellen Kooperation zwischen Österreich und Ungarn," Forschungsberichte des Wiener Institutes für Internationale Wirtschaftsvergleiche, July 1972, no. 2.

A Czech study reports 271 cases of deliveries of complete industrial plants and licenses from the West to the East in 1967; most of them were ordered by Romania and the USSR and delivered by France and the FRG (Table 30). These projects are not completely in line with the concept of cooperation, although they do fit in broad terms.

According to ECE estimates the number of cooperation agreements in mid-1972 was about 600; most of them, however, were with Yugoslavia. The other Eastern countries (excepting the USSR) had over 300 cooperation agreements, with Hungary leading the field (164).[6] In 1974 the USSR had 160 cooperation agreements with the West according to its own figures, and of them most involved

Table 30

Eastern European Imports of Complete Industrial Plants and Licenses
from the West, Country of Destination and Country of Origin, 1967

Exporting country	Importing country							Total	In %
	USSR	Romania	Poland	CSSR	Bulgaria	Hungary	GDR		
	Number of items								
FRG	9	22	10	7	7	9	8	72	26.6
France	10	16	4	6	4	4	4	48	17.7
Great Britain	4	13	9	1	2	2	2	33	12.2
Italy	7	12	3	1	5	3	—	31	11.1
Austria	2	2	2	10	2	3	2	23	8.5
Japan	17	1	1	—	—	—	1	20	7.4
Switzerland and Liechtenstein	3	4	3	2	2	2	—	16	5.9
Sweden	1	2	1	—	1	—	3	8	3.0
Belgium	1	3	1	—	1	—	1	7	2.6
Netherlands	—	1	—	3	—	—	1	5	1.8
Denmark	1	—	1	1	—	—	1	4	1.5
USA	—	1	1	—	—	—	—	2	0.7
Finland	2	—	—	—	—	—	—	2	0.7
Total	57	77	36	31	24	23	23	271	100.0
In %	21.0	28.4	13.3	11.4	8.9	8.5	8.5	100.0	

Source: F. Mette, Informace o moderním zařízení, výrobních postupech,
technické dokumentaci a licencích, zakoupených socialistickými státy v kapitalistických státech v roce 1967, Prague, UVTEIN, 1969.

cooperation in research and development and were concluded by
the State Committee for Science and Technology. According to the
deputy chairman of the State Committee, Gvishiani, most of these
agreements were with large multinational firms (including 33 with
the United States). By the end of 1975 the State Committee had 170
agreements with Western firms [7], over one third of them with
the United States.

McMillan [5] estimates the total number of cooperation agreements between Western countries (excluding the United States) and
the Eastern countries at 724 on the basis of records kept by him
personally up to the beginning of 1975 (his file data were verified
by direct questioning of the Western firms concerned) (Table 31).
Of them 390 involved interfirm cooperation without joint ventures,[7]
8 were joint ventures in the East, 163 were joint ventures in the
West,[8] and 192 between Western firms and government agencies of
the Eastern countries; in this group the USSR is by far the most

169

Table 31

Cooperation Agreements between the West (without the USA) and Eastern Countries, 1975

	Interenterprise cooperation without joint ventures		Joint ventures		Cooperation between government agencies in the East and firms in the West	Total
		in %	in the East	in the West		
			Estimated total number of agreements			
Bulgaria	22	(5.6)	0	10	—	—
CSSR	35	(9.0)	0	12	—	—
GDR	9	(2.3)	0	6	—	—
Hungary	134	(34.4)	2	32	—	—
Poland	112	(28.7)	0	33	—	—
Romania	39	(10.3)	6	22	—	—
USSR	39	(10.0)	0	48	—	—
Eastern countries total	390	(100.0)	8	163	192	753

Source: C. H. McMillan, "Forms and Dimensions of East-West Inter-firm cooperation," East-West Cooperation in Business: Inter-firm Studies, East-West European Economic Interaction, Workshop Papers, vol. 2, Vienna, 1977.

170

Table 32

Cooperation Statistics of
Eastern Countries, 1965-75

	1965-67	1972	1973	1974	End of 1975
Country	Number of cooperation agreements with Western industrial countries				
Hungary	43	164	300	600‖	400††
Poland	41	55*	200	250#	
Romania	9	36	49‡		250‡‡
Bulgaria	9	18	50		
USSR	5			160**	
CSSR	20	33	25§	27	
GDR	7	13			
CMEA	134	(319)†	ca. 600	ca. 1,000	over 1,000

Sources: E. Sárosi, "Zur industriellen Kooperation zwischen Österreich und Ungarn," Forschungsberichte des Wiener Institutes für Internationale Wirtschaftsvergleiche, 1972, no. 2; Zahraniční obchod (Prague), 1975, no. 10, p. 11; Cooperation (Essen) 1976, no. 2, p. 18; J. Anusz, "Expansion of Industrial Co-operation between Poland and Developed Capitalist Countries," in Foreign Trade Research Institute, East-West Economic Relations, Warsaw, 1973; B. Bojkó, "Results and Problems in Co-operation with Western Firms in Hungarian Light Industry," in East-West Cooperation in Business: Inter-firm Studies, East-West European Economic Interaction, Workshop Papers, vol. 2, Vienna, 1977; P. J. Nichols, "Western Investment in Eastern Europe, the Jugoslav Example," in Joint Economic Committee, Congress of the United States, Reorientation and Commercial Relations of the Economies of Eastern Europe, Washington, U.S.G.P.O., 1974; and various press reports.

*According to J. Anusz, at the end of 1971 Poland had 180 cooperation agreements with Western firms.

†Without the USSR.

‡Total number of cooperation agreements with East and West: 200, of which, 49 in 1973 (most of the agreements were concluded with Western firms).

§Another 118 agreements with developing countries.

‖Of which, 356 active.

#Of which, 90 with the FRG, and according to other sources, as many as 140.

**Of which, 33 with the USA.

††Only effective agreements.

‡‡Another 500 in the negotiating stage.

Table 33

Cooperation Statistics of Western Industrial Countries

Reporting country	Year	CMEA	Hungary	Poland	Romania	Bulgaria	USSR	CSSR	GDR
				Number of cooperation agreements					
West (without USA)	1975	753							
USA	mid-1975 A	389†	32	71	50	23	136	34	13
	B	791‡	63	125	97	56	248	47	18
Austria	1968	30	16	6	1	2	2	2	3
	end of 1974	ca. 110	75	10	2	8	12*	4	—
	end of 1975	122	80	12	5	8	12*	4	1
FRG	1973	214	111	52	20	7	14*	10	—
	1974	232	133	55	26	7	?	11	—
	end of 1974	350	150						

Sources: The U.S. Perspective on East-West Industrial Cooperation (preliminary), Bloomington, Industrial Development Research Center of Indiana University, Team of Researchers, 1976; W. von Lingelsheim-Seibicke, Kooperation mit Unternehmen in Staatshandelsländern Osteuropas. Eine Einführung in die Praxis, Cologne, 1974, p. 25; Die Presse, (Vienna), October 27, 1975; Bundeskammer der gewerblichen Wirtschaft (Vienna); Business International, Eastern Europe Report, 1974, no. 25, p. 372; C. H. McMillan, "Forms and Dimensions of East-West Inter-firm Co-operation," East-West Cooperation in Business: Inter-firm Studies, East-West European Economic Interaction, Workshop Papers, vol. 2, Vienna, 1977.

*Scientific-technical cooperation.

†In 30 cases the country of the cooperation partner is unknown. In 70 cases the cooperation is indirect, i.e., concluded by a foreign subsidiary of a U.S. firm.

‡In 137 cases the Eastern country is unknown. In 96 cases the cooperation is indirect, i.e., concluded by a foreign subsidiary of a U.S. firm.

A — concluded agreements and agreements currently in force.

B — concluded, current, and in negotiating stage.

preponderant (agreements of the State Committee), although government agencies of the other Eastern countries (particularly Romania and Poland) have also concluded cooperation agreements with Western firms.

McMillan's statistics may be supplemented with data gathered by a group led by P. Marer [8] on American cooperative undertakings with the East, the number of which has increased markedly in the past few years. According to this source there have been 389 cooperation agreements between the United States and the Eastern nations. It should be borne in mind, however, that the American figures include agreements which otherwise would not be considered cooperation. Table 32 summarizes Eastern statistics on cooperative undertakings with the West; Table 33 gives some Western figures for cooperation with the East.

The number of East-West cooperative undertakings was about 600 at the end of 1973, and in 1975 it passed the 1,000 mark. This estimate also agrees with the ECE figure [9].

The ECE study shows the participation of individual Western countries in cooperative undertakings with the East. Of those agreements recorded in the ECE statistics (see the third section of Chapter 3), the FRG and France were each involved in 27%, Austria was involved in 12.1%, Italy and Sweden were involved in 8.7%, the United States had 2.7%, and Japan had 6.3%.

Table 34 contains more detailed statistics on American cooperation agreements. About three fifths (156) of the 253 American firms cooperating with the East and providing information have agreements with only one Eastern country; the others have agreements with two or more. Fifty-six of the 156 cooperating with only one country deal with the USSR, clearly illustrating the American preference for the leading Eastern power. It may be supposed that many of these U.S. firms are "newcomers" in Eastern business whose interest in the Soviet market was aroused by the new turn in U.S. Eastern policy. Romania was second, and Poland third, on the list. Only two U.S. firms cooperated with Czechoslovakia, and only one with the GDR. Forty-one firms are engaged in two Eastern markets, with a clear preference for the Soviet Union and Poland. Those firms dealing with Hungary, Czechoslovakia, and the GDR are for the most part firms operating on several Eastern markets and hence having long experience in that regard.

Hungarian statistics (Table 35) show that 1968 was the first year that cooperation agreements with the West reached any significant proportions; this was after introduction of the Hungarian reforms.

173

Table 34

Frequency of Cooperation Agreements of U.S. Firms with Eastern Countries, 1975

The following number of U.S. firms	had cooperative undertakings with... Eastern countries	Total	Of which, with								
			Hungary	Poland	Romania	Bulgaria	USSR	CSSR	GDR	not known
			Number of cooperative ventures								
156	1	156	8	15	16	11	56	2	1	47
41	2	82	8	16	8	7	29	5	2	7
18	3	54	6	13	10	4	16	4	0	1
12	4	48	9	11	6	4	12	3	2	1
10	5	50	7	10	8	4	10	9	2	0
10	6	60	11	8	10	9	10	9	3	0
6	7	42	6	6	6	6	6	6	6	0
253	—	492	55	79	64	45	139	38	16	56

Source: The U.S. Perspective on East-West Industrial Cooperation (preliminary), Bloomington, International Development Research Center of Indiana University, Team of Researchers, 1975.

Table 35

Hungary's Agreements on East-West Industrial Cooperation, by Partner Country

| Partner country | Number of agreements concluded in period/year | | | | Number of agreements in force | | | | |
	1963-67	1968	1969	1970	End of 1970	Mid-1972	in %	End of 1974	in %
FRG	9	11	12	8	40	55	(33.6)	140	(39)
Austria	4	5	7	4	20	24	(14.7)	54	(15)
France	1	1	5	1	8	16	(9.8)	26	(7)
Great Britain	2	1	4	1	8	11	(7.0)	21	(6)
Switzerland	2	–	4	1	7	12	(7.5)	21	(6)
Sweden	4	1	–	4	9	12	(7.5)	25	(7)
Italy	–	2	4	4	10	17	(10.2)	30	(8)
Netherlands	3	–	2	2	7	6	(3.6)	36	(10)
Other countries	2	5	–	2	9	11	(6.1)	13	(3)
Total	27	26	38	27	118	164	(100.0)	ca. 356	(100)

Sources: E. Sárosi, "Zur industriellen Kooperation zwischen Österreich und Ungarn," Forschungsberichte des Wiener Institutes für Internationale Wirtschaftsvergleiche, July 1972, no. 2; F. Horchler, "The Future of Austro-Hungarian Foreign Trade," Forschungsberichte des Wiener Institutes für Internationale Wirtschaftsvergleiche, June 1975, no. 27; Technisches Leben (Budapest), 1976, no. 1; various press reports.

There has been a sharp upswing since 1973. Hungary's most important cooperation partners by far are the FRG and Austria, countries with which Hungary has maintained close economic relations for many years.

The Monetary Value of East-West Cooperative Undertakings

Only Polish statistics provide any relatively detailed information on the value of deliveries stemming from cooperative undertakings [6, 10]. Thus in 1969 Polish exports from such undertakings to Western industrial nations (excepting Finland) amounted to $1.9 million (7.7 million foreign exchange zlotys), with another $1.3 million going to Finland. In 1970 the figure had risen to $6.5 million (27 million foreign exchange zlotys) to the West (excepting Finland), and in 1971 to $16 million (64.5 million zlotys)(Table 36). In 1969 Great Britain was the biggest customer for Polish exports from cooperative undertakings; in 1970 and 1971 it was the FRG.

Table 36

Industrial Cooperation in Poland's Exports to the West

Country	Polish exports under cooperation agreements with Western countries				Share of cooperation exports in export of capital goods	
	1969	1970	1971		1969	1970
	in $1,000			in %	in %	
	(1)	(2)	(3)	(4)	(5)	(6)
FRG	564	4,022	7,392	46.2	11.5	71.0
Great Britain	713	728	1,472	9.2	35.7	23.2
Italy	81	786	400	2.5	1.9	20.5
Sweden	231	431	1,632	10.2	10.5	26.5
Denmark	101	207	592	3.7	13.2	15.9
France	100	166	160	1.0	2.1	3.5
Belgium	33	115	224	1.4	5.6	14.0
Austria	78	49	624	3.9	5.9	3.0
Switzerland	29	17	2,640	16.5	5.8	0.5
Total	1,902	6,521	16,000	100.0	4.5	14.0
Finland	1,250	1,545	–	–	32.7	40.0

Sources: Columns 1, 2, 5, and 6: J. Olszynski, "Kooperacja przemysłowa Polski z wysoko rozwiniętymi krajami Europy Zachodniej," Warsaw, SGPiS, Zeszyty naukowe, 1973, no. 94.
Columns 3 and 4: J. Anusz, "Expansion of Industrial Cooperation between Poland and Developed Capitalist Countries," in Foreign Trade Research Institute, East-West Economic Relations, Warsaw, 1973, and our own calculations.

Polish statistics for 1974 show 90 cooperation agreements, with a total estimated worth of $150 million,[9] between the FRG and Poland. Polish deliveries stemming from such agreements amounted to 7% of Polish exports to the FRG; for products of the machine-tool industry the figure was 20% of total 1974 exports [11].

Table 36 shows the share of exports from cooperation agreements in total Polish exports of capital goods to various Western countries for the years 1969 and 1970. In 1969 cooperation exports amounted to 4.5% of total Polish capital goods exports to Western countries, while for 1970 the figure was 14% [10]. According to [6] such exports amounted to 1.5% in 1969, 4.0% in 1970, and 6.5% in 1971 of the total exports of industrial finished products (including consumer goods). About half of exports from cooperative undertakings were in mechanical engineering, and another 30% were in other branches of heavy industry. In 1971, 25% of the exports of the Polish foreign trade enterprise Elektrim (dealing with the electrical engineering industry), 13% of the Polimex-Cekop firm (complete plants), and 11% of the Bumar firm (construction machinery) were products from cooperative undertakings.

According to Bulgarian estimates, about 2-3% of exports to Western countries at the end of 1973 resulted from cooperation agreements [12]. In Hungary for the same period this figure was about 2% [13]. In 1975, 0.8% of the total output of Hungarian light industry was delivered to the West under cooperation agreements [14]. In Czechoslovakia cooperation exports represent scarcely 1% of total exports to Western countries [35, 36] (in mechanical engineering the figure is less than 1% [2]). In the early seventies deliveries stemming from cooperation agreements were estimated at 5-10% of total East-West trade [15]. Current estimates are more cautious for the most part. The ECE estimates, for example, that deliveries from cooperation agreements comprise 4-5% of trade between Western and Eastern Europe [16].

Concentration of Cooperation in Various Branches

Since cooperative undertakings can only be instituted if the interests of the two partners coincide, it would seem that the East and West have a roughly equal share in determining in what areas this cooperation is to be concentrated. Practice has shown, however, that it is the Eastern nation which takes the initiative in most such undertakings and hence has played the decisive role in determining where efforts were to be concentrated.

Most Eastern imports from the West are capital goods: advanced technology and technical progress, incorporated into machinery, are to promote growth and increased productivity in industry. Within the capital goods industry the main emphasis falls on machine building, chemicals, and electrical engineering, with specific differences occurring from country to country.

This general import pattern is also reflected in industrial cooperation: the Eastern nations replace or supplement commercial imports as far as possible through cooperation agreements in order to save foreign exchange and attain higher efficiency for the imported facilities. This is especially true of plant imports, licensing agreements, and cooperative undertakings in the area of science and technology. Thus these specific points of emphasis have for the most part been determined by the Eastern conception of development. In contrast it is usually the Western partner that leads the way with subcontracts, job processing, and so on. In projects leading to the construction of plant manufacturing for export, or to sales promotion, how the future market situation in the West is appraised is a crucial factor.

In order to see what the trends are in particular branches of industry as far as cooperation agreements are concerned, for comparative purposes we also included an old Czech publication showing Eastern European imports of licenses and complete industrial plants from the West (although the classification is not wholly commensurate with today's concept of cooperation, it is sufficient for a comparison). In 1967 most agreements were in the chemical industry (Table 37). The most important Western supplier in 1967 was the FRG, followed by France and Great Britain.

The cooperation studies of the ECE [9, 17] review the focal points of East-West cooperation in 1972 and 1975. Table 38 shows that between 1972 and 1975 cooperation agreements in the engineering industry and in branches not classified in 1972 (mainly light industry) increased in importance, while agreements in chemicals and electrical machinery waned in number.[10] The most important branch of industry was the engineering industry in both these years (22.3% and 30.0%, respectively). The principal Eastern countries involved in cooperation agreements in the engineering industry were Czechoslovakia and the GDR. Bulgaria had only a few agreements in this area. In the USSR the number of cooperation agreements in the engineering industry increased between 1972 and 1975.

Table 37

Eastern European Imports of Complete Industrial Plants and Licenses from the West, by Industrial Branch, 1967

a. By receiving country

Industrial branch	USSR	Bulgaria	CSSR	GDR	Hungary	Poland	Romania	Eastern countries total	in %
	Number of agreements								
Chemicals	14	9	8	5	1	10	28	75	27.7
Light industry	16	9	2	1	1	2	6	37	13.7
Metallurgy	—	1	4	2	13	—	8	28	10.3
Foodstuffs	4	—	1	1	—	4	2	12	4.4
Electrical machinery and electronics	7	—	1	4	1	3	5	21	7.7
Vehicles	3	—	1	—	2	3	3	12	4.4
Building materials	2	2	2	2	1	1	1	11	4.0
Others	11	3	12	8	4	13	24	75	27.7
All branches	57	24	31	23	23	36	77	271	100.0

b. By delivering country

	FRG	France	Great Britain	Italy	Austria	Japan	Switzerland	Sweden	Other countries
					Number of agreements				
Chemicals	15	13	14	10	5	7	4	1	6
Light industry	11	4	3	3	3	3	6	–	4
Metallurgy	13	7	2	2	4	–	–	–	–
Foodstuffs	4	1	1	1	–	–	–	2	3
Electrical machinery and electronics	7	3	4	2	4	4	–	1	–
Vehicles	2	3	3	2	1	1	–	–	–
Building materials	–	3	1	3	1	1	–	–	2
Others	20	14	5	8	9	4	6	4	5
All branches	72	48	33	31	23	20	16	8	20

Sources: F. Mette, Informace o moderním zařízení, výrobních postupech, technické dokumentaci a licencích zakoupených social-istickými státy v kapitalistických státech v roce 1967, Prague, UVTEIN, 1969.

Table 38

Structure of East-West Cooperation, 1972 and 1975,
by Eastern Country and Branch of Industry

Industrial branch	USSR 1972	USSR 1975	Hungary 1972	Hungary 1975	Poland 1972	Poland 1975	Romania 1972	Romania 1975	Bulgaria 1975	CSSR 1972	CSSR 1975	GDR 1975	Total 1972	Total 1975
	Share of each branch of industry in total number of cooperation agreements in Eastern country, in %													
Machine building	4.6	17.4	29.1	30.8	22.6	28.6	4.8	31.4	12.5	20.0	50.0	66.6	22.3	30.0
Machine tools	9.1	4.3	3.5	7.4	11.3	7.1	10.0	—	12.5	13.3	—	33.3	8.4	5.7
Transport equipment	13.6	4.4	20.9	17.6	11.3	8.9	28.6	22.9	12.5	26.7	28.6	—	17.3	15.0
Electrical	18.2	8.8	18.6	14.7	13.3	10.7	14.3	11.4	12.5	13.3	7.1	—	16.3	11.6
Chemicals	31.8	26.1	14.0	10.3	24.5	10.7	14.3	17.1	12.5	20.0	14.3	—	19.3	13.5
Metallurgy and mining		13.0		1.5		16.2		2.9	—		—	—		6.8
Light industry	22.7	4.3	13.9	11.8	17.0	7.1	28.0	2.9	—	6.7	—	—	16.4	6.8
Foodstuffs		13.0		1.5		3.6		5.7	25.0		—	—		4.8
Other branches*		8.7		4.4		7.1		5.7	12.5		—	—		5.8
Total	100.0	100.0	100.0	100.0	100.0	100.0	100.0	100.0	100.0	100.0	100.0	100.0	100.0	100.0

Source: ECE, Analytical Report on Industrial Co-operation Among ECE Countries, Geneva, 1973. Based on 202 agreements concluded in 1972. ECE, TRADE/R. 320, August 26, 1975.

*Construction, tourism, etc.

Table 39

Structure of East-West Cooperation, 1975, by Industrial Branch and Eastern Country

Industrial branch	USSR	Hungary	Poland	Romania	Bulgaria	CSSR	GDR	Total
	Share of each Eastern country in total number of cooperation agreements in each branch of industry, in %							
Machine building	6.5	33.9	25.8	17.7	1.6	11.3	3.2	100.0
Machine tools	8.3	41.8	33.3	–	8.3	–	8.3	100.0
Transport equipment	3.2	38.8	16.1	25.8	3.2	12.9	–	100.0
Electrical	8.3	41.7	25.0	16.6	4.2	4.2	–	100.0
Chemicals	21.4	25.0	21.4	21.4	3.6	7.2	–	100.0
Metallurgy and mining	21.4	7.1	64.4	7.1	–	–	–	100.0
Light industry	7.1	57.2	28.6	7.1	–	–	–	100.0
Foodstuffs	30.0	10.0	20.0	20.0	20.0	–	–	100.0
Other branches*	16.7	25.0	33.3	16.7	8.3	–	–	100.0
Total	11.1	32.8	27.1	16.9	3.9	6.8	1.4	100.0

Source: ECE, TRADE/R. 320, August 26, 1975.

*Construction, tourism, etc.

Table 40

Structure of East-West Cooperation, 1975,
by Type of Cooperation and Branch of Industry

Industrial branch	Licensing agreement	Delivery of complete plant	Specialization, coproduction	Joint venture	Cooperation in third countries.		Total
					Project planning	Subcontracts	
	Share of industrial branch in total number of agreements per type of cooperation, in %						
Machine building	29.5	2.2	39.2	16.7	42.0	28.6	30.0
Machine tools	11.1	–	7.2	–	–	42.9	5.7
Transport equipment	20.4	4.4	23.2	–	5.3	7.1	15.0
Electrical	7.4	8.9	15.9	33.3	10.5	7.1	11.6
Chemicals	14.8	24.4	7.2	33.3	15.8	–	13.5
Metallurgy and mining	1.9	15.6	2.9	–	21.1	–	6.8
Light industry	5.6	15.6	2.9	–	–	14.3	4.9
Foodstuffs	3.7	11.4	1.5	16.7	–	–	6.8
Other branches*	5.6	17.8	–	–	5.3	–	5.8
Total	100.0	100.0	100.0	100.0	100.0	100.0	100.0

Source: ECE, TRADE/R. 320, August 26, 1975.
*Construction, tourism, etc.

Table 41

Structure of East-West Cooperation, 1972 and 1975, by Industrial Branch and Type of Cooperation

Industrial branch	Year	Licensing agreements	Delivery of complete plants	Specialization coproduction	Total
		Share of type of cooperation in total number of agreements in branch, in %			
Machine building	1975	25.7	1.6	43.5	100.0
	1972	28.9	4.4	48.8	100.0
Transport equipment	1975	35.5	6.4	51.5	100.0
	1972	29.0	5.3	50.0	100.0
Electrical	1975	16.7	16.7	48.5	100.0
Chemicals	1975	28.6	39.2	17.8	100.0
	1972	20.5	23.1	33.3	100.0
Metallurgy and mining	1975	7.3	49.8	14.2	100.0
Total	1975	26.1	21.7	33.3	100.0
	1972	28.2	11.9	37.1	100.0

Sources: ECE, Analytical Report on Industrial Co-operation Among ECE Countries, Geneva, 1973; ECE, TRADE, R. 320, August 26, 1975.

Agreements on transport equipment occupy second place (17.3% and 15%); Czechoslovakia and Romania lead the field in this area. In 1975 only 13.5% of all agreements (19.3% in 1972) were in the chemical industry. In the USSR cooperative undertakings in chemicals were a focal point for both years. The electrical engineering industry was involved in 16.3% and 11.6% of all agreements in 1972 and 1975, respectively. In 1975 about 5% each of all agreements was in metallurgy, light industry, foodstuffs, and other branches.

Table 39 shows the distribution of cooperative undertakings by branches of industry between the Eastern countries. Hungary and Poland, which were involved in 32.8% and 27.1% of all cooperative undertakings, also led the field in most branches of industry.

Table 40 shows the correlation between the forms of cooperation and the different branches of industry. In 1975 licensing agreements followed more or less the same pattern as the branch structure of all East-West cooperation agreements. Deliveries of entire plants were concentrated in the chemical industry, metallurgy, and light industry; joint ventures fell mostly to electrical engineering and chemicals; subcontracts were concentrated in the machinery and machine-tool industries; and third country cooperative ventures also were in machinery. Specialization and coproduction were mainly in the area of machinery and transport equipment.

Table 41 shows the share of the three most important forms of cooperation (licensing agreements, deliveries of plant, specialization/coproduction) by industrial branch; in some cases a comparison between 1972 and 1975 was possible. The percentage of deliveries of complete chemical plants shows an especially sharp increase (from 23% to 39%), while specialization and cooperation agreements in chemicals declined just as sharply (from 33% to 18%).

Tables 42 and 43 show the composition of cooperation agreements between firms in the East and West (without joint ventures and without U.S. undertakings), classified by industrial branch and by broad user categories of the projects for 1975 [5]. More than half of the agreements involved machinery (34.7% nonelectric and 10.4% electric machinery, 7.2% machine tools), and 13.5% were in chemicals. Again, more than half of the cooperation agreements (53.4%) involved capital goods projects, 17.6% intermediate industrial goods, and 25.4% consumer goods.

In the FRG over one third of cooperative ventures in the East in 1972 were in machinery, 19% were in electrical machinery, and 8% were in vehicles. The percentage of cooperation agreements involving the

Table 42

Structure of Interfirm Cooperation Undertakings (without Joint Ventures) between the West (without USA) and the East, by Industrial Branch, 1975

Product or activity	Country							Eastern countries total
	Bulgaria	CSSR	GDR	Hungary	Poland	Romania	USSR	
	Share in %							
Foodstuffs	14.3	–	–	5.5	2.2	7.1	–	4.7
Raw materials and fuels	–	20.0	20.0	2.7	–	7.2	36.4	4.7
Chemicals	7.1	12.5	40.0	12.3	13.1	17.9	9.1	13.5
Transport equipment	7.2	6.3	–	8.2	10.8	17.9	–	9.2
Machine tools	–	–	–	6.8	8.7	10.6	18.2	7.2
Nonelectrical machinery	28.6	68.8	–	32.9	39.1	32.1	9.1	34.7
Electrical machinery	21.4	6.2	–	15.1	8.7	3.6	–	10.4
Other manufactured goods	21.4	6.2	–	15.1	17.4	3.6	18.1	13.5
Other nonclassified products	–	–	40.0	1.4	–	–	9.1	2.1
Total	100.0	100.0	100.0	100.0	100.0	100.0	100.0	100.0

Source: C. H. McMillan, "Forms and Dimensions of East-West Inter-firm Cooperation," in East-West Cooperation in Business: Inter-firm Studies, East-West European Economic Interaction, Workshop Papers, vol. 2, Vienna, 1977.

Table 43

Structure of Interfirm Cooperation Undertakings (without Joint Ventures) between
the West (without USA) and the East, by Purpose, 1975

Country	Investments	Purpose			Total
		Industrial intermediate products	Consumer-oriented projects and products	Others	
		Share in %			
Bulgaria	71.4	7.2	21.4	–	100.0
CSSR	56.3	12.5	31.2	–	100.0
GDR	–	60.0	–	40.0	100.0
Hungary	46.6	11.0	38.3	4.1	100.0
Poland	63.1	21.7	15.2	–	100.0
Romania	57.1	17.9	21.4	3.6	100.0
USSR	45.5	45.5	–	9.0	100.0
Eastern countries, total	53.4	17.6	25.4	3.6	100.0

Source: C. H. McMillan, "Forms and Dimensions of East-West Inter-firm Cooperation," in East-West Cooperation in Business:
Inter-firm Studies, East-West European Economic Interaction, Workshop Papers, vol. 2, Vienna, 1977.

Table 44

FRG Agreements with Eastern Countries on Industrial Cooperation,
by Industrial Branch

Industrial branch	Existing cooperative agreements			(Including projects under negotiation)
	Eastern countries total	of which,		Eastern countries, total
		Hungary	Romania	
	Share in total number of agreements, in %			
Capital goods industries	62	over 75	over 75	(over 50)
Of which,				
machinery	34			
electrical industry	19			
motor vehicle industry	8			
Consumer goods industries*	over 10			(over 20)
Other industrial branches†	ca. 28			(ca. 25)

Source: K. Bolz and P. Plötz, Erfahrungen aus der Ost-West-Kooperation, Hamburg, HWWA-Institut für Wirtschaftsforschung, 1974.
*Mainly textile and leather industries.
†Mainly construction, food, and basic materials.

capital goods industry was 62%, and even as high as 75% for agreements with Hungary and Romania (Table 44). Over 10% of the agreements involved the consumer goods industry (mainly textiles and leather), a good number were in the construction sector, foodstuffs, and the basic industries. If one includes agreements still in the negotiating stage, 20% of the total are in the consumer goods industry, and 50% are in the capital goods industries [18]. It may be concluded from these statistics that in the future the Eastern countries will devote more attention also to the consumer goods industry; there should also be some good opportunities for the capital goods industries which deliver plants to the consumer goods industry. According to Lingelsheim-Seibicke [19], of the total number of cooperation agreements concluded by the FRG as of mid-1973, 39% were in machine building, 9% in the vehicle industry, 20% in electrical machinery and precision instruments, 10% each in chemicals and the textile and leather industry, and 6% were in the food industry.

In 1975 almost four fifths (79.3%) of the 426 agreements of U.S. firms[11] on industrial cooperation with the East were in the manufacturing industries (see Table 45). Within this sector machine building and chemicals headed the list, with each having one fifth of the total number of agreements. The electrical machinery and petroleum-processing industries were also important sectors.

Table 45

Cooperation Agreements of U.S. Firms with Eastern Countries, by Industrial Branches, 1975*

Industrial branch	USSR	Bulgaria	CSSR	GDR	Hungary	Poland	Romania	Country unknown	Eastern countries, total	in %
					Number of agreements					
Cooperation agreements										
Manufacturing	83	32	19	4	35	72	44	49	338	79.3
Construction	3	1	2	2	3	7	10	9	37	8.7
Mining	2	1	—	—	—	1	2	—	6	1.4
Hotel and other services	6	1	1	—	1	2	2	4	17	4.0
Transport	3	—	—	—	2	1	5	5	16	3.8
Finances	1	—	—	—	1	1	1	1	5	1.2
Commerce	2	—	—	—	—	—	—	—	2	0.5
Agriculture	2	1	1	—	1	—	—	—	5	1.2
Total	102	36	23	6	43	84	64	68	426	100.0

189

									Total	%
Of which: manufacturing										
Foodstuffs, tobacco	5	4	1	1	2	4	1	2	20	5.9
Textiles	1	–	2	–	1	–	–	–	4	1.2
Lumber, paper	5	–	–	–	–	1	1	–	7	2.1
Chemicals	14	6	2	1	5	13	12	11	64	18.9
Petroleum processing	9	4	5	1	1	6	6	12	44	13.0
Rubber, leather, glass	7	4	–	–	2	7	4	1	25	7.4
Basic metals	2	1	1	–	2	8	2	–	16	4.7
Metal products	2	1	1	1	3	3	–	–	11	3.3
Machine building	23	1	2	–	6	12	8	14	67	19.8
Electronic equipment	9	9	5	–	8	12	5	7	55	16.3
Vehicles	4	2	–	–	4	3	3	1	17	5.0
Various	2	–	–	–	1	3	1	1	8	2.4
Manufacturing	83	32	19	4	35	72	44	49	338	100.0
Total, in %†	28.7	11.1	6.6	1.4	12.1	24.9	15.2	–	–	100.0
Of which, other sectors,	19	4	4	2	8	12	20	19	88	
in %‡	27.5	5.8	5.8	2.9	11.6	17.4	29.0	–	–	100.0

Source: The U.S. Perspective on East-West Industrial Cooperation (preliminary), Bloomington, International Development Research Center of Indiana University, Team of Researchers (not comparable with data in Tables 4 to 9); own calculations.

*Including agreements in negotiating stage. Breakdown partly estimated.
†"Country unknown" is distributed proportionally.
‡Excluding manufacturing.

Table 46

Hungarian Cooperation Agreements with Western Firms, by Industrial Branch

Industrial branch	Number of agreements concluded in the period/year				Number of effective agreements			
	1963-67	1968	1969	1970	End of 1970	Mid-1972	End of 1973	End of 1974
Machinery	23	17	27	20	87	122	ca. 204	235
Heavy industry	–	–	–	–	–	–	ca. 33	32
Chemicals	2	4	8	2	16	13	ca. 27	39
Light industry	–	3	2	1	6	29	ca. 33	46
Foodstuffs	2	2	1	4	9	–	ca. 4	4
Construction	–	–	–	–	–	–	–	–
Total	27	26	38	27	118	164	ca. 300	356

Source: E. Sárosi, "Zur industriellen Kooperation zwischen Österreich und Ungarn," Forschungsberichte des Wiener Institutes für Internationale Wirtschaftsvergleiche, July 1972, no. 2; F. Horchler, "The Future of Austro-Hungarian Foreign Trade," Forschungsberichte des Wiener Institutes für Internationale Wirtschaftsvergleiche, June 1975, no. 27; various press reports. Also see Table 48.

About 5% of each of the agreements was in the vehicle industry, basic metals, and foodstuffs. Most of the U.S. agreements in the manufacturing industries were concluded with the USSR (mainly in the machinery, chemical, and crude oil industries), and with Poland (mainly the chemical industry, electronic machines, machine building, and basic metals). The number of cooperation agreements in economic sectors outside the manufacturing industries is relatively small; almost one third (29%) of these agreements are with Romania, mainly in the construction and transport industries. There are 17 agreements in the hotel sector (especially with the USSR); the number of agreements in mining, agriculture, commerce, and financing is very small.

Hungarian statistics on cooperation (Table 46) show a concentration of agreements with the West in the machine-building industry, with foodstuffs and light industry bringing up a distant rear.

Varying Attitudes of CMEA Countries
toward East-West Cooperation

There are considerable differences among the Eastern countries with regard to their interest in East-West cooperation and to the economic importance of this type of relationship. Both readiness and capacity to enter into cooperation agreements with Western firms depend on the political situation, the type of economic planning, the management of industrial organization, and the economic situation. The importance of East-West cooperation is related to the intensity of foreign trade, particularly trade with the West, of the particular Eastern country, as well as to the number and compass of the agreements. Table 47, "Cooperation and Foreign Trade Indicators," contains figures on the level of total foreign trade and trade with the West for each Eastern country; in some cases these figures at least provide background for explaining why some Eastern countries are more disposed to entering into cooperation agreements than others.

The foreign trade ratio (foreign trade in percentage of the gross national product), foreign trade intensity (export per capita), and the Western trade share are all factors determining the intensity of cooperation. In general one could expect that the intensity of cooperation is positively correlated with the foreign trade ratio and trade share with the West. The number of cooperation agreements also depends on the interest and engagement of the Eastern European managers directly involved. If this is so, then

Table 47

Cooperation and Foreign Trade Indicators of Eastern Countries

Indicator	Year	Bulgaria	CSSR	GDR	Poland	Romania	Hungary	USSR
Intensity of cooperation								
In million $*	1973	19.1	112.4	328.7	28.5	61.5	7.6	69.9 (139.7)
Index †	1973	148.8	25.3	8.6	100.0	46.2	373.9	40.6 (20.3)
Number of cooperation agreements with West‡	1973	50	25	13	200	49	300	160
Foreign trade in % of GNP§								
at domestic prices	1973	32.8	20.2	19.5	25.0	—	34.4	5.7
at foreign prices	1973	(20.3)	(14.8)	(17.0)	(10.8)	(11.4)	(19.6)	(4.2)
Export per capita, in $	1973	382	406	440	193	179	414	85
Foreign trade turnover with West, million $	1973	956.1	2,810.0	4,273.4	5,693.0	3,011.6	2,279.4	11,175.7
Western trade								
in % of exports	1973	13.5	21.8	22.9	34.2	38.8	26.7	23.8
in % of imports	1973	15.8	25.4	32.6	44.4	44.8	30.0	29.5
Centralization of foreign trade‖								
in finished products X	1972	57	51	121	81	30	39	270
M	1972	56	67	100	75	24	29	118
in machinery X	1972	91	95	229	109	44	46	283
M	1972	75	121	116	103	23	24	158

| Employed in agriculture # in % of total employed | 1972 | 32.8 | 16.7 | 12.0 | 35.0 | 44.2 | 25.0 | 25.6 |

Source: Own calculations.

*Foreign trade turnover with West per cooperation agreement in million $ (GDR: 1972; USSR: 1974; value in parentheses — without estimated number of cooperation agreements of the State Committee for Science and Technology). The lower this indicator, the more intensive the cooperation relations with the West.

†Reciprocal of indicator in preceding line (foreign trade with West per cooperation agreement). Index, Poland = 100. GDR: 1972; USSR: 1974.

§Average of exports and imports. Gross national product and foreign trade values converted to comparable domestic prices (in parentheses: foreign trade in convertible currencies, i.e., at foreign prices).

‖Exports (X) and imports (M) per foreign trade organization, in million $.

#Including forestry.

194

there is also a plausible correlation between the degree of centralization of the foreign trade apparatus and the readiness to enter into cooperation agreements. Foreign trade turnover divided by the number of economic units authorized to engage in foreign trade (overall and in the machine-building sector) has been used as an indicator of the degree of centralization of foreign trade. In labor-intensive cooperative undertakings with the West, the interest of the Eastern European partner will depend to a certain extent on the situation on the labor market; countries with a labor reserve are more inclined to participate in labor-intensive cooperative undertakings than those with a labor shortage. The situation on the labor market is roughly reflected by the relative proportion of the manpower engaged in agriculture and forestry (the labor force in these sectors is the most important manpower source for the other sectors).

The number of cooperation agreements with Western countries is not itself a suitable measure of the economic importance of such ventures for the respective Eastern countries; this figure must always be seen in the context of total foreign trade volume. The indicator "cooperation intensity" reflects the value of trade turnover with the West per cooperation agreement for each Eastern country. The intensity will be greater the lower this indicator. An indicator of cooperation intensity that gives the reciprocal value of the above indicator in index form (Poland = 100) is closer to the usual approach. Hungary has the highest cooperation intensity, followed far behind by Bulgaria and Poland, with Czechoslovakia and the GDR bringing up the rear. Romania and the USSR occupy middle positions. The factors determining interest in cooperation play a certain role, but in many cases they are eclipsed by other openly political factors. The following sections discuss the situation in the individual Eastern countries.

Hungary

Hungary is the Eastern European country with the greatest number of cooperation agreements and the highest cooperation intensity. The reasons lie partly with the extensive reforms made in the economic system in 1968, which gave Hungarian enterprises far-reaching decision-making powers also in the area of foreign trade. Foreign trade is important for the Hungarian economy; it amounts to about one third of the gross national product. The Hungarian trade share with the West is around the CMEA average. The

Hungarian foreign trade apparatus is largely decentralized, which is one of the reasons why Hungary has proven so adaptable in cooperative ventures. There are serious signs of a labor shortage, which will probably dampen Hungarian willingness to enter labor-intensive cooperative undertakings in the future (job processing, etc.). As a rule Hungarian enterprises have a direct interest in successful cooperation.

Promotion of industrial cooperation with the West has a high priority in the government's economic policy. Easy-term credits can be obtained for cooperative ventures;[12] customs preferences had been given for capital goods imported for cooperative undertakings, but this provision had to be canceled, since it was contrary to GATT regulations. Certain limits are set, however, by political necessities and other considerations. Thus the establishment of joint ventures with Western participation located in Hungary have been permitted since 1970, but in practice the opportunity was first utilized in 1974, and then only to a limited degree. By the end of 1975 there were four joint ventures in Hungary with Western countries, but none of them involved production in the strict sense. They were:

Hirbow: Bowmar Canada, Ltd., with Hiradastechnika and Elektromodul;

Volcon: Volvo, Sweden, with Csepel and Mogürt (see Case Study 7, Appendix 1);

Sicontact: Siemens, FRG, with several Hungarian firms (see Case Study 8, Appendix 1); and

Radelcor Instruments: Corning Medical, United States, with Metrimpex and the Radelkis Cooperative.[13]

Hungary is also involved in another 63 joint enterprises abroad (46 in Europe, 7 in Asia, and 5 each in Africa and America); 41 of them entail trade, 14 services, and only 8 production [21].

In the German experience [18] 60% of cooperation agreements with Hungary have been encumbered by only minor problems or none at all. Interestingly, a study conducted by Hewett [22] in autumn 1974 in Hungary showed that large Hungarian enterprises have only a very minor interest in any form of cooperation agreements. It is the small and middle-sized firms that are mainly involved in cooperation agreements with the West, and correspondingly they often choose small and middle-sized FRG firms as their partners [18]. Most Hungarian cooperation agreements with the West have been on a minor scale [22].

The foreign trade company Intercooperation AG was founded in

Hungary to initiate and facilitate cooperative undertakings with the West. An interministerial committee sets preferences with regard to cooperation agreements and has a veto right over proposals for such agreements.

Table 48

Hungarian Agreements on Industrial Cooperation, Total and with Austria, End of 1974

	By type of cooperation and branch of industry		
	Share in the number of cooperative undertakings		Austria's share in total Hungarian cooperative un-dertakings with West, in %
	with the West, total	with Austria	
	in %		
Types of cooperation			
Licensing agreements*	43	20	7.2
Coproduction	30	44	22.4
Specialization	19	25	19.1
On third markets	8	11	21.4
Industrial branch			
Machinery	66	30	6.8
Chemicals	9	37	62.5
Light industry	11	9	12.8
Foodstuffs	13	18	21.7
Construction	1	6	75.0
Total	100	100	15.2

Source: F. Horchler, "The Future of Austro-Hungarian Foreign Trade," Forschungsberichte des Wiener Institutes für Internationale Wirtschaftsvergleiche, June 1975, no. 27.
*Repayment with cooperation product.

Cooperative relations between Austrian and Hungarian industry (see [1, 23]) are especially close, owing partly to geographic proximity and partly to the historical ties between the two countries. Table 48 provides a breakdown of Hungarian cooperation agreements with the West by industrial branch and form of cooperation: the structure of Hungarian cooperation agreements with Austria is given for comparison. Cooperation between Hungary and Austria in chemicals and construction has been particularly active; licensing agreements between Austria and Hungary have been relatively rare.

Poland

After Hungary Poland has the next greatest number of cooperation agreements with the West. The intensity of cooperation, however, is much lower than in Hungary in view of the large volume
of Polish trade with the West. In contrast to Hungarian cooperative ventures, which are mostly small, many of the Polish agreements have attained major dimensions, e.g., the agreement between
Steyr-Daimler-Puch and the Polish auto industry, so that the trade
turnover of Poland's cooperative undertakings with the West perhaps exceeds that of Hungary.

In its basic features the Polish economic reform is similar to
the Hungarian reform, although administration of the economy has
not been as extensively decentralized nor have the enterprises
been given such broad powers. Moreover, the Polish reform was
carried out in stages, whereas in Hungary the "New Economic
System" was introduced all at once, after two years of preparation.
Polish industry has been cultivating cooperative relations with the
West since the midsixties. In 1965 Polish heavy industry had 20
agreements with the West. Special units were set up in the Ministry of Foreign Trade and in a number of foreign trade organizations to promote cooperation. Despite some success the overall
result has been modest, for which the Poles think the system of
directive planning is to some extent responsible.

The experience of the FRG in cooperation with Poland has been
just as positive as its experience with Hungary [18]. In general Poland is at a lower technical level than Hungary. Since about 1971
Poland has stepped up its foreign trade with the West; in particular, imports on credit have been pushed (in 1974 and 1975 about
half of Polish imports were from Western nations). The main import has been capital goods; this has been true of cooperative undertakings as well, where deliveries of complete plants and licensing accords, to be paid back later with products from the new plant and
equipment, have been common. Poland has the largest agricultural
labor force among the Eastern nations. The labor market is not
balanced, and regional pockets of temporary hidden unemployment
seem to occur. This circumstance is undoubtedly a factor in Poland's interest in labor-intensive cooperation agreements.

Romania

Romania is a country with many contradictory factors shaping its readiness to enter into cooperation agreements. First, it is economically the most backward of the Eastern countries, and foreign trade plays only a relatively minor role. Although numerous changes have been made in the Romanian economic system, they have hardly amounted to a reform similar to what has taken place in Hungary, Poland, and to a certain extent in the GDR and Czechoslovakia. Instead, powers have merely been shifted back and forth between ministries and "industrial centrals" (concerns) while the directive character of the way the plan is imposed on the enterprises has scarcely been touched. On the other hand, Romania has been trying to steer a course toward some degree of emancipation from the Soviet Union and the CMEA by cultivating closer economic cooperation with the West. Romania is not only a member of GATT but also the only Eastern nation that is a member of the World Bank and the International Monetary Fund. It was also the first Eastern European country to allow the formation of joint companies with Western participation within its borders (see Chapter 6). To date, six joint ventures have begun operations (ten others, including with Shell, Black and Decker, Rolls-Royce, and VFW-Fokker, are in the negotiating stage) [24]:

Romcontrol Data: CDC, United States, with CIETV (see Case Study 5, Appendix 1);

Rifil: Romalfa, Italy, with the Industrial Center for Synthetic Fibers (capital $2.1 million; Romanian shares 52%; manufacture of acrylic fibers);

Resita Renk AG: Zahnräderfabrik Renk, FRG, with Resita and Uzinexport (see Case Study 6, Appendix 1);

Roniprot: Dainippon Ink, Japan, with the Romanian Industrial Center for Dyes (capital 28.6 million DM; Romanian share 57.38%);

Elarom: L'Electronique appliqué, France, and the Romanian Industrial Center for Electronics (capital 10 million F; Romanian share 51%).

Romelite: F. Kohmeier KG, Austria, with the Romanian Industrial Center for Heavy Machinery (capital 120 million schillings; Romanian share 51.7%).

A good portion (about 12%) of Romanian exports to the Western industrial nations and to the developing countries are made by joint ventures abroad with Romanian participation. Romania participates in four such companies in both the FRG and Italy, three in both Lebanon and France, and one each in Switzerland, Austria, Great Britain, Japan, and Peru. The high proportion of the labor force in agriculture and forestry in Romania is an incentive to

Romania's interest in cooperative undertakings. Although Romania
is the most prepared politically to enter into such undertakings with
the West, the economic premises for them are rather meager.

FRG enterprises have encountered a fair number of problems in
their cooperative ventures with Romania; there have been delays
in getting started; there has been a lack of flexibility in decision-
making; and the West German partner has had to get by with insufficient information [18]. The centralized planning system, with
numerous plan objectives expressed in quantitative magnitudes, is
a serious obstacle. The joint ventures now existing in Romania have
experienced their most serious problems in obtaining the necessary supplies. Since the plan contains no provisions for deliveries
to joint companies, it is difficult to procure raw materials and primary products from domestic firms. If they are ordered through
foreign trade enterprises, further delays ensue, as the latter must
first find out the "world trade prices" of the goods in question. Exports of a joint venture to other CMEA countries must be paid in
hard currency, but the CMEA countries often prefer to import directly from the West, even though the product of the joint venture
is cheaper in Romania [25].

Bulgaria

Bulgaria has the closest economic ties of all the Eastern countries to the USSR and also has by far the lowest trade share with
the West. In general Bulgaria is more reticent about cooperative
relations with the West than, say, Romania, Poland, and Hungary,
but it has made notable headway in some areas. It has about the
same number of cooperation agreements with the West as Romania.
About 2-3% of Bulgarian exports are from cooperative ventures.
The founding of joint companies is not permitted in Bulgaria and
will probably not be considered until the Soviet Union makes
the first move in this direction (see the last section of Chapter 6).

Soviet Union

The Soviet notion of industrial cooperation with the West differs
from that of the other Eastern nations [26]. According to A. Bel-
chuk, the director of the "Trends and Prospects of Economic Relations with the Capitalist Countries" Section of the Institute of World
Economy and International Relations of the Academy of Sciences of

the Soviet Union [27], the most important areas of East-West cooperation are:
— international economic cooperation in the form of joint industrial projects, where large-scale projects of hitherto unknown
   size are being constructed or are in preparation. These include, in addition to the delivery of whole plants for the manufacturing industries (automobile factories), projects for the
   joint harnessing of Soviet energy and raw materials (principally in Siberia and the Far East);
— scientific-technical cooperation;
— joint operations on third markets.
   The Soviet Union has so far largely avoided forms of cooperation that would require the direct participation of Soviet production enterprises. This is linked to the fact that in the Soviet Union
the domestic economy is much more shielded from other countries
than in the other Eastern nations. The Soviet Union thus prefers
forms of cooperation for which special regulations may be set up:
for example, scientific-technical cooperation, handled primarily
by the State Committee for Science and Technology, cooperation
on third markets, for which foreign trade organizations are responsible, and large-scale industrial projects, e.g., the construction of an auto factory in Togliattigrad and the truck factory on the
Kama [28], and the tapping of natural resources, e.g., the repeated
natural gas pipeline agreements with the participation of the USSR,
the FRG, and Austria [29]. The Soviet Union has preferred Japanese, FRG, and (at least until the trade agreements were canceled) American enterprises as partners in cooperative undertakings. The Soviet Union has taken a negative view on the establishment of joint enterprises domestically:

It must be supposed that industrial cooperation between the
Soviet Union and the Western countries will continue in the future to be based on forms which will not result in the establishment of property rights by foreign firms to enterprises in the
Soviet Union [27].

Article 8 of the "Agreement on the Further Development of Economic Cooperation," concluded between the USSR and the FRG on
October 30, 1974, in Moscow, speaks explicitly of the "formation
of joint companies, with the participation of Soviet foreign trade
organizations, in the FRG" and of the "establishment of representation of FRG enterprises in the USSR."

According to reports of participants at a conference of econo-
mists from the FRG and the Soviet Union, held in autumn 1974 in
Tbilisi, there were signs of a change in the Soviet attitude toward
Western participation in enterprises in the Soviet Union.[15]

One of Brezhnev's statements at the Twenty-fifth Party Congress,
held in February 1976 in Moscow, implied that the USSR was still, as
always, opposed to direct capital participation (with property
rights for the Western partner).[16] At an East-West conference
organized by the Vienna Institute for Comparative Economic
Studies in June 1976 at Tbilisi, the vice-minister for the machine tool industry, Cheburakov, left the door open for direct investments by Western enterprises, with participation in management, profits, and risk, but without property title [32].

At the Twenty-fifth Party Congress Brezhnev also underscored
the significance of compensation agreements, which he called a
new form of economic relations.[17] He pointed out that the USSR
would henceforth promote compensation agreements in the manufacturing industries in addition to the traditional areas of raw materials and semifinished products. Since then the advantages of
compensation transactions have been extolled in numerous official
Soviet statements [3, 4]. In an American study the volume of
compensation transactions between East and West has been estimated at about 28% of total East-West trade, and at 21% of the
trade between the United States and the Eastern nations (including
17% with the USSR and 38% in trade with the other Eastern nations) [34].

Czechoslovakia

Czechoslovakia, along with the GDR, is the most technically advanced of the Eastern nations. Czechoslovakia's trade share with
the West is the second lowest, but this is due more to political
than economic circumstances. In Czechoslovakia an extensive
economic reform was carried out in 1967-68, but after the Soviet
intervention it was largely withdrawn. Industrial cooperation is
indeed promoted by means of tax concessions, but the results so
far have been much slimmer than in the other Eastern nations;
indeed, this point has also been criticized in official circles. In
mid-1974 an official of the Czechoslovak Foreign Trade Ministry
who was responsible for cooperation agreements stated that in 1973
Czechoslovakia had concluded no new cooperation agreement with any
Western European country with which intergovernmental coopera-

tion agreements already existed. In 1974 only one new cooperation agreement was concluded.

This poor showing is partly ascribable to bureaucratic obstacles in the state administration (where the officials are reluctant to demonstrate a willingness to enter into such arrangements with the West) and partly due to coolness on the part of managerial personnel, who want to take no risks. The FRG has had problems in its cooperative undertakings with Czechoslovakia, e.g., failure to maintain the prescribed quality standards or to meet delivery deadlines [18]. The labor shortage in Czechoslovakia most likely also helps to dampen interest in labor-intensive forms of cooperation.

GDR

Until recently the GDR was the least interested of all Eastern nations in industrial cooperation with the West. As late as 1970 the idea of close cooperation with the West was rejected as "subversion" [37]. The GDR could afford a negative attitude toward cooperation with the West because, thanks to its level of development, it had less need of Western technology than the other Eastern nations, even though it suffered from a severe labor shortage (partly as a result of emigration to the West up until 1961). In addition, because of "internal trade" arrangements with West Germany it has enjoyed several other advantages (special customs and tax arrangements, swing credit arrangements, etc.) [38, 39].

However, in the light of the increasingly positive experience being accumulated by the other Eastern nations, authoritative circles in the GDR began to speculate whether perhaps some real opportunities had not been missed by the rejection of cooperative arrangements [39].

Since about the beginning of 1975 a new attitude in the GDR toward East-West cooperation has been discernible and is sometimes referred to as the "cooperation offensive" [40]. Negotiations are being carried on with Krupp and Hoechst (FRG) on the conclusion of a skeleton agreement establishing a framework for the implementation of particular cooperative ventures on the order of several billion DM. Furthermore East German firms have been showing an increasing interest in cooperative undertakings with Western firms on third markets (especially in the developing countries).[18]

Notes

1. Chapter 3 discusses the different types of cooperation.
2. In some cases Western firms even prefer that their cooperative relations with the Eastern countries remain unknown; this is true, for example, of some producers of trademark articles who have some of their product manufactured in the East.
3. Appendix 2 contains a Hungarian list of cooperative agreements with Austria published in [1].
4. See the third section of Chapter 3. The Helsinki Conference acknowledges these differences in views in that it speaks of both industrial cooperative undertakings and of large-scale projects of common interest (see the last section of chapter seven).
5. Poland has published some figures on the volume of exports stemming from cooperative undertakings, but they do not mention how the figures were arrived at.
6. According to Polish statistics [6], however, Poland already had 180 cooperation agreements with the West by the end of 1971.
7. Hungary and Poland in the East, and the FRG, Austria, France, Great Britain, and Italy in the West, were the main participants in these joint ventures.
8. McMillan's estimates of East-West joint ventures in the West are in some cases lower than the statistics published by the Eastern nations on participation in ventures in the West (see the third section of this chapter).
9. This estimate is based on the total period of validity of the agreements, which is for several years.
10. The recorded percentage shares are based on a selection from agreements filed in the ECE cooperation registry (see the third section of Chapter 3), i.e., on a broad random sampling that therefore may differ from the actual total sum of East-West cooperative undertakings (compare the structure of Hungary's cooperative undertakings by industrial branches in Table 46).
11. The figures on the distribution of the Eastern cooperative undertakings of U.S. firms by industrial branches are taken from an earlier version of an American research report [8] and therefore are not in total agreement with other statistics on American cooperation agreements with the East. Some of the figures are estimates.
12. According to Hungarian observations [20], in many cases traditional trade is dubbed "cooperation" so that the participants can get credits and other advantages that otherwise would not apply.
13. "Radelcor Instruments," established in Budapest on December 9, 1975, will produce instruments for biological research with the know-how of its American partner. The first of these instruments are scheduled to be marketed in 1976, and the socialist countries will presumably be the main markets. "Radelcor" receives special parts from the Corning works in the United States and Great Britain. "Radelkis" is the largest specialized firm for electrochemical instruments in Eastern Europe.
14. "For it should be stated that after the initial period of increased interest in the development of industrial co-operation with capitalist firms there appeared towards the end of 1960's ... a decline in the interest of foreign trade enterprises and industry in completing the agreements already signed. This phenomenon had its roots in the growing conflict between the necessity of introducing new forms of economic relations with foreign countries and traditional, rigid methods of

204

planned management of the economy.... We may assume that the new stage of co-operation between Polish industry and capitalist firms was begun in 1971" [6].

15. Professor Ivanov, of the USA Institute of the Soviet Academy of Sciences, asserted that this question was being reconsidered in the USSR. The Soviet Academy of Sciences had been requested to develop a new concept of cooperation [30].

16. "I have in mind, among other things, compensation agreements under which new plants, belonging entirely to our state (author's emphasis), are built in cooperation with foreign firms" [31].

17. It is interesting that in the most recent Soviet usage, compensation transactions are almost never called a form of cooperation but a variant of "a progressive and effective type of foreign trade agreement" [33].

18. Agreements on joint large-scale projects in Australia, Mauritania, and Cameroon exist between GDR enterprises and the Austrian firm VÖEST-Alpine.

References

[1] F. Horchler, "The Future of Austro-Hungarian Foreign Trade," Forschungsberichte des Wiener Institutes für Internationale Wirtschaftsvergleiche, June 1975, no. 27.

[2] J. Nykryn, "Inter-firm Co-operation in the Machine Building Industry," in East-West Cooperation in Business: Inter-firm Studies, Vienna, East-West European Economic Interaction, Workshop Papers, vol. 2, 1977.

[3] A. Below, "Abkommen auf Kompensationsgrundlage über Grossvorhaben mit kapitalistischen Ländern," Aussenhandel UdSSR, 1976, no. 3, pp. 48-51.

[4] W. Schuschkow, "Über die Zusammenarbeit mit kapitalistischen Ländern beim Bau grosser Industrieobjekte in der UdSSR," Aussenhandel UdSSR, 1976, no. 2, pp. 8-11.

[5] C. H. McMillan, "Forms and Dimensions of East-West Inter-firm Cooperation," in East-West Cooperation in Business: Inter-firm Studies, Vienna, East-West European Economic Interaction, Workshop Papers, vol. 2, 1977.

[6] J. Anusz, "Expansion of Industrial Co-operation Between Poland and Developed Capitalist Countries," in Foreign Trade Research Institute, East-West Economic Relations, Warsaw, 1973.

[7] E. Hoorn, in Die Presse (Vienna), November 15, 1974 and October 27, 1975.

[8] The U.S. Perspective on East-West Industrial Co-operation (preliminary), Bloomington, International Development Research Center of Indiana University, Team of Researchers, January 1975, June 1975.

[9] ECE, "Preparations for the Second Meeting of Experts on Industrial Cooperation," Committee on the Development of Trade, TRADE/R. 320, Geneva, August 26, 1975.

[10] J. Olszynski, "Kooperacja przemysłowa Polski z wysoko rozwiniętymi krajami Europy Zachodniej," SGPiS, Zeszyty naukowe (Warsaw), 1973, no. 94.

[11] Cooperation (Essen), December 1974, no. 4, p. 32.

[12] Business International, Eastern Europe Report, 1974, no. 6.

[13] Business International, Eastern Europe Report, 1974, no. 3, p. 24.

[14] B. Bojkó, "Results and Problems in Co-operation with Western Firms in the Field of Hungarian Light Industry," in East-West Cooperation in Business: Inter-firm Studies, Vienna, East-West European Economic Interaction, Workshop Papers, vol. 2, 1977.

[15] P. Knirsch, "Vom Ost-West-Handel zur Wirtschaftskooperation," Europa-Archiv, 1973, no. 2.

[16] ECE, Economic Bulletin for Europe, vol. 27, Geneva, United Nations, 1975.

[17] ECE, Analytical Report on Industrial Co-operation Among ECE Countries, Geneva, United Nations, 1973.

[18] K. Bolz and P. Plötz, Erfahrungen aus der Ost-West-Kooperation, Hamburg, HWWA-Institut für Wirtschaftsforschung, 1974.

[19] W. von Lingelsheim-Seibicke, Kooperation mit Unternehmen in Staatshandelsländern Osteuropas. Eine Einführung in die Praxis, Cologne, Deutscher Wirtschaftsdienst, 1974.

[20] K. Zborovari, "International Production Co-operation, Several Theoretical and Practical Questions," Vezetőképszés, 1972, no. 4, cited in E. Hewett, "The Economics of East European Technology Imports from the West," American Economic Review, May 1975.

[21] Cooperation (Essen), September 1975, no. 5, p. 14.

[22] E. Hewett, "The Economics of East European Technology Imports from the West," American Economic Review, May 1975.

[23] E. Sárosi, "Zur industriellen Kooperation zwischen Österreich und Ungarn," Forschungsberichte des Wiener Institutes für Internationale Wirtschaftsvergleiche, July 1972, no. 2.

[24] ZVO-Informationen, Rumänien, information bulletin of the Siemens AG (Red. v. Heyking), Munich, August 1975.

[25] Business International, Eastern Europe Report, May 14, 1976.

[26] M. Schmitt, "Probleme der industriellen Ost-West-Kooperation," in G. Leptin, ed., Handelspartner Osteuropa, Berlin, 1974.

[27] A. Beltschuk, "Wirtschaftliche und technisch-wissenschaftliche Kooperationen zwischen der Sowjetunion und der Bundesrepublik Deutschland," Osteuropa Wirtschaft, September 1973, no. 2, p. 111.

[28] Chase World Information Corporation, Kam-AZ — The Billion Dollar Beginning, New York, 1974.

[29] H. P. Linss, "Wirtschaftlich-technische Kooperation am Beispiel des Röhren-Erdgasgeschäftes," in G. Leptin, ed., Handelspartner Osteuropa, Berlin, 1974.

[30] Business International, Eastern Europe Report, 1974, no. 24, p. 367.

[31] L. I. Brezhnev, "Report of the CPSU Central Committee to the 25th Congress of the CPSU in Moscow, Feb. 24, 1976," in Our Course: Peace and Socialism, Moscow, "Novosti" Publishers, 1977, pp. 127-28.

[32] Die Presse, Vienna, July 6, 1976.

[33] I. Russow, "Möglichkeiten des Buntmetallhandels mit Westeuropa," Aussenhandel UdSSR, 1976, no. 2, pp. 23-29.

[34] Chase World Information Corporation, East-West Markets, April 5, 1976.

[35] Business International, Eastern Europe Report, 1974, no. 1, p. 4; 1974, no. 17, p. 262.

[36] Zahraniční obchod (Prague), 1975, no. 10, p. 11.

[37] M. Schmitt, in Wirtschaftswoche, 1970, no. 50, cited in K. H. Standke, "Technologischer Transfer und die Kooperation westlicher Industrieländer mit Ostmitteleuropa," p. 138, in G. Leptin, ed., Handelspartner Osteuropa, Berlin, 1974.

[38] S. Nehring, "Zu den Wirtschaftsbeziehungen zwischen der BRD und der DDR," Die Weltwirtschaft, 1974, no. 2.

[39] DIW, Berlin, DDR-Wirtschaft. Eine Bestandaufnahme, Frankfurt, 1974, pp. 290 ff., 280.

[40] K. Bolz, "Kooperationsoffensive der DDR," HWWA-Wirtschaftsdienst, 1971, no. 2, p. 62.

11

Practical experience with East-West industrial cooperation

The Preparatory Stages [1]

Although the Eastern countries are far more actively engaged in overall propaganda on East-West industrial cooperation than are the Western nations, in many instances the initiative for specific agreements comes from the West. According to reports from the FRG, about half of all cooperation undertakings now come into being as a result of proposals from West German firms. Originally, initiatives from Western partners were by far the most preponderant, but lately a shift has taken place. In particular, some Hungarian firms have manifested a genuine interest in cooperative undertakings and on their own initiative have submitted proposals to Western partners. According to E. Hewett [2], who refers to Hungarian surveys in his report, the initiative for most cooperation agreements in Hungary still comes from Western firms, however. For the other Eastern European countries it is still typical that enterprises take up the question of cooperation only after directives from higher up, and then without having any clear idea of the meaning and purpose of such cooperation.[1]

In many cases, however, initiatives from Western firms are encumbered by a lack of information on technical innovations, focal points of development, capacities, etc., of the Eastern European enterprises.[2] Important information and documentation does, to be sure, often exist, but it is difficult to get at (e.g., in specialized periodicals and staff journals). Language also constitutes a barrier. Market research results occasionally offered by Eastern European institutes are in most cases of doubtful value, and in the West only a few enterprises are capable of conducting really useful market research in the East. Local surveys are difficult or often impossible or risky. International corporations that have their own internal information-gathering system, and firms with many years of experience with Eastern contacts during which they have been

208

able to build up their own information network, sometimes find themselves enjoying important advantages over other competitors.

In many cases special congresses on cooperation, seminars, lecture series, etc., have been useful for preparing the way for cooperation. To overcome this problem of an information shortage, several agencies (e.g., the ECE in Geneva) have contemplated setting up an international center for East-West cooperation. In some countries (e.g., the United States and FRG)[3] information on the possibilities of East-West cooperation is disseminated by national agencies.

The Significance of Traditional Relations

Reports on industrial cooperation repeatedly call attention to the fact that sound cooperation agreements are possible only on the basis of long years of business relations, personal contact, and mutual trust. The cooperation agreement between Honeywell, United States, and Metronex, Poland, on the manufacture of the Vutronik system for controlling industrial processes, was made possible by manifold Honeywell deliveries to Poland in 1956 and by the equipping of a refinery in Gdansk. Long years of contacts (some even before the war) were the foundation for the agreement between Steyr-Daimler-Puch, Austria, and the Hungarian auto industry; this was one of the first major East-West cooperative ventures. The agreement between the Austrian Chemie Linz and Hungary was also made possible by long years of traditional business relations (see [4] and Case Studies 9 and 10, Appendix 1). One Western firm with some of the longest Eastern experience is VÖEST-Alpine, a nationalized enterprise of the Austrian steel industry, which has carried out cooperation projects both in the Eastern countries (USSR, Czechoslovakia, and Hungary) and jointly with them in developing countries. VÖEST recommends beginning with smaller projects and going on to larger projects after some positive experience has been accumulated.

In the FRG a survey showed that in more than half the cases the first contacts for cooperation agreements came from already existing interfirm relations. However, the importance of traditional relations will vary depending on the type of cooperation agreement; in agreements where a market outlet is the primary purpose, previous familiarity with the partner is less important (it is occasionally pointed out that cooperation is one of the ways to open a new market) than in agreements leading to some form of mutual dependence between the two partners. A study of Eastern cooperative under-takings of the British electronics and communications industries [5] showed that most such agreements came out of trade relations in which the personal factor (e.g., a British manager who could speak the language of the Eastern country) played an important role. According to McMillan [6] previous trade contacts had existed in two thirds of all cooperative agreements between East and West (the United States excepted).

Negotiations for Agreements

Since most cooperation agreements pertain to production, what they achieve will depend significantly on the Eastern European producer. However, the first phase of negotiations is usually handled by the competent foreign trade organization or by specialized organizations, or in some cases by representatives of planning offices, ministries, and banks. Representatives of the Eastern European producer are called in only later.

Notable differences exist between the various Eastern nations, and often even between different sectors in the same country. For example, in Hungary the relevant foreign trade organizations, or Intercooperation AG, as well as the particular producer firm (several Hungarian producers are authorized to conduct foreign trade on their own) participate in negotiations. But difficulties often arise when several enterprises or foreign trade companies participate at the same time in a cooperative undertaking, since their divergent interests must often be brought down to a common denominator. Numerous cooperation agreements with Hungary contain, for example, a zero balance clause, stipulating that the respective values of mutual deliveries from East and West must balance each other. If several Eastern enterprises are party to such an accord, a zero balance is often demanded from each, and that can cause considerable difficulties in implementing the cooperative venture (see Case Study 9, Appendix 1). In Romania the Eastern negotiating partner is usually the respective industrial center.

Negotiations on cooperation agreements are in most cases long and drawn out: according to one FRG survey six months to one year in 60%, two years in 24%, and over two years in 15% of the cases. In 15% of the agreements the negotiations were interrupted for six months to three years. In two thirds the Western firm knew

Table 49

Evaluation of Cooperation Negotiations with Eastern Countries by FRG Firms

Country	Rating	Negotiations with Eastern partner	Share of the three rated items in total number of responses, in % of Eastern European partners			Cooperation with top authorities in Eastern countries, in %
			Negotiating skills	Knowledge of technical details and products	Information on market situation	
Eastern countries, total	good	over 50	70	under 45	under 45	35
	satisfactory	over 35	24	under 50	under 30	40
	poor	10	6	under 10	under 30	25
Poland	good	12	40	40	30	almost 100
	satisfactory	75	40	40	20	–
	poor	13	20	20	50	–
Hungary	good	75	85	45	60	25
	satisfactory	25	15	45	15	50
	poor	–	–	–	25	25

Source: K. Bolz and P. Plötz, Erfahrungen aus der Ost-West-Kooperation, Hamburg, HWWA-Institut für Wirtschaftsforschung, 1974.

211

that negotiations were being carried on with other Western firms on the same cooperative venture.

Despite various difficulties Western German firms rated their negotiations with the Eastern countries as good in 50% and as poor in only 10% of the cases. Negotiations with Hungary were rated especially positively, while Poland got a poorer rating. The negotiating skill of the Eastern partner was rated as good in 70% of the cases, and once again Hungarian managers were rated above, and Polish managers as below, average. The Eastern partner's knowledge of technical details was rated as good in only 45% of the cases, while the level of information on the Western market situation came off rather badly (a rating of poor in 30% or, in the case of Poland, even 50% of the cases) (see Table 49).

Marer's study [7] of U.S. cooperative undertakings in the East in the chemical industry showed that American firms regarded negotiations as time consuming, costly, and risky. Difficulties arose from the fact that the negotiations usually took place in the capitals of the Eastern countries and that the Eastern partners in most cases insisted on talks with the top management of the Western firm. The U.S. firm had to show up with a whole team and be empowered to make immediate decisions. On the other hand, the waiting time required for the Eastern Europeans to make decisions was long. The U.S. firms found it particularly annoying that they never knew what criteria would ultimately be used to decide to grant an order or not. In many cases American firms have gotten the impression that their chances were minimal and that they had been invited to tender an offer (costly for them) only because the information they furnished was useful to the Eastern partner in making a decision. The expression "whipsawing" is often used for such a situation.

P. Hardt [8] has pointed out that negotiations occasionally get bogged down by a large number of participants; but at the same time, he stresses that it is necessary for representatives of the producing firm to participate in the negotiations to ensure the success of the project from the outset.

The success rate of cooperation negotiations is variously reported: in most areas only about 5% of all projects contemplated are finalized, and some sources even report a figure of 1-2%. Occasionally, however, it is reported that almost all serious talks end in the conclusion of an agreement. Existing cooperation agreements are in most cases prolonged. For example, the Central Association of German Chambers of Industry and Commerce (Deutscher

Industrie- und Handelstag) reports that of the 150 cooperation agreements in force between West German and Hungarian firms in 1973, only four were not extended after the stipulated expiration date.

Size of Firms Participating in
East-West Cooperative Undertakings

Varying, at times contradictory, statements have been made about the size of Western firms participating in East-West cooperative ventures or preferred by the Eastern countries as partners. Eastern official sources usually stress explicitly that cooperative ventures with smaller Western firms are also welcome.[4]

However, it is the large firms, particularly the multinationals, that engage in the majority of the major large-scale East-West cooperative ventures. Multinational concerns are preferred by the Eastern countries because they have the most advanced technology, because of their financial power, and also because they can usually meet the Eastern demands for counterpurchases better than smaller enterprises.[5] According to J. Wilczynski [10] about half of the 800 multinational concerns maintain relations with the Eastern nations, 200 of them in the form of cooperation agreements. According to Wilczynski multinational firms are involved in four fifths of all East-West cooperation agreements.[6] The Soviet State Committee for Science and Technology has 100 cooperation agreements with multinational concerns. In 1975 multinationals were involved in 76% of American cooperation agreements with all Eastern countries, and 78.5% of those with the USSR [11] (see Table 7).

In the chemical industry large firms, usually multinationals, were involved in 58 of 66 American cooperation projects with Eastern countries [7].[7]

C. H. McMillan's study [6], which does not include American cooperative ventures, showed that in 1975 multinationals were involved in 46.5% of all agreements, half of them going to large and medium-sized multinationals (sales over $500 million or subsidiaries in at least five countries) and half to small multinationals (sales less than $500 million, subsidiaries in one to four countries). The number of multinationals involved in Eastern cooperative undertakings was high in Japan and Italy and relatively low in Switzerland and Great Britain (Table 50).

H. Radice, on the other hand [5], points out that small and

middle-sized firms play a greater role in East-West cooperation than is usually assumed. Cooperation agreements are made with small Western enterprises for the most part when they possess the advanced technology the Eastern country needs.

Table 50

Multinational and State-owned Western Enterprises
Involved in Interfirm East-West Cooperation*

	Share of multinational firms participating in total number of agreements, in %	Share of state-owned Western firms in total number of cooperative agreements, in %
Austria	45.5	45.2
Belgium	33.3	–
Finland	40.0	–
France	30.4	13.0
FRG	56.1	8.8
Great Britain	27.8	5.6
Italy	61.5	53.9
Japan	75.0	–
Sweden	41.7	–
Switzerland	28.6	–
Total	46.5	18.1

Source: C. H. McMillan, "Forms and Dimensions of East-West Inter-firm Co-operation," in East-West Cooperation in Business: Inter-firm Studies, East-West European Economic Interaction, Workshop Papers, vol. 2, Vienna, 1977.
*Without USA; without joint ventures. State-owned enterprises refers to firms in which the state owns at least a 50% share.

Two sources, one from the West and one from the East, list the motives for the interest of small and medium-sized Western firms in Eastern cooperation. The Hungarian B. Bojkó [12] stresses that small Western firms in light industry participate in Eastern cooperative undertakings in order to better withstand competitive pressure from large Western firms. The general manager of the Austrian firm Steyr-Daimler-Puch, M. Malzacher [13], points out that, for example, in the auto industry firms in the smaller Western European countries, which cannot match the size of large firms in the FRG or France, have a special interest in Eastern cooperative undertakings because through them they can specialize their production, reducing the range of products types, while at the same time expanding their sales program with products manufactured partly or entirely by their cooperation partner.

FRG cooperative ventures, in sheer number of agreements, were spread out evenly over all size categories. Small to medium-sized enterprises (250-500 employees), firms employing 500-2,000, and those employing over 2,000 were each involved in one third of all cooperative ventures. Most cooperation agreements of the small to medium-sized enterprises were in respect of licensing, while 60% of the specialization agreements involved firms employing 500 to 2,000 people. Cooperation in research and development is almost the exclusive domain of the largest West German firms (see Table 51). In other Western countries the percentage of large firms involved in Eastern cooperative ventures is stated, in various reports, to be higher than in the FRG.

Table 51

FRG Industrial Cooperation Agreements with Eastern Countries, by Firm Size and Type of Cooperation

Size of FRG firm	All cooperative undertakings	Licenses	Research and development	Specialization
	Share of firms of indicated size in total number of cooperative ventures, in %			
By number of employees				
up to 250	20	}35	—	
250-500	15		ca. 7	
500-2,000	30	35	} ca. 40	60
2,000-5,000	}35	30		
over 5,000		—	50	
By turnover in DM				
up to 20 million	}25	}35		
20-50 million				
50-250 million	35	50		60
250-500 million	20	15		
over 500 million	20	—	50	

Source: K. Bolz and P. Plötz, Erfahrungen aus der Ost-West-Kooperation, HWWA-Institut für Wirtschaftsforschung, Hamburg, 1974.

The Eastern countries sometimes express their preference for large concerns explicitly. In Czechoslovakia the Foreign Trade Ministry recommended that large and medium-sized Western firms be chosen in industrial cooperative ventures, since they were better able to counterpurchase Czechoslovak goods. Polish sources are reporting official interest in joint ventures alone with Western firms that have strong financial backing and the most advanced technology. The Soviet State Committee for Science and Technology has concluded its agreements only with large Western firms. Smaller firms must therefore find other ways to put their know-how to use in the Soviet Union, and without the help of the State Committee this is usually very difficult. Some Western countries have taken steps to make Eastern cooperation easier for smaller firms. For example, an office in the FRG embassy in Moscow was set up especially to facilitate contact between Soviet agencies and small and middle-sized FRG firms. American firms find valuable assistance in the US-USSR Trade and Economic Council, which began operation in Moscow in mid-October of 1974.

The Eastern countries may often prefer Western state-owned enterprises as cooperation partners for ideological reasons, or perhaps because they think that such firms can be more easily motivated to conclude international agreements than Western private firms. Table 50 shows that Western state enterprises are involved in 18.1% of all cooperative ventures with the East, this percentage being disproportionately high in Italy and Austria, undoubtedly because of the large role played by the state sector in "cooperation-intensive" areas in both countries.

Problems in Implementing Cooperation

Only 25% of German firms indicated in a survey that there were no problems in carrying out cooperative ventures. Among the main problems were:

Delays in Start-up

Unexpected delays in starting operations occurred in 25% of all FRG cooperative ventures with the East. This is one of the most frequent complaints (in research and development there were delays in as many as 50% of the cases). In addition to confusion about the interpretation of certain formulations in the agreement and the desire for amendments, there are two other major factors responsible for these delays:

1. In projects in which the cooperative product is to be manufactured in a newly constructed plant, the construction and delivery deadlines are usually not met in Eastern countries. Subcontracts from Eastern European factories are a special and difficult problem: often the Eastern European partner will refuse to subcontract in his own country, but Western deliveries are frequently not possible because of limited foreign exchange funds.[8] Recourse to efficient subcontractors from third Eastern countries may be expedient in

216

some cases. The Austrian branch of the Otto Dürr Co., Stuttgart, obtained a $10 million project for two auto-painting assembly lines at the Skoda Works in Mlada Boleslav in the face of tough competition by transferring the order of plant parts worth $3 million to Poland and Hungary; Czechoslovakia then did not have to use Western currency to pay for these parts.

2. If existing plant is to be used for the cooperative undertaking in the Eastern countries, resistance at the enterprise level may be expected. If a reorganization is necessary, there is always the risk that it will cause temporary premium reductions, and it is therefore often avoided. Other difficulties arise in procuring the necessary intermediate products domestically. AEG-Telefunken reports, for example, a case in which the final assembly of some AEG equipment was to be done in an Eastern country. However, neither the West German nor the Eastern firm had taken into account that only some of the needed switches and fuses of requisite quality were obtainable. There were also problems in trying to achieve the required surface quality by galvanization, phosphating, laquering, etc., since the processing properties of the domestically produced plastic granulate did not meet specifications. More parts than planned had to be produced in the FRG, and the consequence was a cost overrun [14]. To be sure, to promote cooperation the Eastern European partner firms are often placed on priority lists, giving them preference in placing orders for raw materials and other domestic subcontracted articles. But latest reports indicate that these priority lists now offer fewer advantages than they did a few years ago on account of the increasing number of cooperating Eastern European firms.

Quality of Eastern European Products

German firms have complained about the inadequate quality of Eastern European products in only a few cases (20%). In cooperative undertakings in research and development, the poor quality of Eastern European research equipment was criticized by 25% of the West German firms involved in cooperative research and development ventures.

Other reports attach much greater weight to the quality problem.[9] Western firms stress that strict quality controls and precise and detailed agreements with regard to quality guarantees should be part of every cooperation agreement. A Swedish firm which had a cooperation agreement with Romania for adding machines discovered that Romania was not willing to permit young engineers and managers to go to Sweden for training. Because of the lack of qualified specialists, the quality of the Romanian-produced machines was poor, and the Swedish firm had temporarily to withdraw its consent to sell the product under its Swedish name. In another cooperative undertaking in the electrical engineering industry, twenty Eastern European engineers were trained in Western Europe for one year. The result was satisfactory: the quality and delivery times met expectations. After three years, however, the quality of the product had fallen off, and by the end of five years only second-grade material was being produced and delivered. In an enquiry into the causes it was found that most of the specialists who had been trained in the West had been transferred to other plants and ministries, and their successors lacked the required know-how.

Commitments on minimum orders of the Eastern European cooperative product should, in the opinions of Western European firms that have participated in such undertakings, not be made until there is proof of actual quality. However, if the Eastern European product does not completely measure up to expectations, yet the discrepancy is not enough to warrant a charge of breach of contract, these sources feel that it is not advisable to reject the product and to pay the penalties provided in the agreement. It is also important that precise conditions and terms be spelled out for guarantee cases when third markets are turned to. In the West it is recommended that where possible, the Western partner should include a damage claim paragraph in quality clauses in addition to the right to reject defective products if inadequate or delayed Eastern European products jeopardize its own delivery commitments.

Other Problems

West German firms named insufficient flexibility in decision-making as a serious obstacle in 20% of the cases; in another 20% communications and information problems were mentioned. British firms find that the Eastern European partner is often too cautious [5]. In 20% of the cases FRG firms complained of nonfulfillment of delivery and payments deadlines (in the latter case only in agreements with Hungary). Other major and frequent problems are: nonobservance of market territories, quantities, or norms; difficulties in selling the Eastern European product; inadequate delimitation of responsibilities; lack of important spare parts;

218

understaffing; financial and foreign exchange problems; long transport times; deficient initiative of personnel; frequent change of personnel; difficulties in calculating the share of performance of each party; and unauthorized use of licenses. Lately the desire of the Eastern countries to be allowed to make compensation in unrelated products has been a serious obstacle to cooperation [5, 7].

In the experience of Western firms, precise specification of all points of a contract is very important in cooperative ventures. Often the contract contains sections on which the partners are in accord, so that a precise written formulation is not deemed necessary. However, occasionally the Eastern European firm acquires new management, which then might interpret differently the text of the contract. In general, job rotation of managerial and technical personnel in the East is more frequent than in the West [8].

Since the perceptible rise in the price of fuel and raw materials in intra-CMEA trade after January 1, 1975, there have been increasing reports that the rise in production costs in Eastern Europe is interfering with the functioning of East-West cooperation agreements. For this reason a number of agreements have come to a standstill [16].

Problems by Type of Cooperation and by Country

According to FRG experience most problems in cooperative undertakings are encountered in research and development and in specialization agreements, i.e., in cases where the partners cooperate on a relatively close basis. Licensing agreements and job processings, on the other hand, are carried out fairly smoothly.

Most ventures with Hungary proceed with only a few problems, although there have been cases in which difficulties have abounded. This was especially the case in 1969, the first year after introduction of the economic reform. More recently fewer problems were encountered. Cooperative ventures with Poland have proceeded relatively smoothly in about half the cases. Experience has been mainly negative with Romania (almost all the cited problems occur), Czechoslovakia (particularly failure to meet quality specifications and delivery deadlines), and the Soviet Union [1].

Contacts with Central Authorities and Officials

Reports on the behavior of central authorities and officials from

Eastern countries in the preparation and execution of cooperative undertakings are somewhat contradictory. Distinctions must be made between the different levels of the bureaucracy and between the different countries. Industrial cooperation with the West is now encouraged by top officials of the administrative and party apparatus, and not only with words but deeds. In cases of difficulty it often helps to go to the top. Not infrequently the Western partner is encouraged by its immediate Eastern partner to make such a move. Specialized organizations that some Eastern nations have set up to promote cooperation (e.g., Intercooperation in Hungary and the State Committee for Science and Technology in the USSR) show initiative and flexibility. However, occasionally considerable difficulties arise in negotiations at lower administrative levels, where officials are reported in a variety of sources to behave bureaucratically, to shun any responsibility, and hence to force a tedious, time-consuming, and complicated wandering from one office to another. Local authorities, whose intentions often differ from those of the central authorities, also cause problems.

For instance, bureaucratic difficulties often arise when the cooperative undertaking entails temporary supply of Western machinery and equipment to the Eastern European partner (e.g., leasing). Not infrequently it takes a year to obtain the Eastern European permissions required for a temporary import. If the cooperative agreement was originally intended to bridge a bottleneck in the Western partner's production capacity, the long wait can ruin the whole project.[10] In many cases Western firms are willing to enter into cooperative ventures with Eastern firms only after the latter have given assurances that no competitive product will be manufactured in the Eastern country. According to reports a verbal assurance of this sort cannot always be relied on.

FRG enterprises have had good experience with central authorities in Eastern countries in only about 35% of the cases; in 25% the experience has been demonstrably poor. Cooperation with Polish central authorities is generally rated good, while Hungarian officials get a good rating in only 25% of the cases (see Table 49). This accords with a survey of Hungarian firms, which have also been critical of the conduct of their own central authorities (see the next section). FRG experience with Romanian and Czechoslovak authorities has been predominantly negative. In ventures that are especially important for the Eastern country, official cooperation has usually been good; in ventures in third countries cooperation is given a relatively poor rating.

Experiences of Hungarian Firms in East-West Cooperation

A survey conducted by the Hungarian Chamber of Commerce on the goals and problems of Hungarian firms in cooperative undertakings with the West yields some interesting insights into the inner workings of these ventures [17, 18].

1. Objectives:
— The obviously most important objective of Hungarian firms is import substitution; this has its roots in foreign exchange problems. In many cases the question of whether the venture is economical or not goes out the window; indeed, "import replacement at any price" becomes the real guideline.
— Since many Hungarian firms have for some time had labor problems, especially in transport and packaging, cooperative ventures are meant to alleviate the labor shortage.
— More and more enterprises regard the saving of investment costs as one of the advantages of cooperation. In many instances it is realized that investments through cooperation cost less than starting out with one's own investment without experience. Hungarian enterprises also hope to save planning and development costs by means of cooperative ventures. They therefore are usually on the lookout for machinery and technology that has already been tried and proven.
— Some enterprises mention the chance to find out about demand on the world market, especially with regard to quality and modern technology, as one of the advantages of cooperation.

According to the experience of Hungarian enterprises, the preparatory stages of a cooperative agreement last at least two years. In some cases two to four years elapse between the time the first proposals are tendered and the time the contract is finally concluded. The general opinion is that the time spent in finding a partner and in acquiring permission could be reduced.

2. Difficulties:
— Lack of information on contracts already in force, technical development, market situation, etc., are some of the difficulties.
— Several enterprises suggest that the application forms and the formalities required in obtaining a permission could be simplified. Approval could also be accelerated by giving the firm manager more personal responsibility. It is pointed out that even when approval has been delayed, the manager still bears responsibility for the venture. This factor is especially important when the enterprise seeks no assistance. Another criticism

is that the central authorities reserve decision-making powers to themselves even when the project can only be assessed by the respective firm itself.

— The lack of investment credits in Hungary is cited.

— The rather inflexible foreign trade system, which often requires the participation of several foreign trade organizations in the negotiations.

— The prescription of a zero balance, i.e., that the foreign exchange needed for the venture be covered by additional foreign exchange earnings. Enterprises feel that in examining the effects of cooperation on the balance of payments, import savings are rarely acknowledged.

— Customs procedures, which are often too complicated (Hungarian customs concessions are granted only on a reciprocal basis, although the Western partner is sometimes not in a position to meet this requirement).

Notes

1. See an interview with Director Berghoff of the West German firm Franz Kirchfeld, Düsseldorf, which is quite experienced in Eastern business: "The partners in the CMEA area are given instructions from above to enter into cooperative ventures, but they do not know exactly how best to proceed. Hence they start out from their own deliveries they have made and ask: 'How can we improve the product if it cannot be sold?' The questions arise: 'Can't we enter into a cooperative venture here? Can't you help us? Can't you give us some know-how? And if we begin with just the veneer' .... Because its goods are often of inferior quality and hence cannot be sold in the West, the East is perforce led to the question of cooperation" [3].

2. The Final Acts of the Helsinki Conference stipulate explicitly an improvement in information about national plans and plan preferences (see Appendix 4).

3. In West Berlin a Center for East-West Cooperation was set up as a limited company in 1975.

4. The need for stronger participation by smaller and middle-sized firms in East-West industrial cooperation was stipulated in the Final Acts of the Helsinki Conference.

5. The willingness to accept delivery of Eastern European goods and to market them worldwide is most likely one of the reasons for the remarkable success of Japanese trading companies in the East [9].

6. This estimate seems somewhat high to the authors.

7. Mentioned in 1975 in Fortune's annual list of largest U.S. firms.

8. The West German firm Berlin-Consult, which leads the field in the construction of complete plants in Eastern Europe, has found that the managers of the new plants would like to import all equipment from the West, whereas the foreign trade organizations, which have the final say, insist on domestic subcontracts.

9. A useful indicator of quality is the discount rate on the sale of Eastern European goods in the West, which varies considerably from country to country and from article to article. It lies between 4-8% (foodstuffs from the USSR, textiles from the GDR) and 10% (machinery from Czechoslovakia and the GDR, chemicals from Romania), to 25% (machinery from the USSR, Bulgaria, and Poland) [15].

10. Leasing (which in many cases can also be seen as a cooperative activity) has so far not played an important role in relations between East and West. The Eastern Europeans often see leasing as an inordinately expensive type of financing. It also causes difficulties with regard to the ownership question and the Eastern European accounting system. The only leasing transactions of any importance so far have concerned containers between Soviet and American and English firms. Soviet banks have participated in the founding of leasing companies in Paris and London, but these deal chiefly with the leasing of Soviet machinery and automobiles in Western Europe.

References

[1] The data in this chapter come primarily from various issues of Business International, Eastern Europe Report, and (especially on the GDR), from K. Bolz and P. Plötz, Erfahrungen aus der Ost-West-Kooperation, Hamburg, HWWA-Institut für Wirtschaftsforschung, 1974, where the groundwork is laid for these reports.

[2] E. Hewett, "The Economics of East European Technology Imports from the West," American Economic Review, May 1975.

[3] Cooperation (Essen), December 1974, no. 4.

[4] E. Sárosi, "Zur industriellen Kooperation zwischen Österreich und Ungarn," Forschungsberichte des Wiener Institutes für Internationale Wirtschaftsvergleiche, July 1972, no. 2.

[5] H. Radice, "Experiences of East-West Industrial Co-operation: A Case Study of U.K. Firms in the Electronics, Telecommunications and Precision Engineering Industries," in East-West Cooperation in Business: Inter-firm Studies, Vienna, East-West European Economic Interaction, Workshop Papers, vol. 2, 1977.

[6] C. H. McMillan, "Forms and Dimensions of East-West Inter-firm Cooperation," in East-West Cooperation in Business: Inter-firm Studies, Vienna, East-West European Economic Interaction, Workshop Papers, vol. 2, 1977.

[7] P. Marer, "U.S.-CMEA Industrial Co-operation in the Chemical Industry," in East-West Cooperation in Business: Inter-firm Studies, Vienna, East-West European Economic Interaction, Workshop Papers, vol. 2, 1977.

[8] R. Hardt, "Looking Back at Ten Years Co-operation of a West German Firm with Polish Machine Tool Builders," in East-West Cooperation in Business: Inter-firm Studies, Vienna, East-West European Economic Interaction, Workshop Papers, vol. 2, 1977.

[9] J. Stankovsky, "Japans wirtschaftliche Beziehungen zur UdSSR und Osteuropa," in A. Lemper, ed., Japan in der Weltwirtschaft, Munich, 1975.

[10] J. Wilczynski, "Multinational Corporations and East-West Technological and Economic Relations," Canberra, January 1975 (manuscript).

[11] The U.S. Perspective on East-West Industrial Co-operation (preliminary), Bloomington, International Development Research Center of Indiana University, Team of Researchers, June 1975.

[12] B. Bojkó, "Results and Problems in Co-operation with Western Firms in the Field of Hungarian Light Industry," in East-West Cooperation in Business: Inter-firm Studies, Vienna, East-West European Economic Interaction, Workshop Papers, vol. 2, 1977.

[13] M. Malzacher, "Practical Aspects of East-West Cooperation Projects for an Austrian Firm," in East-West Cooperation in Business: Inter-firm Studies, Vienna, East-West European Economic Interaction, Workshop Papers, vol. 2, 1977.

[14] M. Schmitt, "Probleme der industriellen Ost-West-Kooperation," in G. Leptin, ed., Handelspartner Osteuropa, Berlin, 1974.

[15] Business International, Eastern Europe Report, May 14, 1976.

[16] Handelsblatt, Business International, Ost-Wirtschaftsreport, February 20, 1976.

[17] Külgazdaság, 1974, no. 8, in Österreichisches Ost- und Südosteuropa-Institut, Presseschau Ostwirtschaft, 1974, no. 12.

[18] Business International, Eastern Europe Report, 1974, no. 21.

12

Evaluation and outlook

Our study of East-West industrial cooperation has pinpointed a number of characteristic features of this form of East-West economic relations. Its relative importance and its potential for further development can be properly assessed only if they are analyzed in light of the development of interfirm cooperation in the market-oriented industrial economies and, further, in relation to all the other forms of East-West economic relations.

After World War II the development of technology in the advanced industrial nations brought about structural transformations that were highlighted by concentration and specialization and the spread of innovations across international boundaries. These new circumstances forced producers to reduce unit costs by increasing output and achieving economies of scale. The concentration of production and the formation of oligopolies in some industrial branches, as well as tariff barriers, other obstacles to trade, and tax burdens that vary from country to country, have pointed up some of the defects of the international market, at the same time as they have cleared the way for new forms of relations other than traditional foreign trade to spring up between firms that have complementary facilities and goals. As a consequence economic relations, capital, and production have largely been internationalized, and industrial organization itself has entered a stage of adaptation marked by interfirm cooperation agreements, mergers, company takeovers, and the emergence and spread of multinational corporations.

The specific forms assumed by international economic relations, i.e., normal foreign trade, interfirm cooperation, or relations within a multinational corporation, depend in the first instance on the cost and benefits of the steering mechanisms employed. Questions of location, investment climate, whether relations are to take place within or outside a tariff-protected economic area, and other factors beyond the direct control of the particular enterprises concerned play a decisive role here.

In Europe's planned economies technical advance has also led to a number of structural changes that have necessitated concentration and specialization on an international scale. In contrast to the West, however, industrial organization is brought into line with such changes by means of administrative measures and plan directives, e.g., coordination of middle-term economic plans, specialization agreements between governments, binding long-term delivery agreements, and more recently, international cooperation agreements, joint planning in selected branches, investment participation in the partner country, and the creation of international economic organizations and large-scale international enterprises.

In both East and West these structural changes have been accompanied by moves toward regional integration. Just as the models and instruments used to reorganize industry vary from East to West, so too the integration mechanisms used in the two regions differ.

Each system is obliged to develop the international division of labor within its own territory by methods congenial to its own setup. On the other hand, the advantages accruing from the international division of labor and from economies of scale, both of European and worldwide scope, cannot be disregarded; and measures have been devised to open new channels and work out new ways to intensify economic relations in both directions. East-West industrial cooperation is a possible supplement and alternative to East-West trade that has developed precipitously over the last fifteen years (up to the 1974-75 recession) despite existing obstacles, although recent trends have cast a cloud over further prospects for its expansion.

East-West industrial cooperation could provide support for ordinary trade by setting up long-term relations and ties at the enterprise level, thereby enabling East-West relations to further expand.

The same cost-benefit calculations applied within each bloc will determine the international division of labor in economic relations between East and West. Institutional differences, however, limit choices in each specific case. For example, capital participation by private foreign companies is not permitted in a number of Eastern nations, and in others it is permitted only with certain restrictions.

The autonomous expansion of multinational corporations through the formation of subsidiaries in the Eastern countries is totally ruled out. Conversely the methods used to implement the international division of labor in the Eastern countries, for example, intergovernmental plan coordination and accompanying organizational changes, cannot be used in the Western market economies. Aside from normal trade, therefore, industrial cooperation agreements concluded between the Western and Eastern firms directly concerned constitute an effective means for expanding mutual economic relations, given the differences that exist between the two economic systems.

Eastern governments prefer cooperation to ordinary trade relations, hoping that by cooperation with Western firms they will be in a better position to absorb Western technology and management methods and thereby to develop their export industries quickly. By such means balance of payments and trade deficits of the Eastern countries, which have long been on the rise, could be controlled and even eliminated without restricting the imports needed for modernization. Finally, the Eastern nations attach great importance to the long-term nature of cooperative relations, since this feature makes them easier to coordinate with the central national five-year plans than ordinary trade transactions, which are dependent on demand and hence introduce an element of hard to assess uncertainty into planning procedures.

In the West both government and private enterprise prefer ordinary trade with the East to cooperation agreements. On the whole, Western firms enter cooperation relations only when it becomes clear to them that they cannot do justice to their interests in the Eastern countries through normal trading transactions. However, our study has shown that the West, too, has an interest in expanding cooperative relations with Eastern partners for general trade policy and political reasons, not to speak of private business interests. Western partners also find cooperation attractive as compared with ordinary trading, since in cooperative ventures it is easier to get around the total separation between foreign trade and the domestic economy which exists in the East, as well as to establish direct relations between supplier and customer (this, however, is so far not true of cooperative relations with the Soviet Union). Hence cooperative undertakings adapt more easily to fluctuating demand than can normal trading transactions, which are carried out almost exclusively by the Eastern foreign trade monopolies.

There have been various attempts to assess the scope of East-

227

West cooperation and to classify it by type or product group in quantitative terms, but all have been attended by difficulties deriving, above all, from the fact that there is no generally accepted notion of how to define, classify, and evaluate East-West cooperation. Although the difficulties in determining even the number of cooperation agreements could be eliminated in the future by means of internationally accepted statistical criteria, the question arises of the extent to which it is even relevant to attach a worth to cooperation agreements in value terms or to log cooperation shipments quantitatively in terms of their share in total foreign trade volume. Cooperation agreements may, in addition to the immediate effect on exports, not only replace imports but, by increasing the efficiency of production enterprises that either supply the firms involved in the cooperation venture or receive its products, help to increase a country's exports in an indirect way. Such an effect could even reduce the share of cooperation sales in a country's total trade volume as exports were generally increasing, although the latter development had only been made possible by the very existence of cooperative undertakings.

Despite certain statistical flaws, our study has clearly shown that industrial cooperation between East and West has increased steadily over recent years. If, nonetheless, it has failed in several respects to completely measure up to expectations, which were somewhat too high originally, this has been because of a number of subjective and objective difficulties that have hampered a more rapid development of this kind of economic tie.

In Western Europe economic integration, of which both the EEC and EFTA are a part, means tariff disadvantages for all third countries, including those in the East; in addition the United States has so far refused to grant most Eastern nations most-favored-nation status. Recently the effects of the 1974-75 recession have created further obstacles to the expansion of East-West cooperation.

In the Eastern countries there are several factors that serve to obstruct the expansion of East-West cooperation: e.g., limits imposed by foreign trade plans, specialization decisions of the CMEA, insufficient decision-making powers of the enterprises, constraints placed on the latter by plan directives, nonconvertible currencies, varying price relations and consequent difficulties in calculating prices, and others. All these factors prevent flexibility in negotiations and impede the rapid conclusion of cooperation agreements; negotiations tions therefore prove costly, especially for Western firms, and only a portion of contemplated cooperative undertakings actually ever see the light of day.

The governments of many Eastern European countries believe that they can increase the effectiveness of their economies by means of interfirm agreements and associated technology transfer without having to go the way of economic reforms; that such reforms are needed, of course, has long been recognized, but because of the political risks they would entail it is hoped they may be avoided. Empirical studies have shown, however, that East-West cooperation has better chances for success in the Eastern countries in which economic reforms have been made than in those that never got beyond the bare beginnings of such reforms. East-West cooperation does not therefore appear to be an alternative to economic reform in the Eastern countries. On the contrary, the further development of cooperation agreements would be promoted if some far-reaching improvements were made in the functioning of the economy, the rights and duties of enterprises and factory associations were expanded, and a rational price system and sensible credit and exchange rates were established.

It must be borne in mind, however, that the external economic conditions for economic reform are now much worse than they were in the sixties, a fact that is all the more regrettable in that the political conditions for an opening up of the East created by détente and the Helsinki agreements are just now beginning to mature. Persisting inflation in the West, the Western monetary crisis, the fluctuations in exchange rates, and the stagnation of demand left by the 1974-75 recession have been stumbling blocks to efforts to establish links between the domestic economies of the Eastern countries and the world economy; such links, however, would be a condition for establishing the necessary framework before taking the next step toward fundamental economic reform. The stability of the Eastern economies is precarious enough for internal reasons without it being further undermined by the repercussions of the crisis in the West, to which central authorities in the East tend to respond defensively and rely even more than they are usually wont to do on directives and prohibitions to shape foreign trade relations rather than trying to steer them with economic instruments.

East-West industrial cooperation should therefore not be seen as an alternative to traditional East-West trade; indeed, its further growth can only take place in coordination with the entire network of East-West economic relations, and it must be assessed in that light. The various forms of East-West economic relations constitute an intricate interlocking network, and cooperation can grow only if East-West trade and finance and credit relations also develop. Conversely, if these relations stagnate, cooperation also suffers.

A long period of recession, stagnation, and inflation in the West could not fail to be detrimental to East-West industrial cooperation. In particular there would always be the risk under such circumstances that the Eastern nations would try to reduce their growing indebtedness to the West by sharp import cutbacks if they find their export possibilities insufficient. They could also attempt to invade the dwindling Western market with products manufactured by the technology obtained from previous cooperation agreements with the West and sold at cut-rate prices. Obviously such a situation would lead to a trade war rather than to further expansion of East-West industrial cooperation.

The further prospects for East-West industrial cooperation thus depend to a quite decisive degree on the growth trends and stability of the world market. In an expanding world market Western markets could absorb Eastern counterpurchases (which make up a sizable portion of East-West industrial cooperation) without too much difficulty. The Eastern nations would be able to meet their earlier commitments, even if they took out more credits to cover the expansion of East-West cooperation. Under favorable circumstances such as these there would also be a greater likelihood that the governments of the socialist countries would turn seriously to the question of much-needed economic reforms or carry further those that have already been instituted. A greater independence of industrial enterprises and a reliance more on economic instruments than on administrative directives to steer the planned economies could serve only to promote new interfirm cooperation agreements. A bright outlook for the world economy would facilitate the establishment of normal relations between the EEC and the CMEA out of which could then develop collaboration between the two economic areas in the common interest of Europe as a whole.

The fate of East-West industrial cooperation is thus linked to political problems, particularly détente. If both sides conscientiously meet all the commitments named in the Final Act of the Helsinki CSCE conference, namely, security, economic and scientific-technical cooperation, improvement in human contacts, and better exchange of information, East-West industrial cooperation, its potential still largely untapped, could provide a new and powerful impulse to the expansion of economic relations in general between East and West.

Appendix 1

<u>Eleven Case Studies</u>

1. <u>Polish Machine Tools — Exports to the West</u>
(Wewag, FRG, and Metalexport, Poland) [1, 2]

The West German machine-tool company Wewag, Düsseldorf
(subsidiary of Hunter Douglas, Ltd., Canada) concluded four cooperation agreements after 1967 with the Polish foreign trade organization Metalexport and various Polish production enterprises,
e.g., Rafamet and Cegielski. As a consequence of these agreements 1,800 Polish machine tools of various types and sizes (price
per unit 20,000 to 250,000 DM) have so far been shipped to the
West, mainly to the FRG.

The agreements provided for the supply of complete technical
documentation, including know-how, by Wewag and the development of a general draft design for developing a new model or modi-
fying an existing one. In all cases the Polish machines are out-
fitted with Wewag components to a value of 15-40% of the sale price
of the complete unit. The Wewag-supplied parts are added either
in Poland or in Düsseldorf. About half of the products are sold
under the commitments of the Western firm to buy (compensation);
the other half are sold at normal terms. For sales in the West the
trade name Wewag Economy is used, with the name of the Polish
partner mentioned. Wewag assumes the full warranty for service
and parts.

One of Wewag's most important experiences in ten years of practical cooperation is that care and circumspection must be exercised
in choosing a partner for cooperation in a production venture. Wewag has had negotiations with twenty-five Polish production enterprises, out of which to date have come only four cooperation agreements.

Some snags have arisen in the implementation of these agreements
as a result of a slump in demand on Western markets. The Polish
enterprises were obliged to fulfill their sales plans and hence turned
to the developing countries (where they can deliver on a bilateral

231

clearing basis) for substitute markets when demand fell in the West. During these years they lost interest in the Western markets, the result of which was missed delivery times (despite reduced demand), a lowering of quality controls, and irregularities in the supply of spare parts. When the West experienced a new upswing, these shortcomings had negative repercussions on their market chances. The difficulties could only be overcome through personal contacts with Polish managers. Polish engineers and salespeople were invited to meetings that take place about eight times yearly in Düsseldorf. The Polish engineers are kept informed about technical developments. The Polish managers are now prepared to ensure that delivery times are met and quality controls maintained even during periods of slump. The establishment of "working groups" for each product or product group, consisting of representatives from Wewag and the Polish partner, has proven to be a useful measure.

2. Soviet Tractors in Canada
(Satra, United States, and Traktoreksport, USSR) [3]

Soviet foreign trade with Canada consists mostly of Canadian wheat deliveries to a value of about $100-300 million Canadian yearly. Otherwise, trade between the two countries is very minor ($10-20 million Canadian in each direction, or less than 0.1% of Canadian exports and imports), so that the USSR has a high trade deficit with Canada on account of the wheat exports. The USSR would like to establish a foothold in the Canadian market with its products, particularly farm tractors. The conditions exist for a successful export venture, since the Soviet Union has a high tractor output, whereas tractors are no longer manufactured in Canada, and consequently no import duty is levied on them. The first efforts of the Soviet foreign trade association Traktoreksport in Canada in 1970, however, ended in failure. The Canadian trading company Twin Lake did sell about fifty Soviet tractors, but it was unable to provide full service. Some of the problems were the lack of familiarity of Canadian mechanics with the Soviet equipment, inadequate supply of spare parts, and a few flaws in the electric system of the tractors. Although all the tractors are still running, the poor service has seriously impaired the Soviet reputation. The second attempt to get into the Canadian market was undertaken

232

by Traktoreksport jointly with the U.S. firm Satra, which has had long years of experience in trade with the Soviet Union (Satra has been importing chromium from the USSR to the United States for twenty years; the sale in the FRG of the Soviet car Lada, manufactured in the Soviet Union on license from Fiat, was managed by a subsidiary of Satra). The two partners established two firms in Canada: Belarus Sales (Satra share 80%, Traktoreksport 20%), which takes care of marketing, and Belarus Equipment (Satra 20%, Traktoreksport 80%), responsible for technical facilities and service. Relatively large investments were required to prepare a sales campaign; in May 1973 the two Soviet-American firms opened showrooms in Toronto with 6,000 sq m floor space and service and storage facilities worth $1 million. This was followed by a somewhat smaller sales and service center in Montreal in February 1974. The Soviet tractors, completely assembled, are fully tested and newly painted in the Toronto center. The work is done jointly by Soviet and Canadian specialists. At the same time, a network of Belarus dealers (forty-three as of February 1974) was set up in five Canadian provinces, and their mechanics were given full training on the Soviet tractors. In 1973, 160 Belarus tractors, mostly smaller to medium-sized units, 25-75 h.p., costing $2,000 to $6,750 Canadian, were sold in Canada, to a large extent overcoming the bad Soviet reputation. One factor, of course, in the sales success was the fact that in 1972-73 farm income in North America rose sharply, and farmers made some large investments. The traditional U.S. suppliers were unable to cover Canada because of the pressure of domestic demand.

This agreement was an East-West joint venture on a third market. For its success the following preconditions were necessary: a receptive market and a suitable product; long years of experience in the East on the part of the Western partner; careful preparation and large initial investments.

3. Intercontinental Hotels (United States) in Eastern Europe [4]

The Intercontinental Hotels Corporation (a subsidiary of PANAM) has concluded cooperation agreements with most Eastern European countries and so far has had positive experience. The Western partner participates in the construction and in the day-to-day management of the hotels, which are connected to the Intercontinental booking system. Since capital participation was not possible, a concession fee is paid for Western know-how (for Hungary this fee is 3-10% of the gross turnover; Hungarian payments were $56,000 in 1970 and $210,000 in 1972). The agreements gave Intercontinental the right to periodically check the quality of the service and to set deadlines for improving any flaws. The following luxury class hotels have been built in the Eastern countries so far: in Hungary the Intercontinental, with 350 beds (January 1, 1970); in Romania the Bukarest Intercontinental, with 428 beds (1971); in Poland a Forum Hotel, with 75 rooms (1974); and in Czechoslovakia the Interprag, with 409 rooms. Negotiations are being carried on with the Soviet Union for the construction of three large hotels in Leningrad, Moscow, and Kiev, with a total of 4,300 beds. Other agreements are in process with Bulgaria and Poland. The construction of the Forum Hotel in Warsaw was turned over to a Swedish firm.

4. Cosmetics in Romania
(Hamol, Switzerland) [5]

Hamol AG (Switzerland) produces its Vitamol cosmetic in eight Western European countries. After positive experience in cooperation agreements with Hungary and licensing agreements with Yugoslavia, Hamol decided to expand operations to Romania, where it saw a prospective market. A three-stage plan was compiled for establishing ties enabling Swiss specialists to become familiar with the situation in Romania and to popularize the trade name Vitamol in Romania. In phase I, begun in 1974, the finished product and its packaging were delivered to Romania to be equipped there with a Romanian label. In phase II only special raw materials and additives plus packaging machinery will be shipped to Romania, where the finished product will be manufactured. During phases I and II Romania need spend no hard currency; payment is in the form of petrochemical products (vaseline, etc.). In phase III, scheduled for around the end of 1975, a joint production enterprise is to be set up in Romania for which Hamol will provide the know-how, machinery, and perfumes. The products will be sold in Romania as well as in some Western and Eastern European countries.

5. Romcontrol Data — A Joint Venture in Romania
(CDC, United States) [6, 7, 8]

In April 1973 an agreement on the establishment of Romcontrol
Data SRL was concluded between the U.S. company Control Data
Corporation of Minneapolis (CDC) and the Romanian Industrial
Central for Electronics and Vacuum Technology (CIETV). The
American partner has a 45% share in the $4 million company
capital. The company produces peripheral instruments for com-
puters (card readers, card printers, and card punchers). Eighty-
seven percent of the output is taken on by the American partner,
which will use it as parts in its own systems or for exports. In 1975,
94% of the components needed for construction were imported
from the United States by CDC; in 1976 this figure should be reduced to 40%. The components comprise 50-60% of the total worth
of the final product.

The agreement between CDC and CIETV contains twenty-nine
supplements of two to thirty pages in which all the important legal
and organizational questions are dealt with. One of the most difficult problems was working out a method of settlement agreeable
to both partners. The agreement was concluded for twenty years.
CDC's contribution consists of technological know-how, equipment
and tools for a few advanced testing facilities, and the assumption
of the costs of training the Romanian personnel in the United States.
The Romanian contribution consists of furnishing the plant grounds,
various pieces of equipment, and cash funds. CDC and the Romanian firm are equally represented in the firm management. As they
have acquired production experience the Romanians have taken
over more and more of the managerial functions, with the agreement of the Western partner, so that by mid-1976 there were only
two Americans left on the management board. Since the beginning
of the joint venture Romanian personnel have increased from 100 to 200.

6. Resita Renk AG — A Joint Venture in Romania
(Zahnräderfabrik Renk, FRG) [9]

The second joint venture agreement in Romania was concluded
in June 1973, between the German Zahnräderfabrik Renk AG (a
subsidiary of the Gutehoffnung Mill) and two Romanian companies
(Resita, with a capital participation of 40%, and the foreign trade

company Uzinexport, with a participation of 11%). The Resita
Renk AG, producing ship engines on German license in Romania,
was founded. Accounting and billing are in German DM; the investment of each partner was 20-22 million DM each. Annual sales of
50 million DM are expected. Half of the output is to be sold in
Romania, 25% in the other Eastern countries, and 25% in the West.
The German share in the company capital is 49%; management is
on a parity basis. For the Western partner the favorable production costs and the improved opportunity to enter the Eastern market were the decisive factors. The staff consists of 150 persons,
five from the FRG. Thus far the expectation of favorable wage
costs has not been fulfilled, since Romania insists that wages and
other costs be paid at world market prices. "Export wages," as
they are called, must be paid into a special fund (including 25%
social security insurance) from which the employees receive only
a portion, and that in Romanian currency. It has proven to be very
expedient to stipulate in agreements (and in Romanian, which is
alone regarded as authoritative in cases of doubt) that export wages
may increase only in the same proportion as official Romanian
wages increase (about 5% per year). The advantages of the venture
in Romania lay in the longer workday and the willingness of the
workers to accept night shifts when necessary. There were snags
in exports to the East caused by the fact that Romania insisted on
delivering products of Resita Renk only if paid in DM and hence
outside the existing bilateral intra-CMEA agreements (which are
generally cleared in transferable rubles).

7. Volcon — A Joint Venture in Hungary
(Volvo, Sweden) [10]

In summer 1974 Volcon Hungary GmbH was founded in Hungary,
with capital participation by the Swedish firm Volvo, the Hungarian
firm Csepel (one of the largest Hungarian industrial firms), and the
foreign trade company Mogürt. The subject of the agreement was
the assembly in Hungary of a small truck type 33-14 (a modified
version of the Swedish Laplander). The joint venture itself is a
relatively small organization that mediates between the Swedish
firm and the Hungarian production enterprise, Csepel. The Swedish contribution to the venture consists of technical documentation, special machinery, etc., furnished by Volcon to Csepel.
The vehicles (an output of 1,000 is planned for the first year) are

to be put together from Hungarian body parts and Swedish motors, transmissions, etc., delivered to Csepel from Volvo via Volcon. Export proceeds of 14-15 million SKr per year are expected, with most exports going to South America. Volcon assumes responsibility for training Hungarian technicians and workers, quality control of the product, and marketing in Hungary and the CMEA countries. Sales in the West will be managed by the Volvo sales network. The general manager of the enterprise is Hungarian; the technical director, a former Volvo employee. The agreement is valid for at least ten years. Negotiations lasted about a year.

Volvo will get 48% of the profits (after deductions and taxes provided by law), and the other 52% will be divided between the Hungarian firms. Business relations have existed for years between Volvo and the Hungarian vehicle industry.

8. Sicontakt — A Joint Venture in Hungary
(Siemens, FRG)

A joint Hungarian-German company, Sicontakt, was founded in the summer of 1974 in Budapest to promote trade between Siemens and Hungarian firms. The capital participations are 51% for the Hungarian firm Intercooperation and 49% for Siemens (total capital $5 million). (Siemens's contribution consists of computer equipment and foreign exchange.) Sicontakt is to service Siemens equipment in Hungary (which means savings in personnel for Siemens) and provide technical assistance to Hungarian firms that have production-cooperation agreements with Siemens. The income of Sicontakt will come from payments by Hungarian firms and subsidies from Siemens. Marketing of Siemens equipment is not envisaged.

The technical director is appointed by Siemens; the sales director, by the Hungarians. The supervisory board consists of three Hungarians and two Germans (unanimity is required for important decisions).

9. Vehicles — Cooperation between Austria and Hungary
(Steyr-Daimler-Puch AG, Austria) [11]

The beginnings of cooperation between Steyr-Daimler-Puch AG (Steyr) and Hungarian firms go back to the fifties, when Csepel-Autogyár began to manufacture truck motors on license from Steyr.

This undertaking, which was advantageous for both partners, created the groundwork for a relationship of mutual trust.

The basis for cooperation relations was established in a five-year skeleton agreement on May 18, 1968, between Steyr and the Hungarian Foreign Trade Bank, followed by agreements with the Vörös Csillag Tractor Factory (1968), Hódmezővásárhelyi Gépjavító Vállalat (1969), and the Ikarus Bus Factory (1970). The Hungarian foreign trade organization Mogürt participated in all these agreements. The interest of Steyr and of the Hungarian firms in cooperation lay first and foremost in the expansion of export opportunities.

Cooperation agreements also included joint research and development. Joint experiments led to the production of a 36 cu m Harmster-Major loading truck,[1] which was developed mainly for the needs of the CMEA countries. The motors, the hydraulic system, and the suspension seat were provided by the Steyr Company; Hungarian firms built the chassis and the cabin.

No other joint development projects have been carried out. In the case of large tractors of 170 to 250 h.p., the partners could not agree on the goals of development. The Steyr Company wanted a traditional design, while Dutra Vörös Csillag Tractor Factory wanted to develop a multipurpose tractor (pinion head design with articulated steering mechanism) suited to be a basic vehicle in construction, forestry, and agriculture. The views of the two firms differed so much that the problem could not be solved even by the delivery of the main parts (velocity gear transmission and drive), since they were not usable for Steyr tractors.

Difficulties arose not only in research and development; they also showed up in production, which is no longer being continued. The following problems have been especially obstructive:

— The Hungarian initiative for cooperation with Steyr in most cases originated with the foreign trade associations or the central authorities for industry, and not with the Hungarian firms; the firms had first to be convinced by these organizations of the advantages of cooperation (i.e., this was necessary in the case of the Ikarus Bus Factory).

— For the Hungarian producers cooperation has tangible advantages only in the long term, e.g., because it absorbs a good portion of the firms' annual allotment of investment funds, and because the high import fees for Western imports to Hungary increase the price of cooperative products and hence impair domestic sales possibilities.

— Cooperation was virgin territory for the Hungarian firm; it lacked practical experience and practiced and responsible specialists. The agreement between the Steyr Company and Csepel-Autogyár could not be brought to completion primarily because the Hungarian partners continually changed their representatives at the negotiations. The Hungarians rarely expressed their intentions clearly; they waited for suggestions from their partner. Responses to the Austrian proposals often came only after considerable delay.

— The cooperation agreement was also hindered by coordination problems among the Hungarians. The centrally managed Steyr concern had to deal with Hungarian firms from different branches of industry, whose proposals had first to be approved by an interim ministerial commission on cooperation. To overcome the continual problems, in December 1969 the Hungarians asked Intercooperation AG to step in. A joint Austrian-Hungarian top-level commission was also formed.

— A special problem in the Steyr cooperation was the demand for a balance in reciprocal deliveries (zero balance). However, the Hungarian firms demanded that this principle apply to every factory, which of course would have caused considerable difficulties.

— Cooperative relations were further jeopardized by the fact that the Hungarian partner fell behind in agreed deliveries to Steyr. For the jointly produced tractors the Steyr concern had received only 95 of the 250 motors ordered in 1970 by mid-November. The quality of the Hungarian parts also often left something to be desired as a result of the poor quality of the raw materials and intermediate products.

— The Austrians showed only lukewarm initiative in selling the cooperation products. Although Austria has a better sales and service network, it has sold fewer of the jointly produced products than Hungary. The sales division of the Steyr concern did not pay sufficient attention to the cooperation products, which made up only about 2% of their sales volume. To overcome these difficulties the Steyr concern even looked into the possibility of building up a special organization for selling the products of the venture.

— The Hungarians thought that some of the prices of the Steyr concern were higher than their Western European competitors'. Hence cooperation was possible only with products for which Austrian and Hungarian markets had been sufficiently receptive

or which could be exported to developing countries.
— The export of Steyr-Ikarus buses to the West was made difficult by the fact that it was not possible to obtain Austrian certificates of origin, despite the fact that over 50% of its worth
had been created in Austria, because the last stage in its manufacture took place in Hungary.
— The high Austrian import fees (customs, turnover equalization
tax) for components obstructed cooperation between Steyr and
Csepel. The Hungarian firm was to produce components for
various Steyr tractors (some no longer in production) for which
Steyr autos were to be delivered to Hungary.
— Often the price system for subcontracted parts for the jointly
produced product was an obstacle to joint production, primarily
because of the different and semisecret accounting systems.
Special products lacked a world market price as a basis of reference, as with mass products. Thus the mass production of
the Haflinger pinionhead Puli crosscountry vehicle, developed by
Steyr, the Hungarian Puli developed by KGMTI, or the light
metal truck developed by Autokut were never produced because
of pricing difficulties.
It was impossible to resolve these difficulties and cooperation
between Steyr and the Hungarian firms came to a halt.

10. Chemicals — Cooperation between Austria and Hungary (Chemie Linz AG, Austria) [11]

The five-year cooperation agreement between Chemie Linz and
the Budapest Chemical Works (BCHW) is a "phase-filling" cooperative venture in production. At BCHW chlorine is produced in
a quantity that exceeds domestic needs as a by-product of the production of caustic soda. To utilize the excess quantity an acid
works would have had to be built at a cost of 14-16 million
forints. It proved more economical, however, to enter into a cooperation agreement with Chemie Linz, on the basis of which the
BCHW is to supply benzene tetrachloride and the Austrian firm is to
deliver 2,4,5-T acid to Hungary for the production of pest control
agents. The exchange factors were adjusted every year in light of
world market prices for the preceding two years. This agreement
offers both partners an opportunity to secure a long-term supply
of basic materials for an optimum output and at the same time
acquire a market for a surplus semifinished product. This coop-

erative venture is also important for Hungarian agriculture, since it helps reduce the shortage of pest control agents.

11. Vehicles — Cooperation between Austria and Poland (Steyr-Daimler-Puch AG, Austria) [12, 13, 14]

The cooperation agreement signed between Steyr-Daimler-Puch (Steyr) and the Polish foreign trade enterprise Polmot at the time of the visit of the Polish Prime Minister Jaroszewicz to Vienna in September 1975 covered the following points:

Austrian commitments:
- Austria will help Poland construct a new motor plant for heavy trucks in Wola and expand the existing factory in Jelcz (a cooperation agreement for medium-sized trucks has existed with Jelcz since 1972). The agreement on scientific-technical cooperation has a period of validity of fifteen years.
- Austrian firms will deliver goods to a value of 3.15 billion schillings by 1980 (Steyr for 2.95 billion S, the other Austrian firms for 0.2 billion S). The Steyr delivery package consists of: 0.39 billion schillings' worth of licenses and know-how, 1.65 billion S for truck parts, and 1.2 billion S for trucks.

Polish commitments:
From 1980 to 1990 Steyr will obtain truck components and heavy diesel engines from Poland worth 5.2 billion S. The Austrian firm has, however, the right to opt out of accepting delivery by paying a penalty of 7.6% of the outstanding sum. The Austrians made express mention of the difficulties that can occur in this respect during a recession. In addition a long-term commitment to accept without an escape clause would actually rule out a basic change in enterprise objectives (e.g., shutting down of truck production). Prices for the Polish deliveries are set a year in advance on the basis of Austrian cost price for the same or a similar product. No stipulations with regard to dividing up the market were agreed upon.

Financing:
- The project is financed with an earmarked financing credit from the Creditanstalt-Bankverein to the Bank Handlowy for 4.3 billion S, with a term of twelve years and carrying interest of 7.5%.

Steyr was competing heavily with Berliet and Volvo in negotiations on this venture. The final decision was made shortly before the agreement was concluded and was said to have been greatly influenced by the Austrian willingness to undertake extensive purchasing commitments. The successful existing agreement for medium-sized trucks has also helped to conclude the cooperation venture.

Notes

1. This Harmster Major extra capacity harvester, an invention of the German farmer E. Weichel, purchased by the Steyr company, is a self-loading, -shredding, transport, and -unloading vehicle.

References

[1] Business International, Eastern Europe Report, 1974, no. 11, pp. 165 ff.
[2] R. Hardt, "Looking Back at Ten Years Co-operation of a West German Firm with Polish Machine Tool Builders," in East-West Cooperation in Business: Inter-firm Studies, Vienna, East-West European Economic Interaction, Workshop Papers, vol. 2, 1977.
[3] R. M. Mansfield, "Belorus Ltd. — A Joint East-West Venture in Canada," Carleton University, Working Paper 5, East-West Commercial Relations Series, Ottawa, 1974.
[4] Business International, Eastern Europe Report, 1974, no. 23, pp. 347 ff.
[5] Business International, Eastern Europe Report, 1974, no. 22, pp. 332 ff.
[6] J. Stankovsky, "Kapitalbeteiligung — Neue Form der Kooperation im Ost-West-Handel?" Vienna, Creditanstalt-Bankverein, Wirtschaftsberichte, 1973, no. 6.
[7] Revista Economica (Bucharest), 1975, no. 31, in Österreichisches Ost- und Südosteuropa Institut, Presseschau Ostwirtschaft, 1976, no. 3, app. 6.
[8] Chase World Information Corporation, East-West Markets, July 12, 1976.
[9] Business International, Eastern Europe Report, 1974, no. 13, pp. 194 ff.
[10] East-West (Brussels), July 12, 1974, no. 111, pp. 1 ff.
[11] E. Sárosi, "Zur industriellen Kooperation zwischen Österreich und Ungarn," Forschungsberichte des Wiener Institutes für Internationale Wirtschaftsvergleiche, July 1972, no. 2.
[12] M. Malzacher, "Practical Aspects of East-West Cooperation Projects for an Austrian Firm," in East-West Cooperation in Business: Inter-firm Studies, Vienna, East-West European Economic Interaction, Workshop Papers, vol. 2, 1977.
[13] Die Presse, September 11, 1975.
[14] Business International, Eastern Europe Report, September 19, 1975.

Appendix 2

<u>List of Industrial Cooperation Agreements</u>
<u>between East and West</u>

Appendix 2 contains a list of agreements, classified by country, on East-West industrial cooperation that have been reported in various press publications from 1974 to 1976 (some important agreements concluded in 1973 are also included in the list). The list makes no claims to completeness; it is merely meant to give a rough idea of the present status of such agreements. Appendix 2 also contains a complete list of cooperation agreements between Austria and Hungary up to the end of 1974, compiled from the Hungarian cooperation registry.

The cooperation agreements are classified as follows:

C — cooperation agreement without further specification

L — licensing agreement without further specification*

L/P — licensing agreement, repayment with the licensed product*

L/C — licensing agreement tied to compensation*

JV — joint ventures

S — skeleton agreement on industrial cooperation

RD — cooperation in research and development

Agreements marked + are described in more detail in Appendix 1 (Case Studies).

---

*In licensing agreements, it is understood that the Eastern partner is the licensee unless explicitly stated otherwise.

BULGARIA

Western country	Announced	Type of agreement	Agreement on	Cooperation partner East	West	Value
FRG	February 1975	C	Communication and automation technology in medicine	Ministry of Electronics and Electrotechnology	Siemens AG	
	August 1974	JV	Joint production plant to plate graphite electrodes in the FRG	Technika	C. Condraty	
	July 1975	L	Manufacture of "Astor" cigarettes in Bulgaria	Bulgartabek	Reemtsma	
	November 1975	L	Manufacture and sales of "HB" cigarettes in Eastern Europe	Tuetuenue-Bulgartabak	Haus Bergmann	
Denmark	January 1975	L/P	Manufacture of forklifts, re-payment by delivery of semi-finished lifts	Balcancar	Je-Lau AS	
GB	January 1974	L	"Karricon" container conveyor and loading equipment	Balcancar	Rubery Owen	
	December 1974	L/C	Construction of factory to produce nonalcoholic beverages in Gurgas, licensed production of nonalcoholic beverages	Alcohol-free beverages and mineral water	Cadbury-Schweppes	
USA	April 1975	L	Manufacture of Meteor-600 burners	Spartak-Works, Burgas	Ray Oil Burner Co.	£ 5-10 mill.

Country	Date	L/C		Bulgarian partner	Foreign partner	
	July 1975		Manufacture and sales of Winston cigarettes in Bulgaria. Technical assistance in cultivation, harvesting, and processing of tobacco	Bulgartabak	Winston-Salem Reynolds Tobacco Co.	
Switzerland	1974	L	Industrial plant	Technokomplekt	BBC	
France	1974	C	Polyethylene plant	Technokomplekt	Technip	$10 million
Japan	1974	C	Condensors for computer and telecommunications industry	Elektroimpex	Nichikon	
	1974	C	Numerical process control	Ekeltroimpex	Fujitsu Fanoc	
Finland	1974	C	Refrigerating equipment	Technoexport	Hurre Comp.	
Austria	September 1975	S	Industrial, technical, and commercial cooperation	Technoexport	VÖEST-Alpine	

CZECHOSLOVAKIA

Western country	Announced	Type of agreement	Agreement on	Cooperation partner East	Cooperation partner • West	Value
Japan	August 1974	L	Acquisition of rotation mold licenses by Japanese firm	Totex Chrastava	Toyo Menka Kaisha	
	August 1974	L	Licensing of jet-driven loom with pneumatic weft insertion, acquisition by Japanese firm	Zbrojovka Vsetín	Nissan Motor Corp.	
	1973	C	Turbines	ČKD Blansko	Toshiba	
Holland	1973	C	Joint production of telephone equipment	Tesla	Philips	20 million hfl
	1973	C	Joint production of diesel locomotives	Škodaworks	Stark-Werkspoor	
Austria	October 1973	C	Delivery of electrical equipment for spinning and weaving mill in Syria	Investa AG	Elektrobau AG Linz	32 million S

246

GERMAN DEMOCRATIC REPUBLIC

Western country	Announced	Type of agreement	Agreement on	Cooperation partner East	West	Value
FRG	September 1974	C, L	Exchange of chemical products, cooperation in licensing and environmental protection	AHB Chemie-Export-Import	Raffinerie-und Petrochemie-Gesellschaft Anic	
GB	January 1974	L	Procedure for manufacturing conveyor belts from rubber or plastic, acquisition by the British firm	AHB Chemie-Export-Import	Greengate Industrial Polymers Ltd.	
Japan	November 1974	S	Cooperation in constructing metallurgical plant and equipment	Schwermaschinen-baukombinat "Ernst Thaelmann"	Nippon Steel Co.	
Austria	December 1974	S	Construction of ethyleneoxide plant by VÖEST; cooperation in mining and enrichment of soft coal in Australia	Maschinenexport	VÖEST-Alpine AG	4 billion S
Italy	September 1975	S	Joint efforts in third countries; commercial and industrial-technical cooperation	Various foreign trade organizations	FIAT	
	October 1975	S	Technical-scientific cooperation; joint initiatives for tapping and exploiting raw material resources	not known	EGAM	

POLAND

Western country	Announced	Type of agreement	Agreement on	Cooperation partner		Value
				East	West	
FRG	August 1974	C	Low tension installation equipment	Elektrim	Brown Boveri et Cie., Mannheim	
Finland	November 1974	C	Design and installation of plant and equipment for ore mining	Centrozap	Metex and Outkumpu	
	November 1974	JV	Joint company Polmot Oy in Finland	Polmot, Dal	Wihuri-Conzern	
France	February 1974	C	Installation of automatic equipment in coal mines	Kopex	Telemeca-nique	
	1973	C	Equipment for metallurgy	Centrozap	Creusot-Loire	
	1973	C	Rapid press	Metronex	Logabax	
	1973	C	Heavy trailers	not known	Nicolas	
	November 1975	C	Joint production of polycarbonates; scientific-technical cooperation in refining and petrochemicals	Polish Chemical Industry	Rhone-Poulence; Institut du Petrole; Ato Chimie	
	January 1976	RD	Joint research and cooperation in servicing, construction of accelerators for medical purposes	Polish nuclear research institute I.B.J.	Comp. Générale de Radiologie	
	October 1976	RD	Cooperation in research and development	UNITRA	Thomson CSF	

Country	Date		Description	Polish partner	Foreign partner	Value
GB	August 1974	C	Electronic equipment for process control	Pnefal, Metronex	Honeywell Ltd.	
	1974	L	Construction of a factory to produce a potato beetle poison		Shell Intern. Petrol.	
	August 1974	C	Tractors, diesel engines; 75,000 tractors annually by 1980 in renovated Ursus Factory near Warsaw	URSUS Tractors, Agromet Motorimport	Massey-Ferguson-Perkins Ltd.	£ 165 mill.
	January 1975	L	Construction of zinc and lead smelting furnace	Centrozap	Imperial Smelting	ca. $4.8-7.2 million
	1973	C	Parts for copying equipment	Polish Optical Works	Rank Xerox	
Italy	December 1974	C	Delivery of spare parts for Fiat 126 to Italy	Bielsko Biala Small Car Factory	Fiat Turin	
Austria	August 1974	C	Coproduction of tractor trucks and new bus models	Polmot	Steyr-Daimler-Puch AG	
	October 1974	S	Melamine plant; design and delivery of production plant and equipment	Polimex-Cekop	VÖEST-Alpine AG	
	August 1975	C	Cooperation in paper manufacture	Paged	Nettingsdorfer-Papier-fabrik AG	
	October 1975	C	+ Manufacture of motors and trucks, licenses and technical-scientific cooperation	Polmot	Steyr-Daimler-Puch AG	3.15 billion S (Austrian delivery) 5.2 billion S (Polish delivery)

Western country	Announced	Type of agreement	Agreement on	Cooperation partner East	Cooperation partner West	Value
Sweden	August 1974	JV	Joint company in Sweden; fishing, fish processing, and marketing	Dalmor	not known	
	August 1974	C	Installation of heavy freight elevators	FSC-Works	Volvo	
	August 1975	L	Data terminals	Metronex; Mera-Elzab	Stansaab Electronic/SAAB-Scania	30 mill. SKr
Switzerland	August 1974	S	Consultation and technical services	Polservice	Gherzi Organisation	
USA	February 1974	L	Licensed manufacture of Singer sewing machines	not known	Singer	
	October 1974	RD	Geological exploration in Upper Silesia and Kraków, lab tests in USA	Warsaw Geological Institute	U.S. Geological Service	
	November 1974	JV	Establishment of joint company "Unitronex Corp." in Delaware; sales of Polish products	Unitra, Metronex, Mera	not known	$30 million sales
	November 1974	C	Production of Combantrin and Mecadox	Polfa	Pfizer	
	1973	C	Hydraulic excavators and depth drill rigs	Bumar	Koehring	

ROMANIA

Western country	Announced	Type of Agreement	Agreement on	Cooperation partner		Value
				East	West	
FRG	1973	JV	+Joint company "Resita Renk"; manufacture of ship engines	Resita Engineering Works (40%) Uzinexport (11%)	Zahnräderfabrik Renk (49%)	20 million DM capital
	1973	C	Mining machinery	Impexim	Krupp	
GB	August 1974	C	Joint production of incubators	Romagrimax	Buckeye-Stephens Ltd.	£ 0.4 mill.
Italy	August 1974	JV	Joint company "Rifil," production of synthetic fibers	Industrial center for synthetic fibers	Ramalfa	$2 million capital
Japan	August 1974	JV	Factory for high-protein yeast, capacity 60,000 t	Industrial center for pharmaceuticals (57.4%)	Dainippon Ink (42.6%)	30 million DM
	September 1975	S, RD	Energy, chemicals, petro-chemicals, mining, machinery, electrical engineering, industrial equipment, agriculture	Council for Science and Technology	Mitsui	
Switzerland	1974	C, (JV)	+Production of cosmetics	not known	Hamol AG	
USA	January 1974	RD	Telecommunications; electric and electromechanical components and consumer goods	Foreign Trade Ministry	ITT	
	1974	JV	+Romcontrol Data. Production of computer software equipment	Industrial center for electronics (55%)	Control Data Corp. (45%)	$4 million capital

USSR

Western country	Announced	Type of agreement	Agreement on	Cooperation partner		Value
				East	West	
FRG	August 1974	S	Planning and construction of foundries for Soviet Kivcet procedure	Litsenzintorg	Klöckner-Humbolt-Deutz-Wedag	
	January 1975	RD	Joint design and production of equipment for textiles	Committee for Science and Technology	Mayer & Co.	
	August 1974	RD	Joint development of radio transmission tube	Svetlana Industrial Combine	Siemens AG	
	August 1974	RD	Cooperation in cryotechnics, development of equipment for chemicals; processing of natural gas	Committee for Science and Technology	Linde AG	
	August 1974	C	Communications center with 3 studios and complete sound equipment	Ostankino Moscow	Robert Bosch Fernsehanlagen GmbH	20 million DM
	October 1974	RD	Cooperation in power plants and light-water reactors, fast breeders and reactors	Committee for Science and Technology	Kraftwerk Union AG	
	January 1974	RD	Exchange of information and services	Committee for Science and Technology	Otto Wolff AG	
	July 1974	C	Typewriter plant in USSR, output 150,000 per year	Prommashimport	Olympia Werke AG	
	1973	C	Mining machinery	Mashinoexport	Rheinstahl	

Country	Date	Type	Description	Soviet Partner	Foreign Partner	Value
	February 1976	L	5 gas-drying plants for fourth expansion stage of natural gas deposit in Orenburg, including supervision of installation and start-up	not known	Davy Power Gas	£ 100 mill.
	February 1976	RD	Magnetic recording technology	Committee for Science and Technology	Wolfgang Bogen GmbH Berlin	
France	October 1975	RD	Conventional power plants, nuclear power plants, air-craft construction	Committee for Science and Technology		
GB	March 1975	C	Wood pulp factory in Western Siberia, repayment with wood pulp	not known	Price and Pierce International	
	August 1975	C	Technical know-how, machinery parts, molds for manufacture of toys in 819 plants in USSR	not known	Dunbee-Combex-Marx Ltd.	
Japan	April 1975	C	Construction of Soviet paper factories	not known	Oji-Paper Co.	
	October 1974	C	Joint use of a container ship on the Japan-Nakhodka line	not known	Yamashita-Shinnihon Steamship Co., Iino Kaiun	
Japan/ Canada	December 1974	RD	Development of technology for hydraulic coal conveyance	Litsenzintorg	Kaiser-Resources, Canada Mitsui Mining, Japan	

Western country	Announced	Type of agreement	Agreement on	Cooperation partner		
				East	West	Value
Austria	October 1975	L	VEW buys Soviet electro slag resmelting procedure	Kiev Paton Institute	Vereinigte Edelstahl-werke AG	
Sweden	August 1974	S	Cooperation in vehicle pro-duction, production of forestry machinery, ship engines, and transport machinery	Committee for Science and Technology	Volvo	
USA	January 1974	C	Industrial design	Litsenzintorg	Raymond Louis-William	
	February 1974	RD	Development of passenger planes, navigation systems, oceanological equipment, and electronics	Committee for Science and Technology	Lockheed	
	October 1974	RD	Motor vehicle construction, aviation technology, electronics, research equipment, automa-tion, and machine tools	Committee for Science and Technology	Bendix Corp.	
	October 1974	RD	Exchange of research results	Committee for Science and Technology	Reichhold Chemicals Inc., Gulf Oil Co.	
	August 1974	RD	Various areas of technology	Committee for Science and Technology	Sperry-Rand Corp.	

254

Date	Type	Description	Soviet Party	Western Company	Value
August 1974	C	Construction of ammonia plants in USSR, delivery of 1 million t superphosphate annually; counterdelivery of ammonia and urea to the USA	not known	Chemico, Occidental Petroleum Corp.	
December 1974	C	Publication of books by Russian authors in English, and American authors in Russian	Soviet Copyright Agency (VAAP)	McGraw-Hill Book Publishing Co.	
March 1974	RD	Technology for nonferrous metals, hydraulic turbines	Committee for Science and Technology	Allis-Chalmers	
November 1974	RD	Processing of crude oil and natural gas, organic chemistry and plastics, environmental protection	Committee for Science and Technology	Universal Oil Products	
1973	C	Compressors	Energomashexport	Elliot	
1973	RD	Computer technology	Committee for Science and Technology	Control Data Corp.	
1973	S	Computer technology	Elektronorgtekhnika	Control Data Corp.	$500 mill.
1973	RD	Energy production (steam and gas turbines, nuclear energy)	Committee for Science and Technology	General Electric	
1973	RD	Electromedicine and measuring instruments, small computers	Committee for Science and Technology	Hewlett Packard	
1973	RD	Exchange of scientific-technical information	Committee for Science and Technology	ITT	

Western country	Announced	Type of agreement	Agreement on	Cooperation partner East	West	Value
	1973	RD	Coal mining	Committee for Science and Technology	Joy Manufacturing Comp.	
	1973	S	Off-shore and deep-sea drilling, instrument technology	Committee for Science and Technology	Dresser Industries	
	August 1975	RD	Chemicals and chemical plant construction	Committee for Science and Technology	H. H. Robertson	
	November 1975	C	Production of chromium dioxide for magnetic tapes in CMEA and India	Tekhmashimport	DuPont; Sumitomo Shoji America Ltd.	
	March 1976	S	Agricultural machinery	Ministry of Agriculture	Deere and Company	
	1973	JV	+Sales and service for Soviet tractors in Canada	Traktorexport	Satra	

HUNGARY

(See pp. 260–64 for agreements with Austria)

Western country	Announced	Type of Agreement	Agreement on	Cooperation partner East	Cooperation partner West	Value
FRG	September 1974	JV	+Joint venture Sicontact in Budapest	Intercooper. (51%)	Siemens AG (49%)	5 mill. Ft. capital
	August 1974	C	Delivery of plant equipment in exchange for parquetry	Intercooperation	Maschinen-fabr. Hildebrand	
	August 1974	C	Commission manufacture of men's trousers	Clothing coop. Vörös Csillag, Szolnok	C. Brühl, Rotenburg	
	October 1974	C	Planning and manufacture of installation equipment	not known	Robert Bosch GmbH Stuttgart	11 mill. DM capital
	September 1974	JV	German–Hungarian trade company Inter–Chemol GmbH in Frankfurt	Chemolimpex (50%)	Metallges. AG (50%)	110,000 DM capital
	March 1975	C	Production of spare parts for hydraulic dredgers	Intercooperation	Mengele	
	1973	C	Magnetic tapes	Polimer Co-op.	BASF	
	August 1975	L/P	Manufacture of BAC soap	Hungarian cosmetics firms	Schwarzkopf	$1 million
	August 1975	L/P	Automatic regulating valves for heating systems	Iklad Machine-tool works	Baelz	3.5–4 mill. DM

257

Western country	Announced	Type of Agreement	Agreement on	Cooperation partner East	Cooperation partner West	Value
	September 1975	C	Construction of 15–20,000 color TVs annually	Elektroimpex, Orion	Standard Elektrik Lorenz	20 million DM
France	November 1974	C	Manufacture of sport shoes	Hungarcoop. Tisza	Adidas-France	15 million fr.
Italy	March 1975	C	Chemicals	Chemolimpex	Montedison	$25 million
Japan	November 1974	K	Electric arc furnaces for ferrous alloys	Building contractor for metals plants	Sumito Shoi Kaisha Ltd.	
	August 1975	L	Hard glass manufacture	Tungsram AG	Nippon Electric Glass Co.	
GB	August 1974	L	Licensed production of shock absorbers	Ujpest Industrial complex	Girling	
	1973	C	Paint bases	Tisza Chemicals	ICI	
NL	November 1974	C	Planning work for streetcar and railroad lines, hospitals, schools, and buildings in the Near East	Intercooperation Medicor	not known	
	February 1975	C	Organ components	Hungarcoop./Közfém	Eminent Bodengraven	300,000 Ft.
Sweden	November 1974	JV	+Joint "Volcon" Co. in Budapest	Csepel, Mogürt	Volvo	
Switzerland	January 1974	L	High tension switches	Transelektro, Ganz	Brown Boveri et Cie.	

Date	Type	Description	Hungarian partner	Western partner
October 1974	S	Cooperation in pharmaceuticals	Hungarian Ministry for Heavy industry	Ciba-Geigy
November 1974	RD	Study of new production methods and technologies, evaluation of market chances for watches and clocks	State Manufacturers' Organization	Swiss Watch-makers' Federation
August 1975	C	Integrated manufacture of manual office typewriters	Hungarian office machine firms	Hermes Precisa
January 1976	S	Exchange of licenses, joint research products	Committee for Technological Development	Brown-Boveri et Cie.
November 1974	L	Gas burners, fluid filters	Csepel Gear and Lacquering Works	Maxon and Romicon (USA)
December 1974	JV	Production of hard-glass containers, factory to produce blood analysis instruments	Metrimpex Budapest	Corning Glass
January 1975	C	High-performance tractors	Györ Car and Machine Works	Steiger-Tractor Works
December 1975	JV	+Joint company "Radelcor Instruments Ltd." instruments for biological research	Metrimpex, Radelkis	Corning Medical

Industrial Cooperation between East and West

HUNGARY: Cooperation agreements with AUSTRIA

According to Hungarian sources* the following cooperation agreements between Austrian and Hungarian firms were in force by the end of 1974:

Subject of agreement	Hungarian partner	Austrian partner†	Year concluded	Duration‡
General skeleton agreement	Metallimpex and 17 Hungarian firms	VÖEST-Alpine	1971	5
General skeleton agreement	Metallimpex and 9 Hungarian firms	VMW Ranshofen-Berndorf		
Utilization of idle capacity	Metallimpex and 3 Hungarian firms	VMW Ranshofen-Berndorf	1973	7
Research and development	Székesfehérvári Könnyűfémmű, Metallimpex	VMW Ranshofen-Berndorf	1973	3
Joint production of buses	IKARUS, Mogürt	Steyr-Daimler-Puch AG	1970	5
Production of electric hydraulic loading and hauling equipment	Technoimpex, Dunamenti	Interhydraulik GmbH	1971	5
Joint production of fittings	Mosonmagyaróvári Fémszerelvény-gyár, Hunicoop	Armaturen-Werke Karl Seidl	1972	10
Joint production of oil and gas burners	Nikex and 4 Hungarian firms	Unitherm GmbH	1971	5
Production of fittings for air-conditioning units	Csőszerelőipari Vállalat, Fűtőber	Karl Weiss	1974	5
Air-conditioning units for pigpens	Mechanikai Mérőmuszerek Gyára, Trans-elektro	Gebr. Trox GmbH	1971	5
Joint production of cash registers	Irodagépipari és Finommechnikai Vállalat	Anker, Graz Anker, Bielefeld, BRD, Závody všeobecného strojírenství, ČSSR	1972	

*F. Horchler, "The Future of Austro-Hungarian Foreign Trade," Forschungsberichte des Wiener Institutes für Internationale Wirtschaftsvergleiche, 1975, no. 27. The agreements marked with a + were taken from various press announcements. †Or partner from third country. ‡Duration of validity in years; X indicates unspecified duration.

260

List of Cooperation Agreements

Subject of agreement	Hungarian partner	Austrian partner	Year concluded	Duration
Joint development of surface finishes	Hunicoop and 2 Hungarian firms	Swarowski GmbH, Vienna	1972	
Joint production of scales	Metripond Mérleggyár	Joseph Florenz AG	1973	5
Production of air compression equipment	Mechanikai Méromüszerek Gyára, Metrimpex	Festo GmbH, Vienna	1973	5
Joint production of small office machines	Irószer Szövetkezet, Chemolimpex Intercoop	Heinrich Sachs Metallwarenfabrik GmbH, Vienna	1969	
Joint production of testing equipment	Elektromodul Irószer	Electrovac, Vienna	1973	1
General skeleton agreement to promote cooperation in chemicals and petrochemicals	Chemolimpex and 7 Hungarian firms	Chemie Linz	1972	5
Exchange of chemicals worth $10 million†	Chemolimpex	Chemie Linz	1974	
Joint trading company	Országos Kőolaj- és Gázipari Tröszt Chemokomplex	Schoeller- Bleckmann Stahlwerke AG	1971	
Joint production of crude oil products	Mineralimpex and 2 Hungarian firms	ÖMV, Schwechat	1968	
Joint production of pesticides and herbicides	Budapesti Vegyimü- vek, Chemolimpex	Chemie Linz	1969	5 + 5
Research and development (pesticides)	Budapesti Vegyimü- vek, Chemolimpex	Chemie Linz	1971	
Research and development (herbicides)	Budapesti Vegyimüvek	Chemie Linz	1972	
Packaging of drugs (Depersolon)	Medimpex Kőbányai Gyógyszerárugyár	Rösch und Handel, Vienna	1960	X

Industrial Cooperation between East and West

Subject of agreement	Hungarian partner	Austrian partner	Year concluded	Duration
Agreement on trademark (Somben)	Medimpex, Chinoin	Rösch und Handel, Vienna	1968	X
Agreement on trademark (vitamin D_2)	Medimpex, Chinoin	Lannacher Heilmittel GmbH	1959	X
Packaging of drugs (Pyramidon)	Medimpex, Chinoin	Gerot Pharmazeutika, Vienna	1964	10
Agreement on pharmaceutical cooperation (Promethazine)	Medimpex, Egyt	Gerot Pharmazeutika, Vienna	1961	15
3 agreements on drug packaging	Medimpex and 2 other Hungarian firms	F. J. Kwizda, Chem. Fabrik, Vienna	1968 and 1972	5
Joint marketing of water purification facilities, technology for mining	Tatabányai Szénbányák	Simmering-Graz-Pauker AG	1968	
Joint production of tires and tire equipment	Taurus Gumiipari Vállalat, Chemolimpex	Semperit AG, Vienna	1970	10
Electricity exchange	Magyar Villamos Művek Tröszt	Österreichische Verbundgesellschaft	1968	10
Joint production and marketing of suntan lotion	KHV, Chemolimpex	Hamol International, Schwechat	1971	6
Writing materials	Pestmegyei Vegyi- és Divatcikkipari Vállalat	Memos, Vienna	1968	2+2+2
Chemical fibers	Hungarotex and 2 Hungarian firms	Chemie Linz	1968	
Joint production of cotton articles	Rábatext, Hungarotex	Getzner Mutter & Cie	1974	5
Joint production of cardboard and pasteboard	Papiripari Vállalat, Lignimpex	Mayr Meinhof Kartonfabrik	1973	4
Wood processing	Mohácsi Farostlemezgyár, Lignimpex	Adolf Funder OHG	1969	

List of Cooperation Agreements

Subject of agreement	Hungarian partner	Austrian partner	Year concluded	Duration
Joint employment of spray technology	Duna Cipőgyár, Interag RT	Polyair GmbH	1973	5
Publication of books	Corvina Könyvkiadó	Copro International		
Joint restaurant management	V. ker, Vendéglátóipari Váll. Terimpex, Monimpex	Primex, Vienna	1971	
Joint enterprise to market honey	Orsz. Méhészeti Szöv, Váll., Monimpex	Bienenkönigin Honigabfüll- and Handels-GmbH	1969	
Joint enterprise to market candies	Monimpex	Petsch, Vienna	1971	
Joint production of cranes for timber industry	Mezőgazdasági Gépgyártó, NIKEX Komplex és Szolg. Váll. Kaposvár	Berger OHG	1972	
Joint production of Harmster trucks	Hódmezővásárhelyi Mezőgéptröszt	Steyr-Daimler- Puch AG	1969	5
Joint production of margarine	Növényolajipari és Mosószergyártó Váll.	Österreichische Unilever GmbH	1972	10
Production of cigarettes	Monimpex, Dohányipari Váll.	Austria Tabakwerke	1972	4
Production of beverages (grape soda)	Badacsonyi Állami Gazdaság, Monimpex	Lenz Moser	1970	5
Production of wafers	Rákóczi Sütő, Komplex	O. Pischinger	1970	
Cooperation in agriculture	Various Hungarian firms	Various Austrian firms		
Production of electromagnetic vibrators	Vasipari Gépjármű, ETI, Intercooperation	IFE-Gesellschaft	1973	
Production of partitions	NIKEX, Intercooperation and 2 other Hungarian firms	Promonta Hof. Co.	1972	2
Joint production of steel shutters	NIKEX and 2 other Hungarian firms	Noe Schaltechnik	1972	

Industrial Cooperation between East and West

Subject of agreement	Hungarian partner	Austrian partner	Year concluded	Duration
Joint company + Intradex in Vienna (production of electric motors, etc.)	Transelektro	W. Elnrieder	1974	
Joint experiments with fungicides +	Nitrogen works Pét	Roehm and Hoes	1975	
Production of the Uncorn 3 N instrument in Hungary	Ganz Instruments	Goerz Elektro	1975	10

Appendix 3

Agreement between the Council of Mutual Economic Assistance
and European Economic Community on Principal Mutual Relations

Draft Proposal*

The Council of Mutual Economic Assistance (hereafter called CMEA) and its
member countries — Bulgaria, Hungary, the GDR, Cuba, Mongolia, Poland, Romania, USSR, and Czechoslovakia — on the one hand, and the European Economic
Community (hereafter called EEC) and its member countries — Belgium, United
Kingdom, Ireland, Denmark, Italy, the FRG, Luxembourg, France, and the Netherlands — on the other hand,

starting from provisions of the Final Act of the Conference on Security and Cooperation in Europe signed in Helsinki on August 1, 1975,

having regard to the progress and development of détente, peaceful coexistence,
and cooperation between countries already achieved in the world, and in particular in Europe in recent years,

underlining the favorable improvements achieved in the development of trade
and in cooperation between the CMEA member countries and the EEC member
countries in different sectors,

willing to make a joint contribution to the broadening and strengthening of
equal and mutually profitable relations between CMEA member countries and
EEC member countries on both a bilateral and multilateral basis,

expressing their readiness to determine the principles of mutual relations between the CMEA and the EEC,

have reached agreement on the following:

Article 1

This Agreement establishes official relations between the CMEA and the EEC.

Article 2

In carrying out the stipulations of this Agreement, the CMEA, its member
countries, the EEC, and its member countries will act in the spirit of the provisions from the Final Act of the Conference on Security and Cooperation in Europe
signed in Helsinki on August 1, 1975, and will in particular observe the principle
of sovereignty, noninterference in internal matters, and cooperation between
governments.

---

*Presented to the president of the EG Council in February 1976 for the CMEA
by the acting prime minister of the GDR. An unauthorized, partially condensed
English translation of the original Russian text appeared in East-West, Brussels,
April 8, 1976, no. 151.

265

Article 3

Relations between CMEA and the EEC will be developed in the following fields:
— improvement of conditions for trade and economic cooperation between CMEA member countries and EEC member countries
— standardization
— protection of the environment
— statistics
— economic forecasting in the sphere of production and consumption under the agreed headings
When necessary, the CMEA and the EEC will, by mutual agreement, lay down other fields of mutual relations.
The CMEA and the EEC will, in accordance with their powers promote and assist in the development of direct cooperation between the member countries of the CMEA and member countries of the EEC in the above-mentioned categories.

Article 4

The relations between the CMEA and the EEC may be realized in particular in the following forms:
— mutual studies and preparation of problems in the fields enumerated in Article 3, as well as other mutually agreed problems; regular exchange of information on these and other questions
— exchange of information on principal directions and current activity of the CMEA and the EEC
— systematic contacts between representatives and collaborators of the CMEA and the EEC
— organization of conferences, seminars and symposia.
When necessary the CMEA and the EEC may determine other forms of relations depending on the concrete problems and the pattern of their solution.

Article 5

The CMEA and the EEC will assist in the constant and balanced growth of trade between the member countries of the CMEA and member countries of the EEC, in diversification of its structure and in assuring favorable conditions for commercial and economic cooperation and full exploitation of possibilities resulting from the development of economies of member countries.

Article 6

On the basis of the principles of this Agreement, the member countries of the CMEA and member countries of the EEC will grant each other most-favored-nation treatment. This will be done on the basis of existing agreements or corresponding agreements which will be concluded between given countries.

Article 7

Member countries of CMEA and member countries of the EEC will construct their relations on the principle of nondiscrimination. In particular, they will abolish all prohibitions or limitations in import and export of any product, if these limitations or prohibitions are not applied to all third countries. They also will not impose them in the future. The CMEA and the EEC will cooperate as much as possible in the realization of these measures.

Article 8

The CMEA and the EEC, member countries of the CMEA and member countries of the EEC will, after mutual consultation, adopt measures which will help mutual trade develop in such a way that it will not cause or establish the possibility of creating serious damages on internal markets for these goods.

Article 9

The CMEA and the EEC will promote trade in agricultural goods between the member countries of the CMEA and the member countries of the EEC. This will develop on a stable, long-term, and just basis. Member countries of the CMEA and member countries of the EEC will not adopt any unilateral measures or limitations on trade with agricultural products which are not applied to all third countries.

Article 10

The CMEA and the EEC, accepting the importance of financial questions for developing trade, consider that it is necessary to study them in order to obtain solutions which will create a balanced growth in trade turnover. From this point, member countries of both organizations will, in particular, grant credits with the best possible conditions.

Article 11

Individual questions of commercial-economic relations for the realization of the provisions of this Agreement related to cooperation between member countries of the CMEA and member countries of the EEC may be regulated by bilateral and multilateral agreements between these countries.

Individual concrete questions may also be solved on the basis of the accepted principles of the Agreement in the way of direct contacts, understandings and agreements between member countries of the CMEA and organs of the European Economic Community, between member countries of the EEC, and organs of the CMEA, and also between the competent economic organizations.

Article 12

The EEC and its member countries will grant to interested member countries of the CMEA, which are less developed, the regime of generalized preferences.

The EEC and its member countries will continue to grant Cuba, a member of "Group 77," corresponding tariff reductions which the EEC and its member countries extend to member countries of "Group 77," as well as those which they have extended or will extend in the future to other developing countries.

Article 13

Provisions of this Agreement do not limit rights and obligations of the CMEA, the EEC, CMEA member countries, and the EEC member countries from existing bilateral and multilateral treaties and agreements, as well as their rights to be included in future similar agreements and treaties.

Article 14

In order to put this Agreement into effect, a Mixed Commission will be established from representatives of the CMEA and its member countries and from representatives of the EEC and its member countries.

The Mixed Commission may also assist in solving the individual concrete questions mentioned in the second part of Article 11 of this Agreement. In order to execute these tasks, the Mixed Commission may establish working groups whose members may be drawn from all member countries of CMEA and the member countries of the EEC or from representatives of interested countries, depending on the character of the observed problem.

The Mixed Commission prepares guidelines for its work. The function of the Mixed Commission will not effect the functions of special commissions existing in the framework of bilateral and multilateral agreements between CMEA member countries and member countries of the EEC.

Article 15 concludes the Agreement with the usual formalities.

Appendix 4

Excerpt from the Final Act of the Conference on Security
and Cooperation in Europe, August 1, 1975

Co-operation in the Field of Economics, of Science and
Technology and of the Environment

2. Industrial cooperation and projects of common interest*

Industrial Cooperation

The participating States,
Considering that industrial cooperation, being motivated by economic considerations, can
— create lasting ties thus strengthening long-term overall economic cooperation,
— contribute to economic growth as well as to the expansion and diversification
of international trade and to a wider utilization of modern technology,
— lead to the mutually advantageous utilization of economic complementarities
through better use of all factors of production, and
— accelerate the industrial development of all those who take part in such cooperation,
propose to encourage the development of industrial cooperation between the
competent organizations, enterprises, and firms of their countries;
consider that industrial cooperation may be facilitated by means of intergovernmental and other bilateral and multilateral agreements between the interested
parties;
note that in promoting industrial cooperation they should bear in mind the economic structures and the development levels of their countries;
note that industrial cooperation is implemented by means of contracts concluded
between competent organizations, enterprises, and firms on the basis of economic
considerations;
express their willingness to promote measures designed to create favorable
conditions for industrial cooperation;
recognize that industrial cooperation covers a number of forms of economic
relations going beyond the framework of conventional trade, and that in concluding
contracts on industrial cooperation the partners will determine jointly the appropriate forms and conditions of cooperation, taking into account their mutual interests and capabilities;
recognize further that, if it is in their mutual interest, concrete forms such as
the following may be useful for the development of industrial cooperation: joint
production and sale, specialization in production and sale, construction, adaptation and modernization of industrial plants, cooperation for the setting up of complete industrial installations with a view to thus obtaining part of the resultant
products, mixed companies, exchanges of "know-how," of technical information,
of patents, and of licences, and joint industrial research within the framework
of specific cooperation projects;

*Department of State Bulletin, September 1, 1975, pp. 331-33.

269

recognize that new forms of industrial cooperation can be applied with a view to meeting specific needs;

note the importance of economic, commercial, technical, and administrative information such as to ensure the development of industrial cooperation;

Consider it desirable:

— to improve the quality and quantity of information relevant to industrial cooperation, in particular the laws and regulations, including those relating to foreign exchange, general orientation of national economic plans and programmes, as well as programme priorities and economic conditions of the market; and

— to disseminate as quickly as possible published documentation thereon;

will encourage all forms of exchange of information and communication of experience relevant to industrial cooperation, including through contacts between potential partners and, where appropriate, through joint commissions for economic, industrial, scientific and technical cooperation, national and joint chambers of commerce, and other suitable bodies;

consider it desirable, with a view to expanding industrial cooperation, to encourage the exploration of cooperation possibilities and the implementation of cooperation projects and will take measures to this end, inter alia, by facilitating and increasing all forms of business contacts between competent organizations, enterprises, and firms and between their respective qualified personnel;

note that the provisions adopted by the Conference relating to business contacts in the economic and commercial fields also apply to foreign organizations, enterprises, and firms engaged in industrial cooperation, taking into account the specific conditions of this cooperation, and will endeavour to ensure, in particular, the existence of appropriate working conditions for personnel engaged in the implementation of cooperation projects;

consider it desirable that proposals for industrial cooperation projects should be sufficiently specific and should contain the necessary economic and technical data, in particular preliminary estimates of the cost of the project, information on the form of cooperation envisaged, and market possibilities, to enable potential partners to proceed with initial studies and to arrive at decisions in the shortest possible time;

will encourage the parties concerned with industrial cooperation to take measures to accelerate the conduct of negotiations for the conclusion of cooperation contracts;

recommend further the continued examination — for example within the framework of the United Nations Economic Commission for Europe — of means of improving the provision of information to those concerned on general conditions of industrial cooperation and guidance on the preparation of contracts in this field;

consider it desirable to further improve conditions for the implementation of industrial cooperation projects, in particular with respect to:

— the protection of the interests of the partners in industrial cooperation projects, including the legal protection of the various kinds of property involved;

— the consideration, in ways that are compatible with the economic systems, of the needs and possibilities of industrial cooperation within the framework of economic policy and particularly in national economic plans and programmes;

consider it desirable that the partners, when concluding industrial cooperation contracts, should devote due attention to provisions concerning the extension of the necessary mutual assistance and the provision of the necessary information during the implementation of these contracts, in particular with a view to attaining the required technical level and quality of the products resulting from such cooperation;

recognize the usefulness of an increased participation of small and medium sized firms in industrial cooperation projects.

Projects of Common Interest

The participating States,

Considering that their economic potential and their natural resources permit, through common efforts, long-term cooperation in the implementation, including at the regional or subregional level, of major projects of common interest, and that these may contribute to the speeding-up of the economic development of the countries participating therein,

Considering it desirable that the competent organizations, enterprises, and firms of all countries should be given the possibility of indicating their interest in participating in such projects, and, in case of agreement, of taking part in their implementation,

Noting that the provisions adopted by the Conference relating to industrial cooperation are also applicable to projects of common interest,

regard it as necessary to encourage, where appropriate, the investigation by competent and interested organizations, enterprises and firms of the possibilities for the carrying out of projects of common interest in the fields of energy resources and of the exploitation of raw materials, as well as of transport and communications;

regard it as desirable that organizations, enterprises and firms exploring the possibilities of taking part in projects of common interest exchange with their potential partners, through the appropriate channels, the requisite economic, legal, financial and technical information pertaining to these projects;

consider that the fields of energy resources, in particular, petroleum, natural gas and coal, and the extraction and processing of mineral raw materials, in particular, iron ore and bauxite, are suitable ones for strengthening long-term economic cooperation and for the development of trade which could result;

consider that possibilities for projects of common interest with a view to long-term economic cooperation also exist in the following fields:

— exchanges of electrical energy within Europe with a view to utilizing the capacity of the electrical power stations as rationally as possible;

— cooperation in research for new sources of energy and, in particular, in the field of nuclear energy;

— development of road networks and cooperation aimed at establishing a coherent navigable network in Europe;

— cooperation in research and the perfecting of equipment for multimodal transport operations and for the handling of containers;

recommend that the States interested in projects of common interest should consider under what conditions it would be possible to establish them, and if they so desire, create the necessary conditions for their actual implementation.

3. Provisions concerning trade and industrial cooperation

Harmonization of standards

The participating States,

Recognizing the development of international harmonization of standards and technical regulations and of international cooperation in the field of certification as an important means of eliminating technical obstacles to international trade and industrial cooperation, thereby facilitating their development and increasing productivity,

reaffirm their interest to achieve the widest possible international harmonization of standards and technical regulations;

express their readiness to promote international agreements and other appropriate arrangements on acceptance of certificates of conformity with standards and technical regulations;

consider it desirable to increase international cooperation on standardization, in particular by supporting the activities of intergovernmental and other appropriate organizations in this field.

Arbitration

The participating States,

Considering that the prompt and equitable settlement of disputes which may arise from commercial transactions relating to goods and services and contracts for industrial cooperation would contribute to expanding and facilitating trade and cooperation,

Considering that arbitration is an appropriate means of settling such disputes,

recommend, where appropriate, to organizations, enterprises, and firms in their countries, to include arbitration clauses in commercial contracts and industrial cooperation contracts, or in special agreements;

recommend that the provisions on arbitration should provide for arbitration under a mutually acceptable set of arbitration rules, and permit arbitration in a third country, taking into account existing intergovernmental and other agreements in this field.

Specific Bilateral Arrangements

The participating States,

Conscious of the need to facilitate trade and to promote the application of new forms of industrial cooperation,

will consider favorably the conclusion, in appropriate cases, of specific bilateral agreements concerning various problems of mutual interest in the fields of commercial exchanges and industrial cooperation, in particular with a view to avoiding double taxation and to facilitating the transfer of profits and the return of the value of the assets invested.

Bibliography

Publications of International Organizations,
Government Sources, and Other Documents

Basic Law on the Associated Chambers of Commerce and Economic Cooperation
in the Economy (Yugoslavia).
Basic Law on the SFRJ, 1965, republished in 1973 as the Law on the Founding
and Registration of Organizations of Associated Labor, Službeni list SFRJ,
1973, no. 19.
Brezhnev, L. I., "Report of the CPSU Central Committee to the 25th Congress of
the Communist Party of the Soviet Union, Held in Moscow, Feb. 24, 1976," in
Our Course: Peace and Socialism (Collected Speeches by General Secretary
of the CPSU Central Committee L. I. Brezhnev [1975-1976]), "Novosti" Pub-
lishers, Moscow, 1977.
Commission Proposals for the Inclusion of Cooperation Agreements of Member
Nations with the Eastern Countries in Community Procedures, Europa-
Documents, Brussels, no. 766, September 23, 1973.
Comprehensive Programme for the Further Extension and Improvement of Co-
operation and the Development of Socialist Economic Integration by the CMEA
Member-Countries, CMEA Secretariat, Moscow, 1971.
CSSR Cooperation Principles, Hospodářske noviny, no. 41, December 10, 1973.
CSSR Law no. 85, 1972, on Procedures in Concluding Agreements on Economic
Cooperation with Foreign Countries, govt. Gazette, no. 25.
Decision of the Czechoslovak Federal Government no. 273, October 2, 1975, on
the Approval of Guidelines for the Further Development of Economic Coopera-
tion with Nonsocialist Countries, in O. Henyš and J. Krupka, "Hospodářská ko-
operace ČSSR s kapitalistickými státy — tendence k vyšším formám," Hospo-
dářské noviny, Prague, January 30, 1976, no. 5.
Decree No. 1196 of the Bulgarian State Council on Economic, Productive, and
Technical Cooperation with Foreign Legal and Physical Persons, Duržaven
vestnik, 1974, no. 46.
Decree of the Bulgarian Council of Ministers, no. 85, 1974, on the Approval of
the Guidelines for the Application of the Order on Economic, Productive, and
Technical Cooperation with Foreign Juridical and Physical Persons, Duržaven
vestnik, 1974, no. 73.
Decree of the Bulgarian Council of Ministers, No. 85, 1974; Guidelines for the
Application of Order No. 1196, Österreichisches Ost- und Südosteuropa-
Institut, Presseschau Ostwirtschaft, 1974, no. 11, appendix 5.
Decree of the Federal Ministry of Foreign Trade of the CSSR, no. 125, Novem-
ber 1975, on the Foreign Trade Activities for Foreign Enterprises within the
CSSR, govt. Gazette, no. 29.
Decree of the Hungarian Ministry of Finances and Ministry of Foreign Trade,
no. 4, 1975, III, 27-KkM-PM.

Decree of the Polish Council of Ministers, no. 123, May 14, 1976, on the Approval for Foreign Legal and Physical Persons to Engage in Certain Economic Activities, Dziennik Uslaw, 1976, no. 19.

Decree of the Romanian Council of Ministers, on the Authorization and Regulation of Commercial Representatives of Foreign Firms and Economic Organization within Romania, no. 15, January 25, 1971, Official Bulletin, 1971, no. 10.

Decree on the Founding, Organization, and Activity of Mixed Enterprises in the Socialist Republic of Romania, no. 424, November 2, 1972.

Decree on Long-term Agreements on Cooperation in Production between Domestic Organizations of Associated Labor and Foreign Persons, no. 7, February 1973, Službeni list SFRJ.

Decree on Taxing Profits of Mixed Enterprises in the Socialist Republic of Romania, no. 425 of November 2, 1972, in Austrian Eastern and Southeastern Europe Institute, Presseschau Ostwirtschaft, no. 2, 1973.

ECE, Analytical Report on Industrial Co-operation Among ECE Countries, United Nations, Geneva, 1973.

ECE, Analytical Report on the State of Intra-European Trade, United Nations, New York, 1970.

ECE, "A Review of East-West Commercial Policy Developments, 1968 to 1973," Economic Bulletin for Europe, vol. 25, United Nations, Geneva, 1974.

ECE, Commission on Transnational Corporations, National Legislation and Regulations relating to Transnational Corporations, 1976.

ECE Documents — TRADE/202 add. 1, September 9, 1968.

ECE, Economic Bulletin for Europe, vol. 27, United Nations, Geneva, 1975.

ECE, Economic Bulletin for Europe, vol. 23, no. 2, United Nations, New York, 1972.

ECE, "Industrial co-operation," Economic Bulletin for Europe, vol. 21, no. 1, United Nations, New York, 1970.

ECE, "Industrial Organisation and Policy," Economic Survey of Europe in 1970, part 1, chap. 2, provisional version (mimeo).

ECE, "Institutional Changes," Economic Survey of Europe in 1968, chap. II, 2, United Nations, New York, 1969.

ECE, Practical Measures to Remove Obstacles to Intra-Regional Trade and to Promote and Diversify Trade. Addendum: Long-term Agreements on Economic Co-operation and Trade, TRADE/R. 302/25, October 1974 and TRADE/R. 217/Add. 1/Corr. 1, November 20, 1975.

ECE, "Preparations for the Second Meeting of Experts on Industrial Co-operation," Committee on the Development of Trade, TRADE/R. 320, United Nations, Geneva, August 26, 1975 (mimeo).

ECE, "Recent Changes in Europe's Trade," Economic Bulletin for Europe, vol. 27, United Nations, New York, 1975.

ECE, "Recent Changes in the Organization of Foreign Trade in the Centrally Planned Economies," Economic Bulletin for Europe, vol. 24, no. 1, United Nations, New York, 1973.

ECE, "Some Factors in the Fluctuation of the Industrial Growth Rate," Economic Survey of Europe in 1968, United Nations, New York, 1969.

ECE, "The European Economy from the 1950's to the 1970's," Economic Survey of Europe in 1971, Part 1, United Nations, New York 1972.

EEC, Official Journal of the, 1969-75:
    — Council Decision, December 16, 1969, on the Gradual Standardization of

Bibliography

Agreements on Trade Relations between Member Nations and Third Countries and on the Negotiation of Community Agreements, Off. J., no. L326/39, December 29, 1969.
— Council Decision, July 22, 1974, on the Introduction of a Consultational Procedure for Cooperation Agreements of Member Nations with Third Countries, Off. J., no. L208/23, July 30, 1974.
— Council Decision, March 27, on Autonomous Import Regulations from Eastern Countries, Off. J., no. L99, April 21, 1975.
— Council Ordinance no. 3054/74 for Specific Products with Origin in Developing Countries (Romania), Off. J., no. L329/70, December 9, 1974.
— Ordinance Establishing Common Regulations for Imports from Eastern Countries, VO 109/70, December 19, 1969, Off. J., no. L19, January 26, 1970.
— Proposal for a Council Decision on the Introduction of a Consultation Procedure for Cooperation Agreements of Member Nations with Third Countries (presented by the Commission to the Council on October 8, 1973), Off. J., no. C106/22, December 6, 1973.
— EGKS, EWG, EAG-Kommission, Achter Gesamtbericht über die Tätigkeit der Europäischen Gemeinschaften — 1974, Brussels-Luxembourg, 1975.
— EGKS, EWG, EAG-Kommission, Neunter Gesamtbericht über die Tätigkeit der Europäischen Gemeinschaften — 1975, Brussels-Luxembourg, 1976.
— "Initiative des RGW bei der Gemeinschaft," EG-Bulletin, no. 2, 1976.
— Kommission der EG, Information — Auswärtige Beziehungen, 91/75: "The European Economy and the Eastern European Countries."
"Ekonomické zásady pro hospodářskou kooperaci," Hospodářské noviny, 1973, no. 48.
Final Act (Signed at Helsinki on August 1, 1975), Conference on Security and Cooperation in Europe: The Department of State Bulletin, vol. LXXIII, no. 188, Washington D.C., September 1, 1975.
GATT, International Trade 1973/74, 1974/75, Geneva 1974, 1975.
Hungarian Law on Foreign Trade, no. III, 1974; Resolution of the Council of Ministers on the Enactment of Law No. III, 1974, on Foreign Trade, no. 1053, October 17, 1974; Decree of the Minister of Foreign Trade, no. 7, 1974, October 17, 1974.
Implementation Order of the Hungarian Minister of Finance on Economic Associations with Foreign Participation, no. 28, 1972.
Kosygin, A. N., "Hauptrichtungen der Entwicklung der Volkswirtschaft der UdSSR in den Jahren 1976-1980," XXV. Parteitag der KPdSU, Moscow, 1976.
Law on Banks and Credit and on Banking, 1971 (Yugoslavia).
Law on Cooperation in the Hungarian Economy, Legislative Ordinance no. 19, 1970.
Law on Credit Operations with Foreign Enterprises — Promulgated in 1960, with Alterations and Supplements in 1972 and 1973 (Yugoslavia).
Law on Foreign Exchange Operations, with Annual Supplements and Alterations (Yugoslavia).
Law on Foreign Trade and Economic and Technical-Scientific Cooperation in the Socialist Republic of Romania, March 1971.
Law on Profit Taxes for Foreign Investors in Domestic Economic Organizations with Respect to Joint Ventures — Promulgated in 1967, with Numerous Alterations and Supplements (Yugoslavia).

Industrial Cooperation between East and West

Law on the Assets of Organizations of Associated Labor, 1967, with Annual Supplements and Alterations (Yugoslavia).
Law on the Investment of Resources of Foreign Persons in Domestic Organizations of Associated Labor, No. 22, April 1973, Službeni list SFRJ.
Law on the Procurement of Foreign Exchange of the CSSR, no. 142, 1970, govt. Gazette.
OECD, Foreign Investment in Yugoslavia, Paris, 1973.
Statisticheskii ezhgodnik stran-chlenov Soveta ekonomicheskoi vzaimopomoshchi 1974, Moscow 1974.
Statutes of the CMEA, December 14, 1974, in the June 11, 1974, version; also Convention on Legal Competence, Privileges, and Immunities of the CMEA, December 14, 1974, in the June 21, 1974, version, CMEA Information Bulletin, 1975, no. 1 (as quoted in German translation, including comment, in Europa Archiv, 1975, no. 11).
UNCTAD, W. Hendricks, "Banking and Financial Aspects of Tripartite Industrial Co-operation," Discussion Paper, TAD/SEM. 1/4, Geneva, 1975.
UNCTAD, "Innovations in the Practice of Trade and Economic Co-operation between the Socialist Countries of Eastern Europe and the Developing Countries," Geneva, 1970.
UNCTAD, Tripartite Industrial Co-operation, UNCTAD Secretariat, TAD/SEM. 1/2, Geneva, November 25, 1975.
UNIDO, "International Industrial Co-operation," ID/132, August 1974.
United Nations, Economic and Social Council, Commission on Transnational Corporations, "National Legislation and Regulations Relating to Transnational Corporations," E/C. 10/8/Add. 1, January 26, 1976.
United Nations, World Economic Survey 1974, part one, New York, 1975.

Books and Monographs

G. Adler-Karlsson, The Political Economy of East-West-South Co-operation, Studien über Wirtschafts- und Systemvergleiche, vol. 7, Vienna-New York, Springer Verlag, 1976.
G. Adler-Karlsson, Western Economic Warfare 1947-1967, Stockholm, 1968.
I. Apostolov and Y. Laskov, "The People's Republic of Bulgaria," in R. Starr ed., East-West Business Transactions, New York-London, Praeger Publishers, 1974.
M. Baumer, W. Beitel, H. D. Jacobsen, F. Müller, J. Nötzold, and J. Sláma, Modalitäten der wirtschaftlichen Zusammenarbeit der BRD mit den Staaten Osteuropas und der Sowjetunion, Stiftung Wissenschaft und Politik-AZ 2031, Ebenhausen, 1974.
M. Baumer and H. Jacobsen, Internationale Wirtschaftsorganisationen und Ost-West-Kooperation, Stiftung Wissenschaft und Politik, Ebenhausen, 1975.
W. Beitel, "Die wirtschaftlich-technische Kooperation aus sowjetischer Sicht," in G. Leptin ed., Handelspartner Osteuropa, Berlin, Duncker & Humblot, 1974.
Benisch, Kooperationsfibel — Bundesrepublik und EG, 3rd ed., 1969.
J. Bethkenhagen and H. Machowski, Integration im Rat für gegenseitige Wirtschaftshilfe, Berlin, 1976.
E. Boettcher, Kooperation und Demokratie in der Wirtschaft, Tübingen, J. C. B. Mohr, 1974.
O. Bogomolov, "East-West Economic Relations: Economic Interests of the Socialist and Capitalist Countries of Europe," in World Economy and East-West Trade, East-West European Economic Interaction, Workshop Papers, vol. 1, Vienna, 1976.

Bibliography

B. Bojkó, "Results and Problems in Co-operation with Western Firms in Hungarian Light Industry," in East-West Cooperation in Business: Inter-firm Studies, East-West European Economic Interaction, Workshop Papers, vol. 2, Vienna, 1976.

K. Bolz and P. Plötz, Erfahrungen aus der Ost-West-Kooperation, Hamburg, HWWA-Institut für Wirtschaftsforschung, 1974.

U. Bosch, Meistbegünstigung und Staatshandel. Zur Technik der Handelsverträge mit dem Osten unter besonderer Berücksichtigung des GATT, Berlin, 1971.

A. Bródy, "The Rate of Economic Growth in Hungary, 1924-1965," in M. Bronfenbrenner ed., Is the Business Cycle Obsolete, New York, 1969.

A. A. Brown and E. Neuberger eds., International Trade and Central Planning, Berkeley, Los Angeles, 1968.

J. A. Burgess, "The Socialist Republic of Romania," in R. Starr ed., East-West Business Transaction, New York-London, Praeger Publishers, 1974.

R. Campbell and P. Marer eds., East-West Trade and Technology Transfer, Bloomington, Indiana University, 1974.

CEPES/RKW, Grenzüberschreitende Unternehmenskooperation in der EWG, Stuttgart, 1968.

J. C. Conner and J. R. Offutt, "Joint Venture in Eastern Europe," in R. Starr ed., East-West Business Transactions, New York-London, Praeger Publishers, 1974.

DIW, Berlin, DDR-Wirtschaft. Eine Bestandaufnahme, Frankfurt, 1974.

H. Giersch, ed., Die Möglichkeiten und Grenzen einer Verbesserung des Ost-West-Handels und der Ost-West-Kooperation, Tübingen, 1974.

J. Goldmann, "Fluctuations in the Growth Rate in a Socialist Economy and the Inventory Cycle," in M. Bronfenbrenner ed., Is the Business Cycle Obsolete, New York, 1969.

J. Goldmann and K. Kouba, Economic Growth in Czechoslovakia, White Plains, International Arts and Sciences Press, 1969.

K. Grzybowski, "The Polish People's Republic," in R. Starr ed., East-West Business Transactions, New York-London, Praeger Publishers, 1974.

K. Grzybowski ed., East-West Trade, New York, 1974.

Ph. Hanson, "The European Community's Commercial Relations with the CMEA Countries: Problems and Prospects," in C. H. McMillan ed., Changing Perspectives in East-West-Commerce, Toronto-London, Lexington Books, 1974.

R. Hardt, "Looking Back at Ten Years Co-operation of a West German Firm with Polish Machine Tool Builders," in East-West Cooperation in Business: Inter-firm Studies, East-West European Economic Interaction, Workshop Papers, vol. 2, Vienna, 1977.

K. Herman, "The Czechoslovak Socialist-Republic," in R. Starr ed., East-West Business Transactions, New York-London, Praeger Publishers, 1974.

H. D. Jacobsen, Die Entwicklung der wirtschaftlichen Ost-West-Beziehungen als Problem der westeuropäischen und atlantischen Gemeinschaft, Stiftung Wissenschaft und Politik, Ebenhausen, September 1975.

H. D. Jacobsen, Die Internationalisierung der Produktion und ihre Bedeutung für die Ost-West-Wirtschaftsbeziehungen. Vom Handel zur Kooperation, Stiftung Wissenschaft und Politik, Ebenhausen, 1976.

H. D. Jacobsen, Die wirtschaftlichen Beziehungen zwischen West und Ost, Hamburg, Rowohlt Verlag, 1975.

M. Kaser, Comecon, 2nd ed., London, New York, Toronto, Oxford University Press, 1967.

A. Kiralfy, "The Union of Soviet Socialist Republics," in R. Starr ed., East-West Business Transactions, New York-London, Praeger Publishers, 1974.

J. Kosta, H. Kramer, and J. Sláma, Der technologische Fortschritt in Österreich und in der Tschechoslowakei, Studien über Wirtschafts- und Systemvergleiche, vol. 2, Vienna, 1971.

E. A. A. M. Lamers, Yugoslavia: A Labour-Managed Market Economy with Special Reference to Joint Ventures Between Yugoslav and Foreign Enterprises, Universitaire Pers Tilburg, 1975.

H. Lange-Prollius, Ost-West-Handel für die 70er Jahre, Bad Homburg, 1971.

G. P. Lauter and P. M. Dickie, Multinational Corporations and East European Socialist Economies, New York, 1975.

G. Leptin, Handelspartner Osteuropa, Berlin, Duncker & Humblot, 1974.

F. Levcik, "Die Vergesellschaftung der Produktionsmittei und Wirtschaftsdemokratie; Thesen," in A. Rauscher ed., Kapitalismuskritik im Widerstreit, Cologne, 1973.

F. Levcik, "Technischer Fortschritt in Osteuropa," in G. Friedrich ed., Computer und Angestellte, Frankfurt on Main, 1971.

F. Levcik, "Zum Problem der Wirtschaftsreform in der CSSR," in E. Schreiber ed., Rationale Wirtschaftspolitik und Planung in der Wirtschaft von heute, Berlin, 1967.

W. von Lingelsheim-Seibicke, Kooperation mit Unternehmen in Staatshandelsländern Osteuropas. Eine Einführung in die Praxis, Cologne, Deutscher Wirtschaftsdienst, 1974.

H. P. Linss, "Wirtschaftlich-technische Kooperation am Beispiel des Röhren-Erdgasgeschäftes," in G. Leptin eds., Handelspartner Osteuropa, Berlin, 1974.

L. A. Litvak and C. H. McMillan, "Intergovernmental Co-operation Agreements as a Framework for East-West Trade and Technology Transfer," in C. H. McMillan ed., Changing Perspectives in East-West Commerce, Toronto-London, Lexington Books, 1974.

H. Machowski, "Entwicklung und Bestimmungsgründe des Ost-West-Handels," in H. Giersch ed., Möglichkeiten und Grenzen einer Verbesserung des Ost-West-Handels und der Ost-West-Kooperation, Tübingen, J. C. B. Mohr, 1974.

H. Machowski, "Länder des Rates für gegenseitige Wirtschaftshilfe," in Aussenpolitische Perspektiven des westdeutschen Staates, Munich, 1972.

C. H. McMillan, "Forms and Dimensions of East-West Inter-firm Co-operation," in East-West Cooperation in Business: Inter-firm Studies, East-West European Economic Interaction, Workshop Papers, vol. 2, Vienna, 1977.

C. H. McMillan and D. P. St. Charles, "Joint East-West Ventures in Production and Marketing — A Three Country Comparison," Institute of Soviet and East European Studies, Carleton University, Ottawa, Working Paper, no. 1, August 1973.

C. H. McMillan and D. P. St. Charles, Joint Ventures in Eastern Europe: A Three Country Comparison, Canadian Economic Committee, Montreal, 1974.

A. Maizels, Industrial Growth and World Trade, Cambridge University Press, 1965.

M. Malzacher, "Practical Aspects of East-West Cooperation Projects for an Austrian Firm," in East-West Cooperation in Business: Inter-firm Studies, East-West European Economic Interaction, Workshop Papers, vol. 2, Vienna, 1977.

P. Marer, Soviet and East European Foreign Trade, 1946-1969, Bloomington and London, 1972.

P. Marer, "U.S.-CMEA Industrial Co-operation in the Chemical Industry," in

Bibliography

East-West Cooperation in Business: Inter-firm Studies, East-West European
Economic Interaction, Workshop Papers, vol. 2, Vienna, 1977.

M. M. Maximova, "Industrial Co-operation Between Socialist and Capitalist
Countries: Forms, Trends and Problems," in East-West Cooperation in Business: Inter-firm Studies, East-West European Economic Interaction, Workshop Papers, vol. 2, Vienna, 1977.

H. Mayrzedt and H. Romé eds., Die westeuropäische Integration aus osteuropäischer Sicht, Vienna, 1968.

F. Mette, Informace o moderním zařízení výbrobních postupech, technické dokumentaci a licencích, zakoupených socialistickými státy v kapitalistických
státech v roce 1967, ÚVTEIN, Prague, 1969.

T. Morva, "Planning in Hungary," in M. Bornstein ed., Economic Planning, East
and West, Cambridge, Mass., 1975.

V. Nešvera, Investitionen in Österreich und in der Tschechoslowakei, Studien
über Wirtschafts- und Systemvergleiche, vol. 1, Vienna, 1971.

P. J. Nichols, "Western Investment in Eastern Europe: the Jugoslav Example,"
in Joint Economic Committee, Congress of the United States, Reorientation
and Commercial Relations of the Economies of Eastern Europe, U.S.G.P.O.,
Washington, D.C., 1974.

J. Nykryn, "Inter-firm Co-operation in the Machine Building Industry," in East-
West Cooperation in Business: Inter-firm Studies, East-West European Economic Interaction, Workshop Papers, vol. 2, Vienna, 1977.

J. Nykryn, Mezinárodní průmyslová kooperace, Prague, 1973.

F.-J. Pascaly, Internationale Arbeitsteilung in EWG und COMECON, Munich, 1973.

K. Porvit, "Planning in Poland," in M. Bornstein ed., Economic Planning East and
West, Cambridge, Mass., 1975.

B. M. Pounds and M. F. Levine, "Legislative, Institutional, and Negotiating As-
pects of United States — East European Trade and Economic Relations," in
J. P. Hardt ed., Reorientation and Commercial Relations of the Economies of
Eastern Europe, Joint Economic Committee, Congress of the United States,
U.S.G.P.O., Washington, D.C., 1974.

F. L. Pryor, The Communist Foreign Trade System, London, 1963.

H. Radice, "Experiences of East-West Industrial Co-operation: A Case Study of
U.K. Firms in the Electronics, Telecommunications and Precision Engineering
Industries," in East-West Cooperation in Business: Inter-firm Studies, East-
West European Economic Interaction, Workshop Papers, vol. 2, Vienna, 1977.

C. Ransom, The European Community and Eastern Europe, London, 1973.

R. C. Ribi, Das Comecon, Polygraphischer Verlag Zürich and St. Gallen, 1970.

D. P. St. Charles, "East-West Business Arrangements: A Typology," in C. H.
McMillan ed., Changing Perspectives in East-West Commerce, Toronto-
London, Lexington Books, 1974.

C. T. Saunders, From Free Trade to Integration in Western Europe, London,
Chatham House, PEP, 1975.

C. T. Saunders ed., East-West Cooperation in Business: Inter-firm Studies,
East-West European Economic Interaction, Workshop Papers, vol. 2, Vienna,
1977.

M. Schmitt, Industrielle Ost-West-Kooperation, Stuttgart, 1974.

M. Schmitt, "Probleme der industriellen Ost-West-Kooperation," in G. Leptin ed.,
Handelspartner Osteuropa, Berlin, 1974.

M. Selucká, Erosion of Monopolistic Position of Eastern European Foreign Trade
Enterprises: Legal Aspects," in C. H. McMillan ed., Changing Perspectives

in East-West Commerce, Toronto-London, Lexington Books, 1974.

R. Selucký, "East-West Economic Relations: The Eastern European Policy Perspective," in C. H. McMillan ed., Changing Perspectives in East-West Commerce, Toronto-London, Lexington Books, 1974.

O. Šik, Ökonomie — Interessen — Politik, Berlin (DDR), Dietz-Verlag, 1966.

Solving East European Business Problems, Business International S. A., Geneva, 1973.

H. Spetter, Inward-Looking versus Outward-Oriented Growth in the Strategy of Industrial Development, Inaugural Dissertation, Hochschule für Ökonomie, Berlin (East), 1971.

I. Spigler, Direct Western Investment in East Europe, Oxford, 1975.

K. H. Standke, Der Handel mit dem Osten, Baden-Baden, 1972.

K. H. Standke, "Technologischer Transfer und die Kooperation westlicher Industrieländer mit Ostmitteleuropa," in G. Leptin ed., Handelspartner Osteuropa, Berlin, Duncker & Humblot, 1974.

J. Stankovsky, "Japans wirtschaftliche Beziehungen zur UdSSR und Osteuropa," in A. Lemper ed., Japan in der Weltwirtschaft, Munich, 1975.

R. Starr, "Evolving Patterns of East-West Business Transactions: Introductory Note on Co-operation Agreements," and "Introductory Note on Contracting with Enterprises in State-Planned Economies," in R. Starr ed., East-West Business Transactions, New York-London, Praeger Publishers, 1974.

E. Tabaczyński, Kooperacja przemysłowa z zangranica, Warsaw, Państwowe Wydawnictwo Ekonomiczne, 1976.

J. Teneda, "The System of Trade between Japan and East European Countries, including the Soviet Union," in K. Grzybowski ed., East-West Trade, New York, 1974.

A. Uschakow, Der Ostmarkt im Comecon, Baden-Baden, Nomos Verlagsgesellschaft, 1972.

"U.S.-Soviet Commercial Relations," in The Soviet Economic Prospects for the Seventies, U.S.G.P.O., Washington, D.C., 1973.

J. Varró, "The Hungarian People's Republic," in R. Starr ed., East-West Business Transactions, New York-London, Praeger Publishers, 1974.

S. Wasowski ed., East-West Trade and the Technology Gap, New York, 1970.

J. Wilczynski, The Economics and Politics of East-West Trade, New York, 1969.

P. J. D. Wiles, Communist International Economics, Oxford, Basil Blackwell, 1968.

T. A. Wolf, U.S. East-West Trade Policy, Economic Warfare vs. Economic Welfare, Lexington-London, 1973.

A. Zwass, Zur Problematik der Währungsbeziehungen zwischen Ost und West, Studien über Wirtschafts- und Systemvergleiche, vol. 5, Vienna, 1974.

Contributions to Scholarly Conferences, Research Reports, Magazine Articles, and Newspaper Reports

"(Der) Abschluss der Konferenz über Sicherheit und Zusammenarbeit in Europa," Europa-Archiv, 1975, no. 17, D 43.

J. Anusz, "Expansion of Industrial Co-operation Between Poland and Developed Capitalist Countries," in Foreign Trade Research Institute, East-West Economic Relations, Warsaw, 1973.

B. Askanas, H. Askanas and F. Levcik, "Die Wirtschaft in den RGW-Ländern 1976 bis 1980: Verschlechterung der Wachstumsbedingungen," Monatsberichte

Bibliography

des Österreichischen Institutes für Wirtschaftsforschung, 1976, no. 12.

B. Askanas, H. Askanas, and F. Levcik, "Structural Developments in CMEA Foreign Trade over the Last Fifteen Years (1960-1974)," Forschungsberichte des Wiener Institutes für Internationale Wirtschaftsvergleiche, 1975, no. 23.

"Ausländische Tungsram-Unternehmen fördern ungarischen Export," Österreichisches Ost- und Südosteuropa-Institut, Presseschau Ostwirtschaft, 1974, no. 12, suppl. 8.

A. Bajt, "Fluctuations and Trends in Growth Rates in Socialist Countries," Ekonomska analiza, 1969, no. 3-4.

A. Bajt, "Investment Cycles in European Socialist Economies: A Review Article," Journal of Economic Literature, March 1971.

B. Balassa, "Types of Economic Integration," paper presented at the Fourth World Congress of the International Economic Association, Budapest, August 19-24, 1975.

W. Beitel, "Ansätze für die Auslagerung von Produktionen aus der BRD nach Osteuropa," Osteuropa Wirtschaft, 1975.

A. Below, "Abkommen auf Kompensationsgrundlage über Grossvorhaben mit kapitalistischen Ländern," Aussenhandel UdSSR, 1976, no. 3.

A. Beltschuk, "Wirtschaftliche und technisch-wissenschaftliche Kooperationen zwischen der Sowjetunion und der Bundesrepublik Deutschland," Osteuropa Wirtschaft, September 1973, no. 2.

Berliner Bank, Mitteilungen für den Aussenhandel, 1973, 1974.

J. Bethgenhagen and H. Machowski, "Entwicklung und Struktur des Ost-West-Handels im Jahrzehnt 1960-1970," DIW Wochenbericht, 10, 1973, of March 2, 1972.

H. Boller, "Die Kooperationsabkommen Österreichs," West-Ost-Journal, Vienna, 1973, no. 6.

K. Bolz, "Kooperationsoffensive der DDR," HWWA-Wirtschaftsdienst, 1971, no. 2.

K. Bolz, "The Prospects of Tripartite Cooperation," Intereconomics, 1976, no. 11.

K. Bolz and P. Plötz, Bericht über die industriellen Kooperationsbeziehungen zwischen der BRD, den sozialistischen Ländern Osteuropas und den Entwicklungsländern, Hamburg, HWWA-Institut fur Wirtschaftsforschung, 1975.

K. Bolz and P. Plötz, "Participation in Tripartite Co-operation," Intereconomics, 1975, no. 9.

K. Bolz and P. Plötz, "Technology- and Marketing-Transfer by Tripartite Co-operation," Intereconomics, 1976, no. 1.

L. Brainard, "A Model of Cyclical Fluctuations under Socialism," Journal of Economic Issues, March 1974.

A. Bródy, "Cycles and Equilibrium," European Economic Review, 1969, no. 2.

W. Brzost, "Podstawowe cele i warunki realizacji polityki licencyjnej Polski w latach 1966-1970," SGPiS, Zeszyty Naukowe, Warsaw, 1973, no. 94.

"Bundesrepublik Deutschland: Deutsche Auslandsinvestitionen/Auslandsinvestitionen in Deutschland," Berliner Bank, Mitteilungen für den Aussenhandel, 1974, no. 5.

Business International, Eastern Europe Report, 1974-1976:

— "A Hungarian Interpretation of Joint Venture Questions," Business International, Eastern Europe Report, 1975, vol. 4, no. 5.

— "Bulgaria Okays Western Offices," Business International, Eastern European Report, 1976, no. 2.

— "East European Co-operation with the West Draws Soviet Criticism," Business

Industrial Cooperation between East and West

International, Eastern Europe Report, April 1976, no. 15.

"Business Week," February 23, 1976, in Moscow Narodny Bank, Press Bulletin, February 25, 1976.

Chase World Information Corporation, East-West Markets, 1974-76.

Chase World Information Corporation, East-West-Markets, May 17, 1976.

Chase World Information Corporation, Kam-AZ — The Billion Dollar Beginning, New York, 1974.

L. Ciamaga, "Co-operation Between the East and the West (Introductory Comments)," in Collective Study of Foreign Trade Institute, East-West Economic Relations, Warsaw, 1973.

Cooperation, Essen, 1974-76.

I. Davidov, "Rechtliche Regelung der Produktionskooperation mit nichtsozialistichen Ländern," Bulgarischer Aussenhandel, 1975, no. 1.

East-West, Brussels, 1974-76.

EG-Bulletin, Brussels, 1975 and 1976.

E. Foltermayer, "The Hyperinflation in Plant Construction," Fortune, November 1975.

F. Franzmayer and H. Machowski, "Willensbildung und Entscheidungsprozesse in der Europaischen Gemeinschaft und im Rat für gegenseitige Wirtschaftshilfe," Europa-Archiv, Folge 2, 1975.

M. Gamarnikow, "Industrial Cooperation: East Europe Looks West," Problems of Communism, May-June 1971.

"(Die) gemischten Gesellschaften — wirksame Förderungsform der rumänischen Warenexporte und -importe," Mitteilungen des Österreichischen Büros für den Ost-West-Handel, Vienna, June 1975.

J. Goldmann, "Fluctuation and Trend in the Rate of Economic Growth in Some Socialist Countries," Economics of Planning, 1966, no. 2.

J. Goldmann, "Tempo růstu a opakující se výkyvy v ekonomice některých socialistických zemí," Plánované hospodářství, Prague, 1964, no. 9; "Tempo růstu v některých socialistických zemích a model řízení národního hospodářství," Plánované hospodářství, Prague, 1964, no. 11.

J. Grabowski and E. Tabaczyński, "Międzynarodowe przedsiewziecia inwestycyjno produkcyjne Wschód-Zachód," Handel Zagraniczny, 1974, no. 1.

H. Haase, "Das Aussenhandelspreissystem im Rat für gegenseitige Wirtschaftshilfe," Osteuropa-Wirtschaft, 1975, no. 3.

M. Haendcke-Hoppe, "Zur Rolle des Lizenzhandels in der DDR — Sorgenkind Lizenzhandel," Forschungsstelle für wirtschaftliche und soziale Fragen, Berlin, 1974.

Handelsblatt. Business International, Ost-Wirtschaftsreport, 1976.

P. Hermes, "Die wirtschaftlichen Implikationen der KSZE," Wirtschaftsdienst, 1975, no. 8.

E. Hewett, "The Economics of East European Technology Imports from the West," American Economic Review, May 1975.

F. Horchler, "The Future of Austro-Hungarian Foreign Trade," Forschungsberichte des Wiener Institutes für Internationale Wirtschaftsvergleiche, June 1975, no. 27.

M. Hrnčíř, "Devizový kurs při zdokonalování soustav plánovitého řízení," Politická ekonomie, Prague, 1973, no. 7.

J. Jezbera, "Efektivnost vývozu a optimalisace," Zahraniční obchod, Prague, 1975, no. 7.

Z. Kamecki, "Niektóre ogólne problemy kooperacji przemysłoweij Wschód-Zachód," Handel Zagraniczny, 1973, no. 12.

Bibliography

E. Kemenes, "Einige juristische und finanzielle Aspekte der industriellen Kooperation," Marketing in Ungarn, 1974, no. 3.

B. Klümper and N. Leise, "Lizenzgeschäfte mit Staatshandelsländern," Forschungsbericht, no. 6, Hamburg, Institute für Aussenhandel und Überseewirtschaft, 1976.

P. Knirsch, "Möglichkeiten zur Förderung der Ost-West-Kooperation," Neue Zürcher Zeitung, November 10, 1971.

P. Knirsch, "Vom Ost-West-Handel zur Wirtschaftskooperation," Europa-Archiv, 1973, no. 2.

R. Kobza, "Ekonomické zásady pro hospodářskou kooperaci," Hospodářské noviny, Prague, November 30, 1973, no. 48.

R. Kobza, "Hospodářská kooperace s kapitalistickými státy," Hospodářské noviny, Prague, October 12, 1973, no. 41.

Ju. Kormnov and I. Petrov, "Razriadka napriazhennosti i khoziaistvennoe sotrudnichestvo," Voprosy ekonomiki, 1976, no. 2.

"K teorii vnějších ekonomických vztahú," Politicka ekonomie, Prague, 1973, no. 11.

Külgazdaság, 1974, no. 8, in Österreichisches Ost- und Südosteuropa-Institut, Presseschau Ostwirtschaft, 1974, no. 12.

O. Kýn, W. Schrettel and J. Sláma, "Growth Cycles in Centrally Planned Economies. An Empirical Test," Osteuropa-Institut, Munich, Workshop Paper, no. 7, August 1975.

A. Lebahn, "Die Position des Rates für Gegenseitige Wirtschaftshilfe (RGW) gegenüber den Europäischen Gemeinschaften (EG)," Archiv des öffentlichen Rechtes, 1975, no. 4.

F. Levcik, "East-West Trade and Economic Development in Eastern and Western Europe," in l'Est, Quaderni n. 5, CESES, Mailand 1974.

F. Levcik, "The Role of the International Economic Organization in the Integration Process of the CMEA Countries," in New Aspects of Economic Relations Between the Two Integration Groups in Europe, publication of the International Institute for Peace, Vienna, Gazetta Publishing House, 1977.

D. A. Loeber, "Kapitalbeteiligung an Unternehmen in der UdSSR?" Recht der Internationalen Wirtschaft, July-August 1976, book 7-8.

H. Machowski, "Abbau des Ungleichgewichtes im Ost-West-Handel," DIW-Wochenbericht, 1976, no. 39.

H. Machowski, "Beschleunigtes Wachstum des Ost-West-Handels," DIW-Wochenbericht, 1973, no. 46.

C. H. McMillan, "The International Organization of Inter-firm Co-operation (with Special Reference to East-West relationship)," IEA Conference on "Economic Relations between East and West," Dresden, June 29-July 3, 1976 (mimeo).

R. M. Mansfield, "Belorus Ltd. — A Joint East-West Venture in Canada," Carleton University, Working Paper 5, East-West Commercial Relations Series, Ottawa, 1974.

E. Mansfield, "International Technology Transfer: Forms, Resource Requirements, and Policies," American Economic Review, May 1975.

J. M. Michal, "Price Structures and Implicit Dollar-Rubel Ratios in East-European Trade," Weltwirtschaftliches Archiv, 1971, vol. 107(1).

H. J. Moecke, "Einfache und erweiterte West-Ost-Kooperation — Vertragsprobleme und Vertragsgestaltung," West-Ost Journal, Vienna, 1975, no. 2, and 1975, no. 3.

Industrial Cooperation between East and West

R. Moronits, "Der innerdeutsche Handel und die EWG nach dem Grundvertrag," Europa-Archiv, 1973, no. 10.

S. Nehring, "Zu den Wirtschaftsbeziehungen zwischen der BRD und der DDR," Die Weltwirtschaft, 1974, no. 2.

F. Nemschak, "Perspektiven und Probleme des Ost-West-Handels unter besonderer Berücksichtigung Österreichs," Der Donauraum, 1973, no. 4.

Neue Zürcher Zeitung, 1974:
— "Die französisch-sowjetische Kooperation vor neuen Aufgaben. Neue Möglichkeiten der industriellen Zusammenarbeit," Neue Zürcher Zeitung, July 16, 1974.

J. Nykryn, "Pojem a funkce mezinárodní prúmyslové kooperace," Zahraniční obchod, 1971, no. 6.

J. H. G. Olivera, "Cyclical Growth under Collectivism," Kyklos, 1960, vol. 13.

J. Olszynski, "Kooperacja przemysłowa Polski z wysoko rozwiniętymi krajami Europy Zachodniej," SGPiS, Zeszyty Naukowe, Warsaw, 1973, no. 94.

Die Presse, Vienna, 1974-76:
— E. Hoorn, in Die Presse, Vienna, November 15, 1974, and October 27, 1975.

V. Přibyl and J. Šťouračová, "Řízení vnějších ekonomických vztahú v zemích RVHP," Politická ekonomie, Prague, 1974, no. 1.

K. P. Prodromidis, "Greek Disaggregated Import and Export Demand Functions," Weltwirtschaftliches Archiv, 1975, no. 2.

Revista Economica, Bucharest, 1975, no. 31, in Österreichisches Ost- und Südosteuropa Institut, Presseschau Ostwirtschaft, 1976, no. 3, suppl. 6.

F. Romig, Theorie der wirtschaftlichen Zusammenarbeit, Berlin 1966, cited in Institut für Gewerbeforschung, Wirtschaftliche Zusammenarbeit zwischen Gewerbe und Industrie in Österreich, Vienna, 1973.

K. Rothschild, " 'Push' und 'Pull' im Export," Welwirtschaftliches Archiv, 1966, no. 2.

"Rumänische Gesellschaften im Ausland," Österreichisches Ost- und Südosteuropa-Institut, Presseschau Ostwirtschaft, 1974, no. 12, suppl. 10.

I. Russow, "Möglichkeiten des Buntmetallhandels mit Westeuropa," Aussenhandel UdSSR, 1976, no. 2.

E. Sárosi, "Zur industriellen Kooperation zwischen Österreich und Ungarn," Forschungsberichte des Wiener Institutes für Internationale Wirtschaftsvergleiche, July 1972, no. 2.

Ch. Sasse, "Kooperationsabkommen und EG-Handelspolitik. Parallelität oder Konflikt?" Europa-Archiv, 1974, no. 20.

H. Schaefer, "Kommunistische Westpolitik und die EWG," Osteuropäische Rundschau, February 1971 and March 1971; "Osteuropa revidiert Einstellung zum Gemeinsamen Markt," Osteuropäische Rundschau, June 1972.

K. E. Schenk, "Perspektiven der industriellen Ost-West-Kooperation," Wirtschaftsdienst, 1975, no. 12.

S. Schultz, "Osthandel der Entwicklungsländer. Kooperation also Mittel der Handelsförderung?" DIW-Wochenbericht, 1976, no. 10.

W. Schuschkow, "Über die Zusammenarbeit mit kapitalistischen Ländern beim Bau grosser Industrieobjekte in der UdSSR," Aussenhandel UdSSR, 1976, no. 2.

N. P. Shmelyov, "Scope for Industrial, Scientific and Technical Co-operation Between East and West," IEA Conference on "Economic Relations Between East and West," Dresden, June 29-July 3, 1976 (mimeo).

K. Šilpoch, "Místo a úloha mezinárodních ekonomických organizací v procesu

Bibliography

socialistické ekonomické integrace," Zahraniční obchod, 1975, no. 1.

G. J. Staller, "Fluctuations in Economic Activity: Planned and Free-Market Economies 1950-1960," American Economic Review, June 1964.

J. Stankovsky, "Austria's Foreign Trade. The Legal Regulation of Trade with East and West," Journal of World Trade Law, November 1969.

J. Stankovsky, "Bestimmungsgründe im Handel zwischen Ost und West," Forschungsberichte des Wiener Institutes für Internationale Wirtschaftsvergleiche, 1972, no. 7.

J. Stankovsky, "Determinant Factors of East-West Trade," Soviet and Eastern European Foreign Trade, 1973, no. 2.

J. Stankovsky, "Die Handelspolitik der Europäischen Gemeinschaften gegenüber den Oststaaten," Quartalshefte der Girozentrale, Vienna, 1973, no. 1-2.

J. Stankovsky, "Kapitalbeteiligung — Neue Form der Kooperation im Ost-West-Handel?" Creditanstalt-Bankverein, Vienna, Wirtschaftsberichte, 1973, no. 6.

J. Stankovsky, "Der österreichische Transithandel," Quartalshefte der Girozentrale, Vienna, 1972, no. 3.

J. Stankovsky, "Ost-West-Handel — Dimensionen, Probleme, Perspektiven," Europäische Rundschau, 1976, no. 2.

J. Stankovsky, "Ost-West-Kooperation im Konjunkturverlauf," in D. Cornelsen, H. Machowski, and K.-E. Schenk eds., Perspektiven und Probleme wirtschaftlicher Zusammenarbeit zwischen Ost- und Westeuropa, Berlin, DIW-Deutsches Institut für Wirtschaftsforschung, 1976, special no. 114.

J. Stankovsky, "Problems of Integration in COMECON," Soviet and Eastern European Foreign Trade, 1971, no. 3-4.

M. Sukijasovic, "Investment of Foreign Capital in the Yugoslav Economy," Yugoslav Survey, 1973, vol. 14, no. 4.

J. Szita, "On Intra-European Economic Cooperation and East-West Trade," Acta Oeconomica, 1974, vol. 13, no. 3-4.

The Times, London, 1976.

I. Toldy-Ösz, "Joint Ventures mit ausländischer Beteiligung," Marketing in Ungarn, 1974, no. 3.

R. Treviranus, "Der Handelsaustausch zwischen der BRD und der DDR unter dem Aspekt der Finanzierung," Ost-Panorama, 1974.

The U.S. Perspective on East-West Industrial Co-operation (preliminary), International Research Center of Indiana University, Team of Researchers, Bloomington, January 1975-June 1975.

V. Válek, "Hospodářská kooperace mezi socialistickými a kapitalistickými státy," Zahraniční obchod, 1975, no. 1.

G. Varga, "Közös Strategia Kidolgozása," Figyelö, Budapest, June 1973, no. 26.

V. Vetrov and V. Kazakevich, in Vneschniaia torgovlia, 1972, no. 11, cited in "Mitteilung der Kommission an den Rat," über die Kooperationsabkommen zwischen den Mitgliedsstaaten der Gemeinschaft und den osteuropäischen Ländern, Europe-Dokumente, Brussels, October 23, 1973, no. 766.

K. Wessely, Analyse der Entwicklung der österreichischen Ostimporte und Ostexporte, Österreichisches Ost- und Südosteuropa-Institut, Vienna, 1974 (mimeo).

G. Wettig, "Zum Ergebnis der KSZE," Berichte des Bundesinstitutes für Ostwissenschaftliche und Internationale Studien, Cologne, 1975, no. 42.

J.Wilczynski, "Joint East-West Ventures and Rights of Ownership," Institute of Soviet and East European Studies, Carleton University, Ottawa, Working Paper, no. 6, 1975.

Industrial Cooperation between East and West

J. Wilczynski, "Multinational Corporations and East-West Technological and Economic Relations," Canberra, January 1975 (manuscript).

"Wirtschaftsorganisationen mit internationalem Status im RGW," report on symposium in Prague, June 1973 and a conference in Sofia, December 1973, in Ikonomičeski život, December 1973, no. 52, and Magyar Hirlap, March 1974, no. 84, cited in Österreichisches Ost- und Südosteuropa-Institut, Presseschau Ostwirtschaft, 1974, no. 9.

A. Wolf, "Licence Trade with CMEA States," Intereconomics, 1975, no. 11.

T. A. Wolf, "The Effects of Liberalization of Austrian Quantitative Restrictions on Imports from CMEA Countries," Empirica, Vienna, 1976, no. 2.

T. A. Wolf, "The Impact of Elimination of West German Quantitative Restrictions on Imports from Centrally Planned Economies," Weltwirtschaftliches Archiv, Kiel, 1976, no. 2.

World Bank, Annual Report, 1975.

Zahraniční obchod, Prague, 1975, no. 10.

Julia Zala, "1958-1967: The Economic Trends of Decade," Acta Oeconomica, 1968, no. 2.

K. Zborovári, "International Production Co-operation, Several Theoretical and Practical Questions," Vezetőképzés, 1972, no. 4, cited in E. Hewett, "The Economics of East European Technology imports from the West," American Economic Review, May 1975.

L. Zurawicki, "Korporacje międzynarodowe a kraje socjalistyczne," Sprawy międzynarodowe, Warsaw, 1975, no. 1.

ZVO-Informationen, Rumänien, Informationsdienst der Siemens AG (Red. v. Heyking), Munich, August 1975.

ZVO-Informationen, UdSSR, I, II, Informationsdienst der Siemens AG (Red. v. Heyking), Munich, 1974.

About the Authors

Friedrich Levcik is the director of the Institut für Internationale Wirtschaftsvergleiche, Vienna. He has a profound knowledge of the economies of both the East and West and has published studies covering a broad range of problems, including economic planning, the labor market, and comparative analysis of economic processes and systems.

Jan Stankovsky is on the staff of the Österreichischen Institutes für Wirtschaftsforschung. An economist, his special interest is in Austrian trade with the East.